THE TRIUMPH OF PROPAGANDA

Film and National Socialism, 1933–1945

THE TRIUMPH OF PROPAGANDA

Film and National Socialism, 1933–1945

Hilmar Hoffmann

Translated by

John A. Broadwin

and

V. R. Berghahn

Berghahn Books
Providence • Oxford

Published in 1996 by

Berghahn Books

© 1996, 1997 of the English-language edition, Berghahn Books, Inc.
© 1988 of the German-language edition, Fischer Taschenbuch Verlag
GmbH, Frankfurt am Main
Originally published as "Und die Fahne führt uns in die Ewigkeit"

Library of Congress Cataloging-in-Publication Data
Hoffmann, Hilmar.
  [Fahne führt uns in die Ewigkeit. English]
  The triumph of propaganda : film and national socialism,
  1933–1945 / by Hilmar Hoffmann.
      p.   cm.
  Includes bibliographical references and index.
  (v. 1 : alk. paper)
  1. National socialism and motion pictures. 2. Motion pictures in
propaganda--Germany--History. 3. Propaganda, German--History--
20th century. 4. Motion pictures--Germany--History.   I. Title.
PN1995.9.N36H6413   1995   95-36005
791.43'658--dc20   CIP
              ISBN 1-57181-066-8 hardback
              ISBN 1-57181-122-2 paperback

British Library Cataloguing in Publication Data
A catalogue record for this book is available from
the British Library.

Printed in the United States on acid-free paper.

CONTENTS

PREFACE

In comparison with the other arts, film has a particularly forceful and lasting psychological and propagandistic impact because of its effect not on the intellect, but principally on the emotions and the visual sense. [Film] does not aim to influence the views of an elite coterie of art experts. Rather, it seeks to seize the attention of the broad masses. As a result, film can exercise an influence on society that is more enduring than that achieved by church or school or, for that matter, literature, the press or radio. Hence, for reasons that lie outside the realm of art, it would be negligent and reckless (and not in the interest of the arts themselves) for a responsible government to relinquish its leadership role in this important area.

Fritz Hippler[1]

Film was doubtless the most influential among the mass media in the Third Reich. It was also the means of artistic communication that Hitler used to greatest effect in bringing his political ideas to a mass audience. Compared to the emotional persuasiveness of moving pictures, radio and the press were less successful in conveying and spreading the message of the new ideology. Within the context of Goebbels's propaganda strategy, however, they were indispensable factors in any concerted and universal campaign of indoctrination, particularly in light of the fact that film lacked the up-to-dateness of radio and the daily newspaper.

Before Hitler came to power, during the so-called time of struggle (*Kampfzeit*), and before the Nazis had subordinated the medium of film to their own purposes, they made clever use of radio to deliver the messages of Dr. Goebbels, the ranting reporter, and Hitler, the neurotic rhetorician. What distinguished their delivery from the generally tedious speeches of democratic politicians was their forcefulness, vision, and mesmerizing emotionalism. The responsiveness to their demagogic language among broad segments of the population was an indication of the degree of social alienation prevailing at the time. Against the backdrop of the growing social problems and identity crises plaguing the Weimar republic, the aggressiveness of the Nazis was a totally new phenomenon. It was a sign of a strong hand at the helm, of an alternative to the uncontrolled proliferation of political parties, and of a renewed awareness of German power.

The optimistic language of the new redeemers promised to inaugurate a new age, to establish a millennial Reich, to lead the way to an exciting and meaningful future. The National Socialists were skillful in coopting concepts to describe this improved future.

It was no mere coincidence that there were six million unemployed in Germany as the Weimar republic was collapsing in 1932. Inevitably, the Depression and the radicalization of domestic politics resulted in new elections that same year (31 July 1932), elections in which the Nazis received 13.5 million votes and emerged the clear winners, their votes having come not only from the army of the socially disadvantaged but mostly from the conservatively minded middle class. Using social demagoguery to trumpet his idea of a future "national community" (*Volksgemeinschaft*) as a cure for Germany's ills, vowing to avenge the shame of Versailles, and offering a formula for the restoration of order, Hitler and his tightly organized party proceeded to build a mass movement. The artful dialectics of Dr. Goebbels had entered the homes of the electorate in 1932 through the loudspeakers of 4.25 million radios. Skilled in the uses of psychology, his voice cracking, Goebbels instilled in the hearts and minds of the broad masses the idea of the Führer as the new messiah. The spoken word and songs substituted for a political program. As Wilhelm Frick put it on 19 February 1933 in Dresden: "They say we don't have a program; but the name Hitler is program enough."[2] Propaganda was the program of the NSDAP, and that is where it focused its energies.

It was this "program" that dictated the ceaseless staging of mass rallies and parades, the intoxication with flags, the pylons of smoking torches, and the echo of martial music, with all its attendant vulgar "ballyhoo." "The art of propaganda," Hitler sensed in 1924, "lies in understanding the emotional ideas of the great masses and finding, through a psychologically correct form, the way to the attention and thence to the heart of the broad masses."[3]

Immediately after the Nazis came to power on 30 January 1933, the newly established Ministry for Popular Enlightenment and Propaganda proceeded to take over the film industry. With the creation of the Reich Film Chamber on 22 September 1933, the NSDAP assumed complete control of the motion-picture industry. The first year of production under the Nazis resulted in a kind of film trilogy on the theme of martyrdom: *SA-Mann Brand* (Storm Trooper Brand, 1933), *Hitlerjunge Quex* (Hitler Youth Quex, 1933), and *Hans Westmar* (1933). The purpose of these films was to raise the unknown Storm Trooper and the murdered Nazi heroes Herbert Norkus and Horst Wessel to the status of role models.

But that same year Goebbels realized how counterproductive it would be in the long run to have Brown Shirts constantly marching not only in the streets but across the silver screen as well. "What we are seeking is more than a dramatization of the Party program. The ideal that we have in mind is a profound union of the spirit of the heroic life and the eternal laws of art," said Goebbels in 1933.[4] Consequently, Nazis in uniform, swastika flags, and the obligatory fascist salute were largely banished from the screen, in any event until the beginning of the war. After the war broke out, the government, as Goebbels said in a speech delivered on 12 October 1941, would once again "decide on the educational and ideological [willensmäßigen] message" of feature films.

The Nazis never ceased using film for the purpose of mass persuasion. Instead, they shifted direct indoctrination from feature films to documentaries and newsreels. According to the subsequent implementation statutes of the Reich Cinema Law of 16 February 1934, every feature film was to be preceded by the showing of a "supporting program" consisting of newsreels and documentaries. The clear differentiation of propagandistic function by film genre showed the Nazis' surprising sensitivity to the various means for effectively influencing the masses. Even feature films that were primarily sources of popular entertainment were never entirely nonpolitical. Like many of Ufa's (Universum-Film-Aktiengesellschaft) productions, feature films transformed entertainment into an artistic event, with an eye to creating the illusion of normalcy during the darkest of hours. To quote Goebbels before the Reich Film Chamber on 15 February 1941: "Even entertainment sometimes has the task of arming the nation to fight for its existence, of providing it with the requisite spiritual uplift, entertainment, and relaxation as the dramatic events of the day unfold." Besides their important function as a diversion, entertainment films were a particularly effective means for disseminating certain topics among the population in a seemingly neutral fashion and without being too heavy-handed or using treasonous terms. The Tobis film Ich klage an (I Accuse, 1941), directed by Wolfgang Liebeneiner, is a classic example. Popular actors of the day whose appearance inspired confidence, such as Heidemarie Hatheyer, Paul Hartmann, Mathias Wiemann, and Harald Paulsen, were enlisted to popularize the euthanasia program that was already under way.

However, Goebbels also regarded historical films about a figure such as Frederick the Great, with an established identity, as a proven way to appropriate some of the Prussian monarch's genius as a leader of the nation and victorious military commander, thereby providing a backdrop for the Hitler cult and making the Führer appear as the legitimate heir to Prussia's virtues and traditions.

Films about Frederick the Great, such as *Der alte und der junge König* (The Old King and the Young King, 1930), directed by Hans Steinhoff, and *Der große König* (The Great King, 1942), directed by Veit Harlan, had less to do with Prussia's rebirth under Frederick than with its revival under National Socialism. The actor Otto Gebühr declaimed the ringing phrases of the Prussian king to an audience of nearly 18.6 million moviegoers as though he were reciting passages from the Führer's harangues. Reenactments of Frederick's defeats, such as the battle of Kunersdorf, were meant to show how in the face of a defeat like Stalingrad metaphysical hope could generate expectations of victory and an iron will lead to final victory—if only everyone fervently believed in the Führer!

The documentary film in the Third Reich lived up to the expectations Nazi propagandists harbored for their message of hate. To convey it effectively, the new regime was obliged to seek replacements for former Ufa writers who wanted to indulge their taste for pedestrian *Kulturfilme* filled with spectacular imagery.

Leni Riefenstahl's hour-long film of the 1933 Nazi Party congress, *Sieg des Glaubens* (Victory of Faith), marked the beginning of a new branch of aesthetics that would persist into the future—the aesthetic of the fascist film. In time, all art would be measured against the standards she had set. Her standards of aesthetic composition would govern the presentation in documentaries of the Party's authoritarian principle of order (*Ordnungsprinzip*) and the rigid canon of Nazi beliefs. Documentary filmmaking was guided by the mandate that "the cinema will deal only with subjects of benefit to the Party." Leni Riefenstahl's Party congress films provided filmmakers with an aesthetic model to guide them in observing the Party's principle of order with maximum vigor. Her creative achievement lay in the general stylistic changes she introduced into the Nazi documentary. She demonstrated in exemplary fashion how individual "physiological identity disappears behind the allure of a technical valorization,"[5] and how the individual as an element of the mass is reified and absorbed as an anonymous part of the greater whole. "The individual is freed and absorbed into the community of the faithful,"[6] which is kept in perpetual motion in Riefenstahl's films. The worship of movement *per se* transformed Nazi ideas into [symmetrical] forms, and these forms were in turn endowed with dynamic movement. At the same time, Riefenstahl's theory of aesthetics explicitly negated the existence of the social nexus.

Though only a tiny minority of directors achieved the high degree of aesthetic quality and controlled scene composition attained by Riefenstahl, they generally managed, using a kitsch aesthetic (*trivialisierte Inhaltsästhetik*), to generate a cinematic apotheosis of Nazi ideas, even if it was just by trotting out the swastika flag as a symbol.

Like the Nazis in general, Leni Riefenstahl made the swastika flag her leitmotif. It appears everywhere in her films; she constantly confronts us with swastika flags waving in the wind as omnipresent reminders of the Führer. The flag symbolizes the Party program; it is the visual epitome of Nazi ideology. The flag "is the new age," the thousand-year Reich. The myth of the flag is a substitute for utopia. The flag is *the* symbol for which there is no substitute. "Yes, the flag means more than death" is a prophetic verse in the Hitler Youth's marching song.

But it is not only Leni Riefenstahl who bombards us with flags. In over 90 percent of Nazi documentary films, the flag figures prominently as an icon-like symbol charged with lofty moral values. It is presented either at the beginning of a film to put the viewer into the right frame of mind or shown toward the end, billowing in the wind as an anodyne for the final apotheosis. Lest anyone forget when a documentary stakes out new territory, the flag also functions as a "fluttering" control point (the point used by surveyors for fixing a boundary).

The first part of this book will investigate the ideological, emotional, and moral significance of the flag in the Third Reich. Was it a brightly colored fetish for the masses that was meant to anchor the Nazi ideology firmly in the deepest recesses of the subconscious? Was it a "psychic infection," to borrow Freud's term in his *Massenpsychologie und Ich-Analyse* (Group Psychology and the Analysis of the Ego). Or an obligatory clichéd image, viewed as the price ambitious directors had to pay in order to be able to bid on the next film contract? Visual incense, a kind of elixir of life, a magic potion to turn one into a hero, to summon up one's courage, to gain confidence? The flag was all that and more: it was a myth for which to die.

"The flag will lead us to eternity"—Fred Zinnemann's film
From Here to Eternity (1953) demythologizes the ideal of "eternity"
with brutal realism, exposing it as militarist cynicism, hell on
earth, the kind of hell that many in the Third Reich suffered in
much more grisly ways.

In presenting a myth to which you have some attachment, you
share in that myth, wrote Elias Canetti. In Hitler's case, this
proved true to the bitter end. Mythic consciousness, using propaganda vehicles such as the flag, early seized the attention of the
"masses" and pointed the way to the disaster that ultimately
befell the Germans and many other nations.

This book is limited to the study of the documentary film in the
so-called Third Reich. A number of works dealing with the Nazi
feature film have already been published. They include such
important contributions as Coutarde and Cadars's *Histoire du
cinéma nazi* (1972),[7] Gerd Albrecht's *Nationalsozialistische Filmpolitik*
(1969),[8] Erwin Leiser's *Deutschland, erwache!* (1968),[9] and Boguslaw
Drewniak's *Der deutsche Film 1938–1945: ein Gesamtüberblick* (1987).
Until now, however, there has been no monographic study of the
documentary film as it relates to that other documentary medium,
the newsreel. This work seeks to fill the gap and at the same time
make a contribution to the history of the genre's popularity.

This volume, a survey of the subject matter, aesthetics, and
development of the documentary film and the newsreel under the
Nazi regime, will be supplemented by two additional parts, cur-
rently in preparation, analyzing individual documentaries produced during the period 1939–1945. The three volumes are
arranged in such a way that the history of the Third Reich and the
anatomy and face of the Nazi spirit can be reconstructed from the
documentaries and newsreels of the period. For this reason, some
films were included to which little importance was attached at the
time they were made but which contain important details for a
study of the Third Reich. Produced under a dictatorship that had
redefined reality and was pledged to uphold the one and only
truth propagated by the Führer, they are an integral part of the
documentary film landscape. When artists forfeit their most
important criterion—truth—out of opportunism, fear, or fanaticism, they give up their independence. This aspect of cinematic
art will be discussed as well.

I have watched over three hundred documentaries and newsreels for this book and the two volumes to follow, and I have analyzed more than half of them in greater depth in volumes two

(1928–1939) and three (1939–1945). I am deeply grateful to the
Bundes-Archiv in Koblenz, in particular to Peter Bucher and
Anneliese Hoffmann-Thielen of the distribution department, for
providing me with copies. I would also like to express my thanks
to Enno Patalas of the Filmmuseum in Munich and Dorothea
Gebauer of the Deutsches Institut für Filmkunde for loaning me
copies. Further, I would like to thank Wolfgang Klaue of the Staat-
liches Filmarchiv of the GDR, Jiri Purs of Ceskoslovensky Film in
Prague, Tom Johnson of America House in Frankfurt am Main,
the Library of Congress in Washington, D.C., and the Film
Library of the Museum of Modern Art in New York for obtaining
copies in my behalf. I owe a special debt of gratitude to the director of the Deutsches Filmmuseum, Walter Schobert, and to Rainer
Schang of the duplication department for their readiness to help
during my frequent visits to the cutting room, including week-
ends. I am grateful to my colleagues Gerd Albrecht and Eberhard
Spieß of the Deutsches Institut für Filmkunde in Frankfurt am
Main for their advice and comments and especially for their
readiness to help at any time in the procurement of documentary
materials. My thanks also go to Alain Lance for his comments.
The efforts of Monika Zehe and Andrea Wölbing in the compilation of the bibliography also deserve mention. I would like to
thank my friends Joachim Gaertner, Willi Köhler, and Dieter
Kramer for critically reviewing my manuscript, and Gudrun Has-
selbacher, Anita Jantzer, Edeltraud Kunze, and Elke Ringel for
converting my manuscript into a well-ordered final copy.

The text is based in part on lectures and seminars I delivered
in 1985, 1986, and 1987 at the Kunstwissenschaftliches Institut of
Philipps-Universität in Marburg and the Faculty of Fine Arts of
the University of Tel-Aviv.

Notes

1. Fritz Hippler, *Film-Kurier* (Berlin), 5 April 1944.

2. Quoted in *Frankfurter Zeitung* (Frankfurt am Main), 21 February 1933.

3. Adolf Hitler, *Mein Kampf*, 2 vols. (Munich, 1925–1927).

4. Joseph Goebbels's speech at the opening of the Reichskulturkammer at Phil-harmonic Hall (Berlin), 15 November 1933, quoted in Gerd Albrecht, ed., *Film im Dritten Reich* (Karlsruhe, 1979), p. 267.

5. Paul Virilio, *Die Ästhetik des Verschwindens* (Berlin, 1986), p. 98, English trans-lation *The Aesthetics of Disappearance* (New York, 1991).

6. Leif Furhammar and Folke Isaksson, *Politik und Film* (Ravensburg, 1974), p. 190, English translation *Politics and Film* (New York, 1971).

7. Francis Courtade and Pierre Cadars, *Histoire du cinéma nazi* (Paris, 1972).

8. Gerd Albrecht, *Nationalsozialistische Filmpolitik* (Stuttgart, 1969).

9. Erwin Leiser, *Deutschland, erwache!* (Reinbek bei Hamburg, 1968), English translation *Nazi Cinema* (New York, 1974).

✦ 1 ✦

THE SYMBOLIC VALUE OF FLAGS
AND STANDARDS

Flags as Symbols

*There are many people today who must realize that with the fall of the
flag, the flag bearer falls as well.—Those who failed to recognize the
[changed] times have no political or cultural or moral right to hoist
another flag. The film industry is marked by a general lack of courage,
a fear to stand up for one's beliefs, and a lack of enthusiasm to make
commitments. The movie producers say "you can clean my plumage,
but don't ruffle my feathers," mollifying themselves by hoisting a new
flag. Most probably some pennant from a bygone era. Intellectual liberalism—which in reality means intellectual chaos—is dead and buried.
To argue that art has no bias (Tendenz) is foolish, naive, and absurd.*

Joseph Goebbels, 28 March 1933[1]

"Flags are wind made visible," wrote Elias Canetti in *Masse und
Macht*,[2] summing up the nature of flags in terms of two basic characteristics: their exposed position, visible from great distances, as
they wave in the breeze above people's heads; and the relationship
between the material from which they are made—cloth or, in the
case of weather vanes, metal—and their immateriality, i.e., their
suitability for expressing abstract ideas, their symbolic function.

Originally, though, flags (a cultural history of flags, standards,
and banners has yet to be written) likely had a utilitarian function.
An encyclopedia of the Middle Ages states that flags were the perfect means for distinguishing "one's own troops from those of the
enemy"[3] and went on to say that for the medieval soldier (and
presumably for those of antiquity and the early modern period as
well), flags were not merely symbols of sovereignty and loyalty.

Rather—as in the case of armies where the wearing of uniforms was not practiced—they were used for the purposes of identification and signaling. Serving for the identification of friend or foe and as a rallying point during engagements between units or individual soldiers, flags afforded protection to those within a unit, ultimately ensuring their survival. The fall of the flag of one's own army meant that chaos would ensue, soldiers running helter skelter across the battlefield or directly into the enemy's arms. Albrecht Altdorfer's monumental painting "Battle of Alexander at Issus" (1529) gives a sense of the vital importance of flags in the conduct of war. The various forces portrayed in this vast panorama of soldiers embroiled in the tumultuous struggle between ancient Greeks and Persians are so intertwined that the different flags are virtually the only way for viewers to orient themselves.

It is probably impossible to determine in which spheres of life flags first came into use. What has come down to us is a report of the magnificent ceremony in which the first flag was formally consecrated when Charlemagne was crowned Holy Roman Emperor in the city of Rome. Ironically, the flag that Pope Leo III granted the secular head of Roman Catholic Christendom in the year 800 A.D. as a sign of his new power was red in color. During war, in seafaring, and in the case of religion, flags were used chiefly as identification signs and as a means to highlight differences. During the crusades, which lasted two hundred years, the number of flags was myriad. They gave courage to the knights of one's own country who were obliged to fight on foreign soil, and they intimidated the natives.

Flags appeared as identification signs on the world's oceans long before Christians took to the sea. The Vikings used them during their sea voyages. With a raven (the symbol of Odin, their god of war and death) painted on their standards, the Vikings brought a reign of terror to the seas. And with martial insignia on the flags flying from their topmasts, William the Conqueror's ships set sail from Normandy in 1066 to invade England at Sussex and defeat the forces of the successor to the throne, Harold II, at Hastings. The Bayeux Tapestry, an embroidered frieze 230 feet in length and a primary cultural and historical document, depicts the lovely cross-emblazoned flags that the Church had granted William in Rome.

Even Richard Wagner was conversant with the role of flags as signals. In his 1865 opera *Tristan and Isolde*, set in the Middle Ages, he makes reference to them through the resonant baritone of Tristan's faithful retainer Kurwenal, when Kurwenal (Act I, Scene 4) informs Isolde, as they sail the Irish Sea, of the upcoming landing on "Cornwall's verdant strand":

> On the mast a flag is flying,
> And gaily waves toward the land
> And in King Mark's castle
> They know the bride is at hand.[4]

For ships the flag is a promise of rescue from peril in the struggle with the forces of nature, just as it is [a promise of salvation] for soldiers embroiled in hand-to-hand combat. Nevertheless the primary function of the flag is not to act as a pledge of good fortune but as a symbol of one's own troops that, when captured, lost sight of, or gone unnoticed, inevitably signals a battle's end, or death. *Unity* under the flag exists only so long as deserting the flag poses a *threat*. This *negative* function of the flag makes it an instrument of repression within the ranks, not the sign of hope that state-controlled propaganda would suggest.

A flag fluttering in the breeze is a symbol of life in the midst of the general threat of death. In other words, it is an ideal instrument for controlling the masses. The dialectic between the promise of good fortune and the risk of death moves the flag into the realm of religion, which helps to explain the use of flags in religious worship. They may appear in the form of the three-tail Easter flag representing the resurrection of Christ or the multi-colored prayer flags found in Tibetan monasteries or the magic streamers carried by American Indians, but they are always intimately associated with the supernatural and with the notion of eternal damnation for those who "fear not God."

The symbol outlined at the beginning of this section in connection with Elias Canetti's definition of the flag is not to be confused with the magical powers of the flag in religious worship. As an object of religious veneration, the faithful considered the flag to be divinely inspired, i.e., sacred. The flag only assumed its symbolic function in the wake of the secularization that accompanied the Enlightenment. Abstract internalized values now gave meaning to life, providing a substitute for religious transcendence. Eugène Delacroix's famous painting "Liberty Leading the People," in which the allegory of Revolution—a woman with bared breast holding a tricolor and a muzzle-loader—leads a band of fighting men onto the stage of history, gives artistic expression to this change. The flag is no longer borne by a soldier but by an abstract allegorical figure, thereby elevating the significance of the scene beyond the actual battle depicted to a higher plane of values.

The flag's transformation from rallying point to revolutionary symbol was rooted in technological change. Since the technological revolution of the nineteeth century, war was no longer a duel between individual soldiers. It was now conducted by mechanical weapons that delivered death and destruction over immense distances. When a soldier was dying or being killed, he no longer looked into the whites of his enemy's eyes; all he saw was the muzzle flash of a gun. The only contact between combatants was that between the telescopic sights of their artillery pieces. This kind of warfare invalidated the flag's role as a true identification sign. Paul Virilio has called modern warfare the "war of light," a mechanized scenario in which target acquisition, "observation," is more important than firepower. In other words, it is primarily perception and observation that decide the outcome of a war; weapons are of secondary importance. In this kind of war scenario it is no longer a question of eliminating the object of perception, the raised flag of medieval warfare. Rather, it is a question of perception itself. The apotheosis of this war is the nuclear flash, where the weapon and the flash of light combine to blind and annihilate the enemy—the consummation and logical consequence of the idea of "blitzkrieg" [lightning or *lighting* war, to use Virilio's play on words—Transl.], a twilight of the gods that gives birth to a race of mutants and zombies. In this twentieth century scenario the flag has no practical use in affording protection. On the contrary, the nerve center of an army—its "flagship"—is the most likely target for destruction. In modern warfare, deserting the flag seems to offer the only true chance of survival. "There is no victory. There are only flags and men who fall," according to Jean-Luc Godard's *Les Carabiniers* (1963).

Nevertheless, the myth of victory and the flag as the symbol of victory persist to this day. As a symbol of the nation, the flag is still considered inviolable. Insulting it is subject to severe punishment under the law. On days of national mourning it stands at half-staff. At state funerals it is draped over the coffin to show that the deceased has been accepted into the immortal community of the nation. It is a symbol that is understood throughout the world like no other. In Paolo and Vittorio Taviani's film *Padre Padrone* (1976/1977) the hero Gavino Ledda is forced to learn: "You must know the name of your flag better than you know your mother's name." Even the novel *Die Katakomben von Odessa*[5] by the Russian writer Valentin Kataev, in which he describes partisan warfare against the German army of occupation in Ukraine, contains a major scene centered on the symbolism of the flag. As he lies dying, a young sapper places a flag under his body so that the liberated citizens of Odessa will later find it, drenched in his blood, and wave it as a sign of victory. This is a desperate attempt to give meaning to "death in battle" in a world devoid of religious transcendence where the "greater good"—the nation—calls for unquestioning obedience under the sign of the flag.

In this sense, the words of Elias Canetti cited at the beginning of this section have a numinous and magical aspect that I will relate below to the imperialist and militarist function of the flag. Flags "are like bits cut from clouds, nearer and more varied in color, tethered and given permanent shape. In their movement they are truly striking. Nations use them to mark the air above them as their own, as though the wind could be partitioned."

Colors and Their Political Significance

I promise that we will hold our flag and our ideas high and carry them with us to our grave. Countless blood witnesses are with us in spirit.

Adolf Hitler[6]

Flags can stand for revolution as well as tyranny and totalitarianism. They may be associated with festivities, prayers, and funerals. Flags—as simple as they are effective—have had an importance in history that has been worth fighting for and waging war over.

Flags by themselves are impartial (though even a plain white flag has a special meaning); and the symbols used in flags are often nothing more than utilitarian. There are whole books written for future sea captains and pilots that are devoted to explaining the shape, color, and positioning of the various naval flags.

Seamen introduced the concept of "flagging" at the beginning of the modern era as a way of differentiating the display of naval flags from that of other types. The English have employed naval flags since 1640. In the German-speaking states their use dates back to 1732 when pilots in the Baltic adopted the term "flagging" to describe the messages conveyed by means of flags.

The complex process of ship-to-ship and ship-to-shore communication gradually gave rise to the development of a sophisticated and standardized flag "language" for the purpose of keeping ships at sea out of harm's way.

A discussion of the makeup of flags becomes a volatile topic whenever we talk about symbols that represent a political ideology or regime. The first documented reference to German flag customs and etiquette dates back to the eighteenth century. The dozens upon dozens of small German states dressed their ships with masthead flags in the livery colors of their respective rulers. After 1848 the black-red-gold flag waved from the masts of German ships. However, it was not recognized universally on the seven seas as a symbol of sovereignty. The British government, in fact, delivered a formal note to the German Confederation stating that Britain would view the Confederation's ships as pirates if they sailed into British waters without flying the sovereign flag of the respective federation member.

In "Dreaming of a Fleet" Ferdinand Freiligrath, Germany's poet of freedom, symbolized the unification of these numerous small states into a single nation-state as black-red-gold storm clouds garlanded across the world's oceans:

> Wave now free Black Red and Gold from every mast
> And flag pole ringing the land!
> The ocean has festooned itself
> In thousands of pennants, oh flag once reviled.[7]

A single flag embracing all members of the North German Confederation existed only after 1866. Bismarck decreed it was to be the Black-White-Red, because this combination of colors "represented not only the black and white of Prussia but the red and white of the Hansa cities and Holstein, i.e., the largest number of non-Prussian ships:"[8]

> The Black-White-Red flies proudly
>   from our ship's mast.
> The flag flies in the face of the enemies who threaten it,
> Who hate its colors.
> It waves back and forth in the wind
>   along the side of the ship,
> and far from the beloved Fatherland
>   upon storm-tossed seas.
> We pledge our loyalty to it.
>   faithful unto death.
> We dedicate our life to the flag,
>   to the Black and White and Red.

Beginning in 1828 the landlocked Austrian monarchy dressed its ships with red-white-red masthead flags bearing an open crown as the emblem of regal power.

The enormous impact of the black-white-red flag even on Germans living outside of Germany is reflected in this rapturous description written by Gustav Freytag and published in the journal *Die Grenzboten* in 1840: "Throughout the entire inhabited world men of German origin—hard-boiled, unemotional German businessmen—waved their hats and shouted for joy, embracing one another with tears in their eyes, because these colors had been raised over their heads in order to release them from their ancient bondage, isolation, and defenselessness and to offer them a shared home away from home and the greatest, most precious masculine pride in their distant German fatherland."[9]

In contrast, Heinrich Heine, writing on the occasion of the 1817 Wartburg festival, used his mordant wit to heap scorn on the shrill declarations issued by members of the ultranationalist student associations and their dream of a unified Germany under the black-white-red flag: "While the past croaked out its dark raven song at the Wartburg festival, a sunrise song about the modern age was sung at Hambach Castle and toasts were drunk to all mankind."[10]

Two weeks after the French established a republic and deposed their king, on 9 March 1848, the National Parliament in Frankfurt am Main adopted "the colors of the former German imperial banner—Black-Red-Gold—as the tricolor of the Germanic Confederation." Intoxicated by the revolution, the composer Robert Schumann gushed: "Black stands for [gun] powder, red for blood, and gold for the lambent flame." And in his London exile Ferdinand Freiligrath wrote the following bellicose verses on "The Revolutionary Colors":

> Aha, fluttering, billowing, a flash of color!
> Hurrah, you Black and Red and Gold!
> It's the former imperial standard,
> Those are the ancient colors!
> This is the banner under which we'll fight and
> Obtain fresh scars.
> You see, we've just begun
> The final battle is yet to come![11]

The National Assembly that was convened in St. Paul's Church—the most highly educated parliament that ever existed

(in the words of Golo Mann)—published the following announcement in the Reich Law Gazette of 12 November 1848: "The German
war ensign shall consist of three horizontal stripes of equal width,
black at the top, red in the middle, and yellow on the bottom. In the
upper left-hand corner the canton shall bear the imperial coat-of-
arms on a rectangular field.... The imperial coat-of-arms consists of
a double-headed eagle displayed sable on a gold field, langued
gules, gold-beaked, and taloned."[12]

The aura of the Black-Red-Gold faded along with the "unfin-
ished German revolution" symbolized by St. Paul's Church. The
young Otto von Bismarck, a delegate to the Diet of the reconstituted German Confederation, quickly dissociated himself from
the colors and their symbolic meaning at the parliament of the
Erfurt Union in 1850. Black-Red-Gold, he said, had never been the
imperial colors; they were symbols of rebellion and the barricade.
Referring to himself in his memoirs *Gedanken und Erinnerungen*,[13]
Bismarck cited an assonant poem written in March 1848 as Prussian troops were withdrawing from Berlin:

> Those were the Prussians, their colors black and white,
> Their flag streaming before them once again,
> As the king's loyal men lay down their lives for him,
> For their king, each one cheering.
> As we watched them carry their dead away
> Without so much as a whimper,
> A shout pierced their loyal hearts,
> You are Prussians no longer—you are Germans now.
>
> Black-Red-Gold is ablaze in the sunlight,
> The desecrated imperial eagle falls;
> This is the end of your glorious history, Hohenzollerns,
> This is where a king fell, though not in battle.
> We take no pleasure
> In watching a falling star.
> You'll regret what you did, Prince [Bismarck],
> None there are who are more loyal than Prussians.[14]

On 9 December 1866 Otto von Bismarck issued the following
decree: "The merchant ships of all Confederation members shall
fly the same black-red-white flag." Not until the following year
did he offer an explanation for the choice of colors—a choice that
he had made entirely on his own: "When we became Prussians, we
adopted the Black and White; the present Black-White-Red was
the result of combining the colors of Prussia with the White-Red of

the Hansa. It was only after I had explained this to old Kaiser Wilhelm that he accepted the adoption of the new colors."[15] The new black-white-red war ensign of the North German Confederation combined the Iron Cross of the wars of liberation, designed by Friedrich Schinkel, with the martial traditions of Prussia. It was Lützow's legendary free corps, organized within the Prussian army, that gave birth to the idea of "unifying Germany by force of arms."

The squabbling over these tradition-laden symbols of state not only generated all sorts of farcical intrigue; it also gave rise to other bizarre behavior, ranging from debates over what was truly German through petty political infighting among the student associations all the way to arguments over the rights of sovereign states—none of which produced anything positive in the end. In his well-researched study titled *Die deutschen Farben* (1955), Paul Wentzcke devoted more than sixty pages to the debates that raged over the question of the new flag from the end of the nineteenth to the beginning of the twentieth century. His discussion illuminates the age-old dichotomy between symbol and reality and indicates the depth of ill-feeling that forms part of the genealogy of the German flag. Hitler wanted his new swastika flag to lead the nation away from the discord of party politics and regional interests as they related to the question of the flag and to stand as an affirmation of the unity of the German fatherland.

In 1870 Chancellor Bismarck put an end to the farce with a touch of sarcasm: "At any other time color combinations wouldn't make any difference to me. I wouldn't care if it was green, yellow and purple, or the flag of Mecklenburg-Strelitz. But the Prussian soldier simply wants no part of the Black, Red, and Gold."

After accepting the Bavarian king Ludwig II's letter offering him the imperial crown, the Prussian king Wilhelm I was acknowledged as German Emperor in a ceremony that took place in the Hall of Mirrors in the palace of Versailles on 18 January 1871. Henceforth, the Black-White-Red of the North German Confederation would be the national flag. A reenactment of the ceremony formed the dramatic high point of the second part of Ernst Wendt's silent movie *Bismarck* (1926)—*the* quintessential German film. The constitution that was ratified that same year made Black-White-Red the official colors of the war ensign and the merchant flag, so that "the black-white-red tricolor now flew over the fortresses of Paris and the palace of Versailles."[16] This was the atmosphere in which the flag was created. Given the popular mood at the time, the flag, because of its ideological claims, had "become the symbol of political unity and strength for thirty million Germans: the black-white-red flag is a permanent fixture among the nations of the world, and it would be pointless, harmful, and criminal to squander the reserves of respect and patriotism that it has built up," wrote Gustav Freytag in a letter from the front. The flag was not only a support for soldiers in uncertain times; it was also ideally suited for subjugating the individual to its symbolic power. This alliance of emotions would unite academics and workers, soldiers and housewives.

After millions of soldiers had died fighting under the Black-White-Red in the First World War and after the unification of Germany under the same flag—"which is still regarded as a great national treasure" (MP Dr. Kahl)—the constitutional committee, following months of tedious deliberation, decided in a roll call vote on 4 June 1919 to adopt the Black, Red, and Gold. The decision was taken in part to ward off the "threat" posed by the Independent Socialists' attempt to force the adoption of "their red Soviet flag." The aversion to the color red was not motivated solely by ideology; it had an irrational component as well. At any rate, the colors Black, Red, and Gold gave rise to a symbiotic love-hate relationship that created the conditions in which the defeated parties could cultivate the idea of taking revenge.

The Social Democratic Interior Minister Eduard David called the "tricolor" the "symbol of a sense of national community" and recommended "maintaining Greater German unity as a lofty ideal and future goal." Indignation at the fact "that our Austrian brothers have been blocked from achieving self-determination and prohibited from becoming part of the Motherland has burned this ideal into the soul of every man who considers himself a German." David expressed the hope that "the anguish will give birth to the strength needed to achieve this new, revived ideal of Greater Germany." "May the black-red-gold banner fly in front of us in all these endeavors."[17] In a little less than twenty years Hitler would realize the dream of a Greater Germany, but in a form very different from that envisioned by David.

Under the Weimar republic the old new colors met with disapproval, especially from right-wing groups such as the veterans' organization called the Stahlhelm. They felt that the colors were a concession to the Social Democrats from whose ranks Reich President Ebert had come. In the eyes of the right, the Black, Red, and Gold stood for a defenseless democracy. They were the colors

of the unrestrained violence of the Revolution of 1848; and—
which was of central importance in the rise of fascism—Black-
Red-Gold became the symbol of the "humiliation of Versailles."
Because the flag that replaced the Black-White-Red of Greater Germany was viewed as a symbol of 1848-style democracy, it came to
represent a "betrayal of the German people," in the same sense as
German nationalists viewed the Treaty of Versailles. For them, the
flag of the Weimar republic became an omnipresent aggravation
and a constant goad to erase Germany's "shame." They invested
all their enthusiasm and affinity for the irrational in one symbol
alone. "And from time immemorial men have fought with greater
ferocity over symbols than over genuine interests. The decision of
the National Assembly gave the opposition on the right a symbol
that in future would arouse all its demonic instincts."[18]

The debate over the flag in the Weimar republic had symbolic
significance. It reflected the strife that existed within the fledgling
democracy. As history has taught us, the disputes over the
national colors and their symbolic meaning was an intermezzo
that ended tragically. Hitler used the debate between the proponents of the Black-White-Red and the supporters of the black-red-
gold flag to incite the masses that would soon rally around him.

The Flag Pledge

*We young people will carry the flag to the front as the young
    prepare to attack.
May it arise and ascend and shoot like a flame into the sky!
We've sworn an oath to the flag for ever and for all time to come!
Damned be he who desecrates the flag!
The flag is our faith in God and people and country!
Rob us of life and limb, if rob us you must, but don't take our flag.
We cherish the flag as dearly as we do our mothers,
For the flag is our tomorrow, our honor, and our courage.*

Eberhard Wolfgang Möller, 1935

When soldiers swore the oath of allegiance to the flag, the flag
attained the status of a sacred shrine. The flag pledge assumed the
function of a religious rite sanctioned by a priest. Enticed by the
"magic implicit in the pledge" (Peter Dade), untold millions of
soldiers have marched to their death throughout history. In mercenary armies the flag pledge was rendered to the commander in

chief as a symbolic seal on a hireling's contract. The custom of touching the flag while rendering a pledge did not come into practice until the seventeenth century.

The question of rendering an oath of allegiance to the state *and* the military has been an issue of controversy in Germany for centuries. In 1834 the members of the German Confederation agreed that the military should not be forced also to swear an oath to the constitution. The Reich Constitution of 1848, however, did require that an oath to the constitution become part of the flag pledge. Then after the Franco-Prussian War (1870–71) the flag pledge became strictly an oath of loyalty to the Emperor as Supreme War Lord. Following World War II the political component was watered down and the flag pledge divided into a military loyalty oath and a specially devised pledge of allegiance to the constitution.

After the death of Reich President Paul von Hindenburg, the Nazis enacted a law on 20 August 1934 transforming the flag pledge into an oath of personal loyalty to the Führer: "I swear before God this sacred oath, that I will yield unconditional obedience to the Führer of the German Reich and people, Adolf Hitler, the Supreme Commander of the Armed Forces, and, as a brave soldier, will be ready at any time to lay down my life for this oath."[19] In contrast to the military, the SS swore an oath of fealty to the "Führer and Chancellor of the Reich," not to the "Führer of the German Reich and people."

The wearing of the national emblem (the Eagle and the Swastika) on their Wehrmacht tunics obliged ordinary soldiers to pledge life and limb to the Führer. The SS—the men with the Death's Head insignia on their caps—were a volunteer force (before the war) that pledged, if need be, to die for Hitler "with faith in their hearts." "We march for Hitler through night and through need ... Yes, the flag means more than death" was the marching song of the Hitler Youth.

From at least 20 July 1944—when military officers opted for moral responsibility in the conflict between their conscience and their oath to Hitler—to the present, the flag pledge has been a subject of debate in the German military.

In the Prusso-German armies and most especially in Hitler's army, defending the flag, even to the point of sacrificing one's life, was considered the ultimate duty imposed on a soldier by his oath of loyalty. Surrendering the flag was tantamount to losing one's honor and brought shame upon the entire regiment. When a unit lost its standard, it lost its soul. On the other hand, a soldier who captured an enemy standard had permission to use his heroic deed as proof of his martial prowess. It was drummed into the head of every member of the Hitler Youth during encampments and field exercises that the loss of even a pennant produced the worst possible stain on one's character. The only song included in the official publication *Pimpf im Dienst*—required reading for the German Jungvolk [the group between the ages of ten and fourteen in the Hitler Youth—Transl.]—was dedicated to the flag:

> Let the flags wave far and wide,
>   we're going over to the attack,
>   true to the mercenary way.
> Let those desperadoes
>   lead the charge,
>   we'll follow in close order formation.[20]

The flag as the imperative! Songs sung together under the flag heightened the sense of fellowship. Psychologists teach us how easy it is to fill an emotional vacuum by forming a powerful affective bond with a leadership figure or a fetish (flag). Refusing to identify with the Weimar republic as their country, many people felt a similar void within themselves—until Hitler offered them a new way of bonding—his way. After relinquishing his individuality, the Nazi Party member was vulnerable to every suggestion put forward by the person "who robbed him of his conscious personality" (Sigmund Freud).

The process of integrating an individual such as the young Quex into the Hitler movement (which shared every attribute of Le Bon's "psychological crowd") would eventually shape the feelings, outlook, and actions of all members of the Hitler Youth, the BDM (*Bund Deutscher Mädel* or League of German Girls), the SA, and the SS.

Professional soldiers and conscripts in the Bundeswehr today no longer swear an oath to an individual or an office. Rather, they render a pledge to the state and the people: "I swear to serve the Federal Republic of Germany loyally and to bravely defend the rights and freedoms of the German People, so help me God." Article 12 of the German Constitution (*Grundgesetz*) specifically includes protection of the flag as a fundamental obligation.

The oath sworn by soldiers of the former German Democratic Republic's *Nationale Volksarmee* was similar to that of the *Bundeswehr*: "I swear to serve the German Democratic Republic, my Fatherland, loyally at all times and at the command of the Workers' and

Peasants' Government to defend it against all enemies. Should I ever violate this my solemn pledge to the flag, may I suffer the harsh punishment provided by the laws of our Republic and be spurned by the working class."[21]

The Swastika Flag

The entry of the flags and standards. Down below, starting at the far end of the Sportpalast, the standards representing Berlin, followed by hundreds of Party flags from Berlin, are moving forward. Little by little the flags are coming up out of the basement vault of the Sportpalast. To the sound of "Deutschland, Deutschland über alles" the flags are borne through the immense hall. The flags are coming closer and closer, the lead flag has just reached the gallery. At the back of the gigantic hall a section has been left unoccupied for the march-past of the flags. The four standards are just beginning to move up to the podium. The flags are moving to the rear, the end section of the hall. Flag after flag keeps coming up out of the basement vault. Every side corridor is packed with bright red swastika flags. The audience throughout the entire Sportpalast has stood up and, with arm raised in the Hitler salute, has joined in the singing of the national anthem.

Joseph Goebbels[22]

The swastika that adorned the flags of the "master race" and would ultimately terrorize the world is a symbol enveloped in mystery. Its earliest recorded use dates back to the Indus civilization around 2500 B.C. Apparently persuaded by what he considered to be the symbolic power of the swastika, the Hindu monk Agehananda Bharatis openly expressed his admiration for Hitler in a "forum" held at the 1986 Frankfurt Book Fair, which had chosen India as its theme that year. Not thinking of the inhumanity that the concept of the master race symbolized to nations forced to live under colonial rule, he claimed that the mass of India's people held views that were very different from those shared by the westernized Indian elite. Hitler, he said, was an "avatar," a deity that had descended to the earth in incarnate form. The swastika, the Indian symbol of salvation, steeped in tradition, had sanctified his mythic mission.[23]

The word swastika is derived from the Sanskrit *svastika*, meaning "salutary sign." *Wan*, the Chinese character for swastika, means "great good luck"; in Greece it was called *hemera* and was the symbol of the sun.

The swastika has taken on a number of meanings over time: Thor's hammer, a sun wheel, a wolf trap, a mill wheel. It has been depicted as crossed lightning bolts, the four "Fs" of Turnvater [father of gymnastics] Jahn (frisch = lively, fromm = devout, fröhlich = cheerful, frei = free), and as a fertility sign. In the twentieth century Kerensky's provisional government in Russia used the swastika on its bank notes as a symbol of independence.

Wilhelm Reich in his *Die Massenpsychologie des Faschismus* (Mass Psychology of Fascism, 1971) added yet another facet to the symbolism of the swastika: the swastika as a copulating couple. In his interpretation of the swastika as a sexual symbol, Reich relied on the representation of a swastika discovered by Bilman and Pegerot dating back to Indo-Germanic times and containing the following inscription: "Hail earth, mother of man. Grow great in the embrace of God, fruitful to nourish mankind." Fertility was represented as the sexual act of Mother-Earth and God-Father. Interviews with people of various backgrounds and of either sex showed "that very few people fail to recognize the meaning of the swastika." Wilhelm Reich concluded that "this symbol depicting two interlocked persons acts as a powerful stimulus on deep layers of the organism, a stimulus that proves to be that much more powerful, the more dissatisfied, the more burning with sexual desire, a person is."[24]

In the context of propaganda, in which the Nazi Party informed the swastika with the symbolism of honor and loyalty, the symbol was also used to make allowances for "the defensive strivings of the moralistic ego," making it correspondingly easier for people to accept. Reich did not, however, feel that this aspect of the swastika's effect on unconscious emotionality accounted for the success of Hitler's mass propaganda; it was "merely" a "powerful aid."

The *völkisch* chauvinist Guido von List in his book *Die Bilderschrift der Ario-Germanen* (The Characters of the Aryo-Germans, 1910)[25] was one of the first to endow the swastika with an ideology and prepare the way for its eventual appropriation by racist ideologues. Various anti-Semitic organizations and Free Corps units soon used the swastika on their battle standards. The swastika became a symbol of reactionary opinion and a sign of race identity directed against Jews and Gypsies, Marxists and intellectuals, the mentally ill and pacifists—against all the outsiders whom Marcel Proust had labeled "la race maudite."

In the cinematic portrait of a city titled *Eger—eine alte deutsche Stadt* (Eger—an Ancient German City, 1938), directed by Rudolf Gutscher, the camera focuses in on swastika motifs in a church dating back to the year 1310 as proof of the claim that Eger [the present-day city of Cheb in the Czech Republic—Transl.] had always been a German city and that the time was long overdue for its return to the Reich.

In his thoughts on "our flag—our program" in his book *Mein Kampf*,[26] Hitler wrote in 1925 that he saw in red the social idea of the movement and in the white disk the national component. In the black swastika he saw "the mission of the struggle for the victory of the Aryan man, and, by the same token, the victory of the idea of creative work, which as such always has been and always will be anti-Semitic." Hitler himself designed the future national flag as far back as 1919. Two years later he also designed the Party standard. As a "special symbol of victory" he included it "among the symbols and battle signs of the National Socialist struggle."

The Nazis appropriated the black, white, and red colors from the former Imperial flag in order to establish a link with Germany's great past and, especially in the early years of the Nazi movement, to win over nationalist groups who considered the Black-Red-Gold nothing but a thorn in their side. Manfred von Killinger stressed this idea of continuity in *Männer und Mächte: Die SA in Wort und Bild* (Men and Powers: the SA in Word and Picture, 1933): "The swastika flag and the war flag were created as a result of [the decision] to continue the use of black and red, which is doubtless the most beautiful color combination ever created."[27]

Hitler's new symbol of the Nazi movement was not to escape the shadows of the past. Although the black, white, and red flag under which he had fought in the war—"these uniquely beautiful colors, in their fresh, youthful combination"—was "sacred and beloved" to him, he was nevertheless adamantly opposed to letting it stand "as a symbol for the struggle for the future." But so long as the venerable old Reich President Paul von Hindenburg continued as the living legend personifying the Battle of Tannenberg, the new regime delayed adoption of the swastika banner as the country's national flag. Thus, on 10 March 1933, the Day of National Mourning, government offices flew only flags with the black, white, and red colors of Prussia.

Just two days later, however, Hindenburg relented and issued a decree on the flag ordering that "until a final settlement is reached regarding the national colors" the black-white-red flag and the swastika flag were to be flown side by side. The decree stated that the traditional symbol represented "the glorious past of the German Reich," while the new flag stood for "the mighty rebirth of the German nation": "Together they embody the *power of the state* and the inner bonds [linking] all the national forces of the *German people.*"[28]

Once before, after having succeeded Friedrich Ebert to the presidency, Hindenburg had taken a similar decision in similar sibylline fashion: at the height of the debate over Black-Red-Gold versus Black-White-Red, he enacted a law ordering that the black, white, and red merchant flag be flown next to the "still valid national colors."

The haste with which the Reichstag passed a new flag law on 16 September 1935, just one year after Hindenburg's death, suggests the importance the Nazi regime attached to mobilizing public opinion under the symbol of the new movement. Reichstag president Hermann Göring desired "a true symbol of the race." In his address to the Reichstag he supported the law in the following grandiose terms:

> Like a magnet, National Socialism attracted to itself whatever resources of iron and steel the German people had within themselves. Similarly, it was our battle standard under which these fighters were assembled, under which they struggled, fought, and, in many cases, died. We must not forget that at decisive moments it was this battle standard that time and again made the weak strong. We must not forget that so long as our Führer held our battle standard—the swastika [flag] with its glorious ancient colors—in his grip, he also held the destiny of the German people in his hands. The swastika has become a sacred symbol for us—the symbol around which all our hopes and dreams revolve, under which we have endured suffering, under which we have fought, sacrificed, and ultimately, for the benefit of the German people, triumphed.

The day before, on 15 September 1935, Hitler issued an order making the swastika flag Germany's official national flag. When he presented the armed forces with their new battle standard, the war ensign, he did not neglect to use the Iron Cross insignia on the swastika flag as an occasion to hark back to the traditions of the World War I Imperial Army:

> May the Swastika be a symbol for you of the unity and purity of the nation, a symbol of the National Socialist world-view (*Weltanschauung*), a token of the freedom and strength of the Reich. I want the

Iron Cross to stand as a reminder to you of the matchless tradition
of the former Imperial Army, of the virtues it embodied, of the
example it set for you. You are under an obligation to the black-
white-red colors of the Reich to perform your duty loyally while
you live and while you die.

Until the beginning of the war in 1939, the old war ensign of the
Bismarck era was officially permitted to be flown once a year on
the anniversary of the 1916 Battle of Jutland, since it had report-
edly stood up so magnificently in this naval battle against the
British. Though there was no victor in this senseless and destructive encounter between the British and German fleets, many
sailors were killed in action. A painting of a sinking cruiser, titled
"Skagerrak," was the focal point of the 1937 Berlin Art Exhibition.
It showed a sailor proudly holding up the flag: "The flag means
more than death"—the Nazis wanted all Germans to inscribe this
slogan on their hearts.

The swastika that Hitler called "a token of freedom" would
soon become a symbol of slavery for all Europe. The flag was
omnipresent in the Third Reich—on the streets, flying from
houses, in documentaries and newsreels. The flag had, as it were,
gotten into the blood of the Germans.

The swastika flag was meant to communicate all the virtues
and symbolic values of the Nazi movement. The blood-red flag
with the mystical swastika emblazoned on a pure white circle was
like no other with regard to its manifold symbolic meanings. It
represented all the amorphous ideas and second-rate virtues in
the Nazi catechism: the Führer, the national community (*Volksgemeinschaft*), the fatherland, the nation; fealty, obedience, a readiness to make sacrifices; race, faith, hope, victory.

The flag was also a sign of the Nazi ideology's irreconcilable
hatreds: anti-Semitism, anti-communism, anti-clericalism, and
later, as the regime prepared for war, its anti-plutocratic campaign. The swastika flag reflected many of the irrational beliefs
that were foisted on millions of Germans through the multiplier-
effect of the weekly newsreels and Party congress films.

Leni Riefenstahl used the flag as an emotional and sentimental
prop with which to orchestrate a dizzying symphony of flags
which disseminated the Nazi world-view in staged aesthetic
events that indicated the "correct" way to regard art. In films such
as *Sieg des Glaubens* (Victory of Faith, 1933) and *Triumph des Willens*
(Triumph of the Will, 1934), she transformed the flag into a fetish.
Riefenstahl liked to show the flag blowing in the wind, as a sign of

movement: the optical opium of the people, forests of flags as a psychological field of force.

The fluttering flag had, of course, already been employed earlier as a symbol of change and freedom, of the resolve to achieve victory. The Nazis exploited it for their own purposes:

> We are the army of the Swastika,
> Raise the red banners high,
> For the German worker
> The way to freedom we shall pave.

The Nazis made skillful use of the emotional content of left-wing revolutionary songs to create their own melodies for the march "into eternity"—with different lyrics, of course.

Roland Barthes in his book *Mythologies* presented the following graphic example of the symbolic significance of the national flag as an illustration of his theory of semiology: "I am at the barber's, and a copy of *Paris-Match* is handed to me. On the cover, a young Black in a French uniform is saluting, with his eyes uplifted, probably fixed on a fold of the tricolor. All of this is the meaning of the picture. But whether naively or not, I see very well what it signifies to me: that France is a great Empire, that all her sons, without regard to color, faithfully serve under her flag, and that there is no better answer to the opponents of an alleged colonialism than the zeal shown by this Black in serving his so-called oppressors."[29]

The Black African's identification with the tricolor in this visual portrayal was meant to suggest an identification, obvious even to the simplest mind, with the ideology it symbolized. Nazi myth-making worked in a similar fashion—albeit with one fundamental difference. Whereas the tricolor is apparently an unknown nationalist quantity to the African, a sacred myth lacking "flesh and blood," to the average Nazi Party member the swastika flag was equated directly with the Führer who was, as it were, present in every fold. The myth of the nation was not an abstraction; it was palpably present in words and in pictures. It was not beyond the masses' comprehension. The flag was Hitler's ubiquitous deputy. Identifying with the flag was synonymous to identifying with the Führer. Nazi propaganda was largely effective because it succeeded in identifying the masses with the Hitler myth. And it was to Leni Riefenstahl that Nazi propaganda owed a debt of gratitude for developing a workable aesthetic formula to elevate the mundane into an apotheosis of the nation.

During the march-past of the flags, anyone attending a rally had to rise from his seat and salute, since flags were viewed as proxies for the Führer. Even when a squad of troopers marched down the street carrying a single flag, passers-by were obliged to honor it by giving the Nazi salute. "The flag arrives: take off your hat! We will be true till death to that!" was a verse in a ballad sung long before by Detlev von Liliencron. At the beginning and end of school holidays, students and teachers had to stand in line for inspection in the schoolyard as the flag was being raised and the Horst Wessel song sung. Starting at an early age, young people were forced to internalize the values represented by the flag:

> At the beginning of school following the end of vacation and at the end of the term before the beginning of the school holiday, the flag must be honored in front of the entire student body, by in the first case raising and in the second lowering the Reich flags while one one verse from "Deutschland, Deutschland über alles" and one from the Horst Wessel song are sung.[30]

The ritual presentation of the ideas associated with the swastika flag was designed to promote "the training of youth for service to the nation and state in the spirit of National Socialism." The flag deprived people of their individuality and made them into the object of another's will. Before the introduction of the Youth Service Ordinance, schools with a 90 percent membership rate in the *Jungvolk*, the Hitler Youth or the corresponding girls' organizations, received a Hitler Youth flag.[31]

The Blood Flag

> *When it comes to marching many do not know*
> *That their enemy is marching at the head.*
> *The voice that gives them their orders*
> *Is their enemy's voice and*
> *The man who speaks of the enemy*
> *Is the enemy himself.*
>
> Bertolt Brecht (German War Primer 1936–1938)[32]

The association of the flag with blood can create a powerful symbol. Ernest, Duke of Bavaria in Friedrich Hebbel's play *Agnes Bernauer* creates just such a symbol when, in a thundering monologue, he invokes not the flag of peace, but the banner of war:

"Look at this banner ... It is woven from the same thread as made the doublet of the last rider who follows it; and one day it will fall apart and turn to dust before the wind in the same fashion! But the German folk has triumphed under it in a thousand battles, and therefore only a cur can pluck it to pieces, only a fool try to patch it, instead of shedding his blood for it and keeping every shred of it holy!"[33]

The Nazis borrowed the idea of the blood flag from the historical past. The concept dated back to the days of the Hohenstaufen dynasty. According to the account in the Song of the Nibelungs, the Burgundians set out from the Rhine along ancient military roads and marched south by way of the Danube under a "blood banner."[34] As the flag of the "holy empire," they bore it in the van of the pennants carried by individual knights. The "fiery banner" made of red silk was a shared symbol valid for all.[35]

What was generally referred to as a blood banner was the (usually) unembellished red flag that until 1806 symbolized the seal on an enfeoffment of imperial land that was tied to a grant of the right to exercise "high justice" [called *Blutbann* or "blood justice" in German, i.e., criminal justice involving capital punishment or mutilation—Transl.]. The blood flag was thus an important symbol in public law. Having been granted the right to exercise high justice, the recipient of a fief was pledged under ancient Germanic law to render unswerving fealty to the lord from whom "justice" was held and to perform unlimited military service on his behalf. Originally, kings alone had the privilege of granting justice. It was not until the expansion of the territorial supremacy of the state in the thirteenth century that this right was also granted to princes and dukes directly subject to the emperor (*reichsunmittelbar*) in their capacity as lords holding lordship over the land, who passed sentence of death in the name of the king.[36]

The right to exercise high justice was later granted as a benefice to the large, free imperial cities as well, at the same time as it was an expression of the juridical authority reserved exclusively for feudal lords. Since the High Middle Ages, the secular "advocates" (*Vögte*), or protectors of churches and monasteries, also functioned as feudal lords, since ecclesiastics with fiefs were precluded from performing secular judicial duties that involved killing or the death sentence ("*ecclesia non sitit sanguinem*").

The Nazis invested the concept of the "blood flag" with a decidedly emotional coloration. "Blood flag" was their name for the swastika flag that had allegedly been drenched with the blood of Andreas Bauriedl who had carried it on 9 November 1923 during the legendary march to the *Feldherrnhalle*, at the time of the Hitler Putsch. At the second Nazi Party congress in Weimar on 4 July 1926, Hitler "bestowed" the flag of this "blood witness" on the then Reichsführer of the SS, Berchtold.

Henceforth, the new standards and flags of the NSDAP and its associated organizations would be consecrated by being ceremoniously touched with the blood flag—always in the presence of a sworn witness to the Hitler Putsch. The *Feldherrnhalle* was turned into an altar to the fallen of the movement, where their names were immortalized:

> We are building the eternal *Feldherrnhallen* of the Reich,
> The steps leading into eternity,
> Until the hammers drop from our hands,
> Then wall us into the breast of these altars.[37]

The Führer's Personal Standard

The art of propaganda lies in understanding the emotional ideas of the great masses and finding, through a psychologically correct form, the way to the attention and thence to the heart of the broad masses.

Adolf Hitler[38]

The "Führer's personal standard" derived from the national service flag and was used for government offices. It was a square containing a large swastika of the cotised and upright variety within a golden wreath and displaying golden eagles in the cantons: two Party badges, a spread eagle in the Art Deco style with heads pointing to the sinister and grasping a wreath containing a swastika and two Army badges, more Roman-style eagles with heads pointing to the dexter and no wreaths. It did not wave or flutter, since it was made of stiffened linen and was similar to a panel painting or, more properly, an icon. The standard was an adaptation of the Roman vexilla. "*Vexilla regis prodeunt*" means literally, "The king's banners go in front," i.e., show the way. Since the second half of the first millennium, this phrase has been the title of a hymn to the Holy Cross written by the most famous Latin poet in Merovingian Gaul, Venantius Fortunatus. Until 1955, it was regularly sung in Good Friday processions; it lives on universally in the recitation of the Divine Office.

The personal standard was a sign of the Führer's *physical* presence. Ordinary flags sufficed to demonstrate his merely metaphorical *omnipresence*; they carried the semantic image of the Führer—to the point of fiction. "This fiction exists in actuality only because it has been invested with a symbolic presence in the form of the Swastika and because the symbol is revered as the sign of a higher purpose. In this way the actual power of government has been duplicated—in the person of the 'Führer' standing at its head and in a notional leader who fits in neatly with Hitler's political decisions and the coercive measures at his disposal to enforce them."[39]

Just in time for the campaign in Russia, the Munich-based Franz Eher Verlag published a book titled *Die Fahne ist mehr als der Tod* (The Flag Means More Than Death, 1940), and subtitled *Das deutsche Fahnenbuch* (The German Flag Book). The first of the eleven vignettes dealing with the flag was devoted to Frederick the Great —"A King Bears the Flag":

> [Against all odds] a man stays [at his post] on the front line. He's a member of the Prince Henry Regiment and is clutching the regimental colors. His eyes seek out the king and speak without talking: I've held on to the flag you entrusted me with, but I'm at the end of my tether. Frederick bends low over him. Gently but firmly he wrests the banner from the man's grip. The standard bearer looks into the face of the king, then collapses without making a sound. The king sits up straight in his saddle, swings the flag up over his head, and calls out amidst the tumult of battle and the shouts of pain: "To the flag and for the flag! Those of you who are brave soldiers, follow me!" The soldiers' eyes are riveted on the king, the regal standard bearer.

And as the battle is in the process of being lost—despite the presence of the regal standard bearer—the king, high atop Mühl Mountain

> casts one more long glance across the vast field already wrapped in the veil of dusk. He mounts his horse. Beaten but unbowed, he turns to his hussars and speaks: "Messieurs, we've held on to the flag. Brave is he who stands the test, and victory goes only to the brave. There it is: With the flag and for the flag."[40]

Predictably, the last contribution is titled: "A Nation Bears the Flag." Here the analogy to Hitler and the reversals of fortune in war is forced upon the reader while at the same time communicating the one certainty that had been drummed into every schoolboy's head: from every defeat Frederick ultimately emerged the victor. The flag was used as a metaphorical instrument to generate confidence of victory.

"The Flag Means More than Death"

Death is always bitter and one only accepts it courageously and without protest when one goes to die for a purpose that is worth giving one's life for.

Joseph Goebbels

Quex the Hitler Youth, Hans Westmar, and Erich Lohner the Hitler Youth in *SA-Mann Brand* are the first deaths portrayed in Nazi films after Hitler assumed power (in the films they were killed before 1933) that were used to justify the myth of dying for Führer and flag. "It is the first death," wrote Elias Canetti, "which infects everyone with the feeling of being threatened. It is impossible to overrate the part played by the first dead man in the kindling of wars. Rulers who want to unleash war know very well that they must procure or invent a first victim.... Nothing matters except his death; and it must be believed that the enemy is responsible for this. Every possible cause of his death is suppressed except one: his membership of the group to which one belongs oneself ... everyone else who feels the same threat attaches himself to the group. Its spirit changes into that of a war pack."[41]

The ritual that the Nazis practiced with the movement's dead was closely tied to the ritual of the flag. Hitler's annual consecration of the flag was the high point of every Party Day. The ceremony, which Leni Riefenstahl extolled in her films *Sieg des Glaubens* and *Triumph des Willens*, was always accompanied by the singing of the Horst Wessel song:

> Hold high the banner! Close the ranks hard serried!
> The Storm Troops march with calm and steady pace.
> Comrades killed by Red Front and Reaction are buried,
> But in spirit keep their place.

In his biography of Hitler, Joachim C. Fest emphasizes Hitler's "talents as stage manager," which reached their climax when the movement's celebrations of death created a mood of hypnotic fascination among the masses: "His pessimistic temperament tirelessly [derived] new lighting effects from the ceremony of death, and the real high points of the artistic demagoguery that he was the first to develop in a systematic fashion came as he strode down a broad avenue between hundreds of thousands to honor the dead on the Königsplatz in Munich or the grounds of the Nuremberg Party congress. In scenes such as these out of a Good Friday celebration—scenes, as was said of Richard Wagner's music, in which magnificence was used to sell death—Hitler's idea of aesthetic politics matches the concept."[42]

Beyond the grave, the fallen continued to live in the community, which availed itself of any opportunity solemnly to invoke their martyrdom. The three martyrs who comprised the 1933 Nazi triumvirate of death were all young heroes, the myths surrounding them well suited to the production of uniquely captivating propaganda. Unvanquished until death, they were transfigured into supernatural beings and lived on in the medium of film: "Only those pure souls enter Hitler's heaven that are, so to speak, *too* pure to remain on this earth for long,"[43] wrote Saul Friedländer. Thus, he said, the young doomed hero was surrounded by a nimbus of complex emotions: "He is the bearer of either one of two banners, one proclaiming an implicit religious tradition, the other that of a cult of primitive and archaic values," and he fights for all the values that his flag symbolizes.

In Hitler's war films the flag served as a symbolic relief from the landscape of war and, more rarely, as a shroud. Contemporaries folded this paradox into the seemingly cynical observation that "after a few marvelous words by Baldur von Schirach [head of the Nazi youth movement—Transl.], nothing seems more alive in Germany than death."[44] The heroic German soul would celebrate its apocalyptic triumph in Stalingrad.

> ... One for all and all for one:
> Bondage has an end!
> Let wave, let wave, whatever can,
> Standard and banner wave!
> Here will we purpose, man for man,
> To grace a hero's grave.
> Advance, ye brave ranks, hardily—
> Your banners wave on high;
> We'll gain freedom's victory,
> Or freedom's death we'll die!
>
> Ernst Moritz Arndt, 1813

The pre-Nazi U-boat film *Morgenrot* (*Dawn*, 1932/33), which was directed by Gustav Ucicky and premiered just after the Nazis came to power, was dedicated to the six thousand sailors who went down to the bottom in their 199 steel coffins: "We Germans don't know much about living, but in death, yes in death, we're fantastic," the U-boat commander said in glowing heroic terms. *Illustrierter Film-Kurier* ended its review of *Morgenrot* in the following inflated terms: "Liers, the major's elderly wife, embraces her last son knowing he will go to sea again and knowing too that he cannot help being the person he is. Losses have to be borne and—even fifty years of night can't blind a German!—again they are off to fight England, the naval ensign fluttering proudly in the sea breeze, for Germany must live. Even if we must die!"[45]

And on 19 May 1933, Goebbels had this to say: "In those days I also tried to clarify the concept of the general line (*Tendenz*), raising objections to the idea that right thinking alone rather than ability should be the decisive factor. We all understood that the word 'art' (Kunst) comes from the word 'can' (können), that not everyone can do what he wants to do. The general line must be viewed in this context insofar as it is not directly related to presenting the events of the day, that is, as I have said elsewhere, we don't want to see our Storm Troopers marching across the screen or the stage. Their job is to march in the streets. This is but one means of giving expression to political life, and this form of expression will be used when it is artistically imperative to do so or, alternatively, when one cannot think of anything better. For as everyone knows, this is the easy way out. Lacking greater skill, people feel obliged to use National Socialist symbols to demonstrate the strength of their convictions."

The Red Flag and the Labor Movement— Excursus on the Indispensability of Symbols

> *Lift our flags into the wind;*
> *Bright as the blazing sun*
> *They bear witness to our faith in*
> *THE GOODNESS OF MANKIND!*

Song of the Young Socialist Workers in the early 1920s

"We filmed a demonstration. The color red came out black in the film. It would have been better to use green flags to get the right shade for red. Our demonstrators—real proletarians from Wedding [a working class district in Berlin—Transl.]—refused to march under green flags. So we had to come up with a different solution."[46]

This story, related by cameraman turned director Piel Jutzi, took place during the filming of one of the most important motion pictures to be set in a working class milieu, *Mutter Krausens Fahrt ins Glück* (Mother Krause's Journey to Happiness, 1929) in which Jutzi used extracts from his documentary *100,000 unter roten Fahnen* (100,000 under Red Flags, 1929). The demonstration he referred to is one of the most impressive scenes in the film. It is not difficult to find additional examples of the (red) flag in leftist films. In *Brüder* (*Brothers*), a Social Democratic film that deals with a strike by Hamburg dockworkers, the flag forms part of the final apotheosis, appearing to the incarcerated workers through prison walls. Art and kitsch, simple straightforward symbolism and phony emotionalism, were not far removed from each other in scenes such as these.

To be sure, it is as wrong here as it is in other instances to speak in pejorative terms about the superficial parallels between Nazi symbols and those used by the labor movement. Even when we quantify the use of identical symbols or compare the results with parallels in other areas, we still find that the most important sources of the symbols used by the Nazis were military and nationalist conservative groups. Of course, the Nazis also intentionally borrowed symbolic and iconographic objects used by the labor movement—which art historians have shown us even included those representing labor itself and "Labor Day"—just as they did in their numerous *contrafacta*, in which they retained the melody of labor songs but replaced the text with completely new words. The reason for this was not simply that these things were relatively public, susceptible to corruption or reinterpretation (which prompted Hanns Eisler's fruitful but by no means convincing attempts to invent an incorruptible musical language). There was another equally important reason. In order to be politically successful and maintain the goodwill of their financial backers in big business, the Nazis had to neutralize the political power of important segments of the working class or win them over to their side. It was not enough to terrorize the labor movement or, after 1933, to crush it. Rather, they mobilized their entire ideological apparatus—from the demagogic linkage of crucial concepts, as, for example, in "National *Socialist* German *Workers'* Party," to the exploitation of signs and symbols, including the flag.

Flags clearly played a significant role in the history of the labor movement. But how did a piece of colored cloth acquire such

importance? Scholarly research evaded this question for quite
some time after 1945. The German public also dissociated itself
from the issue by choosing, as it were, to repress it. The result, as
so often in the past, was that they drew upon conservative myths
or mystical and irrational explanations. Today, however, there are
signs of an attempt to arrive at an understanding of the issue that
goes beyond mere ideological criticism.

Historical symbol research and social historical analyses of
symbols can bring us closer to an understanding of that need for
symbols which Robert Michels long ago perceived in the labor
movement.[47] Because of their "sensory expressivity and emotive
quality," hardly anyone can deny the "significance and influence
of symbolic forms of communication" or the constant reemer-
gence of the archetypal symbolic imagery to which Ernst Bloch
drew our attention when he used the example of the dance around
the liberty tree on the ruins of the Bastille.

Today it is chiefly advertising and the omnipresence of its
essentially frivolous but highly developed imagery that are con-
tinual reminders of the effect of iconographic symbolism.
Strangely, postmodern trendsetters incorporate these empty man-
nerist symbols into their Rococo-like culture.

There is in all human beings a considerable "number of affective factors that go to make up experience." In the history of the
labor movement, as in every other area of political life, "signs,
symbols, and rituals play an important part in structuring political experience, especially in establishing collective identities."

We must, of course, deal with these things, but we need have
no fear of abandoning reason in the process. In fact, there is
greater peril if we close our eyes to these phenomena. "To refer to
the communicative competence of symbolic imagery in the labor
movement is not to argue for a 'paradigm shift.'" It is simply an
indication of a way to broaden our perspective. In the past, greater
importance was attached to the subtle meanings in the written
and spoken language used in the labor movement. Now it would
seem appropriate to give increased attention to sensory and symbolic forms of orientation.

One of the most important symbols in the labor movement is the
red flag which appeared on everything from the logo of the KPD
(Communist Party of Germany) newspaper during the Weimar
republic to the banners carried in the strikes of the 1970s. The history of the red flag is closely tied to the social history of the past
two hundred years, and it is also important as an example of the

supreme confidence with which workers have dealt with the legacy of the national culture and the culture of the ruling class.

Viewed from the perspective of political revolution, the early history of the red flag provides sporadic examples of its appearance during peasant uprisings. The red flag led the way to victory for the bourgeoisie during the French Revolution of 1789. And the Social Democrat Friedrich Wendel[48] attempted to trace the red flag directly back to Germanic and early medieval symbols of communal ownership. At the court of Charlemagne the flag was considered "the sacred symbol of suzerainty" and henceforth became a symbol which the emperor used when he granted the right to exercise "high justice" and pronounce sentence of death (*Blutbann*). According to Wendel's interpretation (more programmatic than analytical), it represented the "affirmation of a social order that was founded on a free people free to work in its own behalf."

So far as we are concerned, all this can remain in the murky past. In 1848 the red flag became an identification sign and a symbol that provoked protest in both France and Germany at the same time. Henceforth, it became the symbol of the "Red Republic," of the socialist and communist movement. Prior to that time, around 1830, it had appeared only sporadically—perhaps more by chance—during a riot of textile workers in Aachen and the revolt of the Silesian weavers in 1844. In the summer of 1848 workers brought out the red flag during demonstrations, on barricades, at political parades, etc., to set it apart from and compete with the Black-Red-Gold of the bourgeois revolutionaries: "Red is now the color of the revolutionary workers' groups." Conditions in France followed a similar pattern after the June Revolution of 1848.

Often—for example, in May 1849 in Wuppertal—the red flag appeared *beside* the black-red-gold tricolor as a sign of the continuing rivalry between workers and the bourgeoisie. According to an anecdote, Friedrich Engels was supposed to have been responsible for making sure at night that there were enough red flags in Wuppertal for maximum visual effect the next day. Consequently, the red flag became a symbol in the chaotic year 1848 that both accompanied protesters and set them apart—over and above any possible inherent properties of the color:

> Thus red acquires historical significance only as a result of political conflict, of its establishment as the symbolic color of the socialist

and communist workers' political movement. Its symbolic meaning does not derive from an emotional association with aggression that, like a genetic trait, is inherent in the color itself, as suggested by the symbol theory of Otto Koenig. Rather, the "aggressive element" in the color red (as in the expressive properties of any color) is the result of its historical and cultural development.[49]

Confidence in dealing with the outward forms of culture gives rise over time to new symbols that suit the needs of the movements that use them:

> The formulation of a proletarian response to prevailing public opinion called for different forms of sensory orientation and communication from those used at political gatherings or discussions in workers' clubs. The red flag was of great importance in the process of developing a public identity. It gave coherence to political demonstrations and laid out limits with regard to other goals and strategies. To quote Georg Simmel, it acted as both a "cause and effect of cohesion."[50]

The flag continued to be a vehicle for nonverbal communication during periods when the labor movement was banned, at funerals, and on other occasions. After 1878 the practice of planting flags in the highest possible and most inaccessible locations was one of the most popular rituals in the proscribed labor movement. During the Nazi era such exercises were also a frequent occurrence. They were always accompanied by a feeling of pride that only workers were capable of mustering the strength, dexterity, and imagination to perform such feats. The same was true of the "*tableaux vivants*" whose techniques were especially in keeping with the "*condition ouvrière*."

The kind of symbolic communication that is a *sine qua non* for all social processes and movements involving large numbers of people developed in a three-step process—"accept, select, modify." Even the Lasalle cult fulfilled an "integrative political function" in holding the socialist movement together—and, of course, in serving as a "transitional ideology" that led to more mature political institutions.

Initially, symbols are neutral—it is only the part they play in history and ideology that changes them into signs of liberation or of totalitarianism. Democratic states also have their symbols. What was significant and historically catastrophic about the Nazis' debasement of flag symbolism was that it responded to latent revanchist and totalitarian fantasies and needs. In this regard, flag symbolism cannot be viewed in isolation; it must be understood within the context of fascist propaganda.

The aesthetic of the Nazi movement that encompassed all spheres of public communication and culminated in the films of Leni Riefenstahl had a *single* objective and a *single* method: the integration and total absorption of the individual into a mighty collective. This aesthetic depicted the collective, the crowd, in ever new and rigorous forms of art, shifting and channeling it into a movement that was to lead the way out of the narrow confines of bourgeois life toward noble and all-embracing goals aimed at achieving a glorious future. It thus channeled the dreams of power and revenge harbored by the humiliated German soldiers who returned from the First World War, realizing that they had been cheated out of their youth, their health, and their lives. They acquired a sense of security in a movement in which they felt themselves to be part of a rising tide that gave new meaning, new direction, new incentives to men who were living in the past, fixated on their wartime experiences. The aesthetic of fascism—with its channeling of the masses, its apotheoses of men and flags marching upward toward the light—was not merely a medium, a "package" for fascist ideas and the fascist message. Rather, the medium was the message. It completely subordinated the individual to the collective and gave the moviegoer, the radio listener, the reader, and the participant in Nazi mass rallies a sense of power, of being one with the collective. In this state of intoxication, the meaning or content of ideas was no longer important. Meaning was submerged in a state of total self-abnegation. Biographical descriptions of the Nazi leadership show that the strategists behind the stage-managing of the masses were themselves unable to remain emotionally detached from the aesthetic. They were part of it, addicted to the masses, just as they would later be increasingly addicted to other drugs.

It is precisely the surrender of one's individuality that distinguishes the fascist aesthetic from the contemporaneous socialist aesthetic. For example, if we compare crowd scenes in Bertolt Brecht's and Slatan Dudow's *Kuhle Wampe* (1933) with Nazi propaganda films, we are struck by the contrast between the streamlined choreography of Leni Riefenstahl's Party congress films and the movements of workers in *Kuhle Wampe*. In the Brecht/Dudow film, the workers almost never move in unison. Instead, they proceed in a disorderly and confused manner with some individuals staying behind, some standing still, and others moving against the crowd. The most famous and impressive example of the contrast between the totalitarian and the subversive proletarian aesthetic is the Odessa Steps sequence in Sergei M. Eisenstein's *Battleship Potemkin* (1925) with its rhythmic montage and richly developed choreographic details, where the Tsar's soldiers walk down the staircase in lockstep and begin firing at the crowd of demonstrators. Anybody standing in the way of their massed momentum, even a mother holding a child in her arms, is shot down mercilessly.

The influence of symbolic and emotive imagery (which is presumably always available for the taking) during a particular historical period is variable. Because of the Germans' experience with fascism, it is not surprising that they have tended to belittle or dismiss this kind of imagery throughout the entire postwar period down to the present day. However, when we realize that the Nazis did not reinvent these symbols but simply exploited them for their own purposes, albeit with the utmost cunning and ruthlessness, we may perhaps arrive at a more impartial approach to flag symbolism and become sensitive to the rapid change in flags. In September 1850 authorities prohibited the flying of the German colors from the tower of St. Paul's Church in Frankfurt am Main. The poet Franz Hoffmann considered this action such an affront that he was moved to write the following poem (later set to music by the Dessau choirmaster and organist Seelmann) with its surprise twist at the end:

> Tattered and torn
> By storm and snow and rain,
> Thus the German flag
> Flutters sadly in front of us;
> Even the staff is split,
> So that the pieces of cloth
> Are barely held together.
>
> Tattered and torn—
> And the staff is still there
> To put a piece of iron on.
> The flag—so pathetically
> Blown to shreds,
> Yet—how quickly
> will another flag be woven!

Today we know: this too was but an episode.

As Hitler's flags inundated Germany on 30 January 1933 in a torrent of red, the Nazi bard Leopold von Schenckendorf wrote the following piece of doggerel:

> Germany must truly understand:
> We intend to raise our banner
> Over German sea and German land.

Flag Miscellany

A march struck up, columns stretching to infinity,
A nation is marching toward its destiny.
Oh how the brilliant rays of suns never before seen
Beat down upon our flag! The mysterious force
Of a single will welding aspiration, suffering and action
Together to create a state.

Gerhard Schumann, 1955[51]

Even today flags are linked to the act of taking possession. We can find examples of this from around the world. I am thinking of the prize-winning World War II photograph of U.S. Marines taken against the light at the precise moment they planted the Stars and Stripes on Iwo Jima after their conquest of that Pacific island. Even a photograph showing a reenactment of the event that was taken several days later and is clearly a simulation is symbolically powerful.

I am also thinking of the space race between the two superpowers: the Apollo 11 crew planting the Stars and Stripes on the moon, and in December 1971 a Soviet space probe sending pictures from Mars to earth of red flags with the hammer and sickle—flags that carry the promise of the galactic expeditions' glorious achievements.

*

To my knowledge, the first film in which the motif of the flag was used dramaturgically as a political metaphor was Sergei M. Eisenstein's *Battleship Potemkin*. After their successful mutiny in the Black Sea, the sailors hoisted the banner of the new age—the red flag of the Soviets. Since color film did not exist at the time, Eisenstein used red paint to hand-color the celluloid frames in which the flag appeared. The revolution was given sensory and emblematic expressivity that went beyond the technical limitations of

black and white film and was imaged onto the viewer's retina
with incomparably greater effectiveness because *Rote Fahnen sieht
man besser* (Red Flags Are Easier To See)—the title of a 1970 documentary directed by Rolf Schübel and Theo Gallehr.

*

Flags also fulfilled a very important dramaturgical function in
Wolfgang Liebeneiner's film *Bismarck* (1940) where the transition
from one emperor to another was symbolized by the dipping and
raising of the flag.

   On 24 January 1934, the anniversary of the birthday of Frederick the Great and the death of the Nazi martyr Herbert Norkus, a
mass rally took place in front of the *Invalidendom* in Potsdam.
Three-hundred forty-two Hitler Youth colors were handed over to
Hitler Youth units.[52]

*

At the same time every year Nazi Party offices would be deluged
with suggestions for organizing the festivities connected with
Hitler's birthday. The recommendations regarding Hitler's fiftieth
birthday are typical. Given the atmosphere surrounding these celebrations, it is impossible to imagine them taking place in the
absence of the flag (following is an excerpt):

> *Speaker:* "Above us the flag and in front of us the Führer!"
> *Refrain:* "Line up your flags on the pole ..."
> *Speaker:* "There are thousands of you behind me,
>   and you are me, and I am you,
>   and we all believe in you, Germany.
>
>   I have never in my life had a thought
>   that has not resonated in your hearts ..."[53]

*

A 1936 anti-fascist sticker: "The times are great/but the portions
are small/what does it avail us that Hitler's banners flutter! /if
here and now millions under these banners/have no freedom and
even less bread and butter."[54]

*

Flyer

Take down the flag, the S.A.'s beer halls are no more,
the Storm Troops no longer march in lock-step pace;
comrades killed by Heini Himmler's black-clad corps
in spirit keep their place.

The trumpet blows its shrill and final blast,
prepared for war and battle they no longer stand;
soon other banners will wave unchecked at last.
Too long has slavery lasted in our land.

And when they've had their fill of strutting, lying,
and when their sacks are full of loot,
they'll do what other desperadoes did before them,
and head for the border, fleet of foot.
Yes, then you'll stand there, betrayed and sighing,
just trying to keep yourselves alive.[55]

*

In the Nevada desert GIs trained for the greatest threat imaginable to American freedom: the power of the Soviet Union. The gigantic "practice range," specially built to support ongoing maneuvers in the desert sands and simulate a real war, is appropriately named "Red Flag." For the Marines who train here the name is similar to a warning signal, triggering Pavlovian responses and creating a combat-ready attitude in every soldier. The enemy defense area is equipped with surface-to-air missiles, anti-aircraft defenses, radar, and electronic communication systems—whether Israeli war booty or old supplies to Egypt. The range creates "a perfectly realistic electronic environment which the American crews are trained to recognize and neutralize. The aerial force participating in such exercises includes an AWACS flying command post and an Aggressor Squadron made up of aircraft whose features are similar to those of the Mig-21 and Mig-23."[56]

*

The U.S. Army will place a soldier under arrest if he allows the sacred Stars and Stripes to touch the ground while it is being lowered and removed from the flag pole.

*

"Hito Hata—Raise the Banner" (1980) is Robert A. Nakamura's biographical semi-documentary about Oda Sok who emigrated to America when he was a child and now lives in the "Little Tokyo" section of Los Angeles. The climax of this touching film is Oda's desperate struggle to survive after he learns that his house is going to be torn down. The film's title refers to an old Japanese parable whose moral is: if you raise a banner, you will prevail. Oda raises the banner.

In Akira Kurosawa's movie *Ran* (1982–85), the Grand Lord Hidetora has just abdicated when Lady Kaede, the ambitious wife of his first son Taro, reminds her spouse of the king's standard—within the very first minute of his newly acquired power. Until that moment, the standard had been displayed on a wall in the royal castle, a decorative symbol of power. "Where is the standard? I do not care about the armor, but the standard!" Consequently, Taro and his retainers rush to reclaim the symbol from the old man. "The standard! ... Give it to us!" However, since the standard represents the last vestige of his faded glory, the Grand Lord refuses to surrender it and, standing at the top of the castle's staircase, he shoots an arrow into the chest of Taro's most zealous retainer, killing him.

The standard, the fetish of sovereignty and unconditional loyalty, would cost the lives of many thousands of Japanese in the wild melee that follows. The very spot where Lady Kaede noticed the absence of the standard would later be adorned with her noble blood, a crimson embellishment bearing witness to the sword stroke that kills her.

In this Kurosawa's last colossal epic, the wide screen is filled with myriad standards, banners, and pennants. From the first sequence to the last, they dominate the film. Soldiers (and extras) numbering in the thousands use red or yellow banners (and toward the end of the film black standards as well), depending on whose side they are on, to identify themselves in the total confusion of battle. The banners also serve as visual markers for the alternating sympathies of the moviegoers. In addition, the banners have symbolic significance. When they are in a vertical position they stand for confidence of victory, and when they are in a horizontal position they symbolize retreat. Red banners that have been dropped are the signs of the vanquished.

The main function of these fluttering pennants attached to long bamboo poles is dramaturgic and aesthetic. In contrast to the columns and forests of flags in Leni Riefenstahl's Party congress films and her film of the Olympic games, Kurosawa's flags rush past the camera, carried by soldiers on horseback as they gallop furiously across seemingly endless fields to attack or to flee for their lives. Kurosawa pushes to the limit the dynamic motif of standard-bearing formations, using overhead shots of riders arranged in parallel lines but moving at varying rates of speed to create an impression of movement within the flow of movement. The effect is heightened since most of these sequences are filmed against fixed vertical backgrounds such as forests, buildings, etc. Carefully calibrated countermovements and regular closeups of horses, flags, falling riders and the banners they carry with them to their death are edited into the flow of movement to increase the momentum. The naturalistic mix of colors produced by the rivers of blood and the host of brightly colored flags is attenuated by the rapid pace of the visuals, blurring what would otherwise be grisly scenes and transforming them into expressive effects—"It was a slaughter, not a battle." The aesthetic components of the film derive principally from the myriad colorful banners that have been woven into a kind of gigantic fluttering rag rug, a monumental period piece made accessible to the senses by the brilliant use of the camera.

*

Earlier in *Kagemusha: the Shadow Warrior* (1979) Kurosawa used flags as aesthetic props which seemed to spread like wildfire through the entire film. He also used the colors red and green in battle scenes to distinguish friend from foe. Every rider and every foot soldier carries a flag. In the Japan of the sixteenth century depicted here, soldiers employed them as lances. The modern filmmaker used them like a brush to add delicate strokes to his historical painting. Filmed in slow motion, the onrushing flags have an emotional impact as they are carried into battle or disappear in clouds of gun powder.

*

Flags are "in" again. Ever since the first closeup of the German presidential standard on the ZDF television channel on 23 May 1977, the national flag has been waving on Germany's TV screens at the end of each broadcast day, to the symphonic strains of the national anthem, as a good night wish from the broadcasters to us. Culture for the soul, or for something else?

*

In the meantime, flags have once again become the favored prop for our clubs and organizations. Why does the flag have to be there at all?

"Now we have a calling card—now we don't have to run around any more like a bunch of nobodies ..." Or: "A flag always shows you where to go, and that's particularly important for us who live in the country." Or "When you're talking about flags, you're talking about honor." These are just a few of the opinions voiced by people interviewed for the 1977 ZDF program titled "With Unswerving Loyalty—Clubs and Their Flags." In Wartenfels near Kulmbach, the mayor and the parish council, the board of the local athletic club, maids and maidens of honor all gathered in church for the consecration of the club's flag. As it had done in Wartenfels, the church bestowed its blessings on flags in the towns of Pottenstein, Eschenbach, Lindenhardt, Ottenhof, and Nitzlbuch, among others. The objectives symbolized in a club's flag are myriad, but loyalty is always part of the symbolic weave. The characteristic title of a 1935 Nazi film was *Unsere Fahne ist die Treue* (Our Flag is Our Pledge of Loyalty).

*

At the convent of Michelfeld near Auerbach in the Upper Palatinate, Head Nurse Peregrina, a member of the Franciscan order, runs a workshop for making flags. She has more orders than she can handle. The many busy hands doing the embroidering belong to deaf-mute women and girls for whom flag making is a form of occupational therapy. Flags thus had a social function before they were assigned a political role. "Many people are upset when they see all these old and new flags. They remind them of the time when flags were used for unscrupulous purposes in the past." The narrator of the television documentary asks, "Are societies that rally around the flag more prone to being misled?" The question is left unanswered.[57] "Always practice loyalty and honesty—until you come to the cold grave!" is a motto stitched in golden letters on one of the flags.

The sad history of flags teaches us that those who carry national and party standards see them only as symbols of their ideas and ideals; whereas their opponents view them in exactly the opposite way, namely as symbols of the enemy, which in Hitler's case meant hatred of and death for Jews, Poles, Russians, and others. The title of a collection of war poems tried to counter the negative image associated with the flag by suggesting, in the words of the original (*Sans haine et sans drapeau*—no hatred and no flag), that songs and poems which dispensed with the usual repertoire of flag symbolism would not erupt into outpourings of hate.[58]

*

Hitler's Germany annexed Austria in 1938, replacing the Austrian national colors with the swastika flag. However, many Austrians, in their mind's eye, superimposed the white stripes of their red-white-red flag on the Nazi banner, envisioning an untainted flag. They then added the white circle with the black swastika. This was their private way of affirming the hope that the Nazi dictatorship would be just a brief interlude.[59]

*

The Fighting Song of the Sappers

Men under black standards
That wave after every victory,
Fighters who clear a path,
When the front no longer moves;
We must blow up the enemy's bridges,
Block the area with bunkers—,
When we arrive, everything'll be fine:
You must break through, sapper!

Men under black standards,
Nothing's too tough or too much for us,
Before the enemy has an inkling,
We'll have reached our objective;
Flamethrowers, hand grenades,
Get a move on, men! We're coming—,
Wherever daring counts:
You must break through, sapper!

Men under black standards
That wave after every victory,
Our comrades—seeds sown by Death—
Remind us:
In struggle alone lies God's bounty
And life's greatest virtue—,
Even if the whole world is against us:
You must break through, sapper!

Notes

1. Joseph Goebbels on 28 March 1933, quoted in Helmut Heiber, ed., *Goebbels Reden*, 2 vols. (Düsseldorf, 1971).

2. Elias Canetti, *Masse und Macht* (Frankfurt am Main, 1960), p. 95, English translation *Crowds and Power* (New York, 1963).

3. J. S. Ersch and J. G. Grube, eds., *Allgemeine Encyclopädie der Wissenschaften und Künste in alphabetischer Reihenfolge von bekannten Schriftstellern* (Leipzig, 1845), p. 119.

4. Richard Wagner, *Tristan und Isolde: vollständiges Buch* (Leipzig, 1941), act 1, scene 4, p. 30.

5. Hoffmann is referring to Valentin Kataev's novel *Za vlast' sovetov* (For the Power of the Soviets) (Moscow, 1950). In 1961 a revised version appeared under the title *Katakomby* (The Catacombs). In 1945 Kataev published a non-fictional account of the underground resistance in Odessa titled *The Catacombs.*—Transl.

6. Adolf Hitler, quoted in Horst Kerutt and Wolfgang M. Wegener, *Die Fahne ist mehr als der Tod: ein deutsches Fahnenbuch* (Munich, 1940; 2d. ed., 1943), p. 143.

7. Ferdinand Feiligrath, *Sämtliche Werke*, ed. by L. Schröder, 10 vols., (Leipzig, 1907).

8. Paul Wentzcke, *Die deutschen Farben* (Heidelberg, 1955), p. 126.

9. Gustav Freytag, *Politische Aufsätze* (Leipzig, 1888), p. 437.

10. Heinrich Heine, *Sämtliche Schriften*, ed. by K. Brigleb (Munich, 1971), vol. 4, p. 88 [Ludwig Börne, eine Denkschrift].

11. Freiligrath, *Sämtliche Werke*, ibid.

12. *Reichsgesetzblatt* (Berlin), 12 November 1848.

13. Otto von Bismarck, *Gedanken und Erinnerungen* (Stuttgart, 1898), vol. 1, pp. 38f., English translation *The Memoirs, Being the Reflections and Reminiscences of Otto, Prince von Bismarck*, 2 vols. (New York, 1966).

14. Paul Wentzcke, *Die deutschen Farben*, pp. 113f.

15. Ibid, pp. 125f.

16. Ibid., pp. 132f.

17. Eduard David, quoted in *Die Geschichte von Schwarz-Rot-Gold: Beiträge zur deutschen Flaggenfrage* (Berlin, 1922).

18. Friedrich C. Sell, *Die Tragödie des deutschen Liberalismus* (Stuttgart, 1953), p. 393.

19. *Reichsgesetzblatt* (Berlin), pt. 1 (Berlin, 1934), p. 785.

20. *Pimpf im Dienst* (Potsdam, 1934), p. 8.

21. *Das neue Fischer-Lexikon in Farbe* (Frankfurt am Main, 1981), vol. 3, p. 1712.

22. Radio report by Joseph Goebbels on a government-sponsored rally in the Berlin Sportpalast on 10 February 1933, quoted in H. Heiber, ed., *Goebbels Reden*, vol. 1, pp. 68f.

23. Hermann Kurzke, "Mafia-Kultur und Yogi Hitler" in *Frankfurter Allgemeine Zeitung*, 18 October 1986.

24. Wilhelm Reich, *Die Massenpsychologie des Faschismus* (Köln, 1971), p. 106, English translation *Mass Psychology of Fascism* (New York, 1970).

25. Guido von List, *Die Bilderschrift der Ario-Germanen* (Leipzig, 1910).

26. Adolf Hitler, *Mein Kampf*, pp. 551ff.

27. Manfred von Killinger, *Die SA in Wort und Bild* (Leipzig, 1934).

28. Paul Wentzcke, *Die deutschen Farben*, p. 158.

29. Roland Barthes, *Mythen des Alltags*, 4th ed. (Frankfurt am Main, 1976), p. 95, English translation *Mythologies* (New York, 1972).

30. Decree of the Reich Interior Minister (1934) in Wolfgang Niess, *Machtergreifung '33* (Stuttgart, 1982), p. 127.

31. Hannsjoachim Wolfgang Koch, *Geschichte der Hitlerjugend* (Percha, 1975), p. 81, English translation *The Hitler Youth: Origins and Development, 1922–1945* (London, 1975).

32. Bertolt Brecht, *Kriegsfibel*, ed. by Ruth Berlau (Berlin, 1955).

33. Friedrich Hebbel, *Agnes Bernauer*, act V, scene 10; cf. Peter Schneider, ... *ein einzig Volk von Brüdern: Recht und Staat in der deutschen Literatur* (Frankfurt am Main, 1987), p. 144.

34. Paul Wentzcke, *Die deutschen Farben*, p. 27.

35. Ibid., p. 36.

36. Johann Fr. Böhmer, "Die Rothe Thüre zu Frankfurt am Main" in *Archiv für Frankfurter Geschichte und Kunst* (Frankfurt am Main), no. 3, 1844, pp. 114f.

37. Klaus Vondung, *Magie und Manipulation: ideologischer Kult und politische Religion des Nationalsozialismus* (Göttingen, 1971), p. 160.

38. Adolf Hitler, *Mein Kampf*, p. 198.

39. Martin Loiperdinger, "Nationalsozialistische Gelöbnisrituale im Parteitagsfilm" in Dirk Berg-Schlosser and Jakob Schissler, eds., *Politische Kultur in Deutschland* (Opladen, 1987), p. 142.

40. Horst Kerutt and Wolfram M. Wegener, *Die Fahne ist mehr als der Tod*, pp. 9–11.

41. Elias Canetti, *Masse und Macht*, p. 156.

42. Joachim C. Fest, *Hitler, eine Biographie* (Frankfurt am Main, 1973), pp. 699f., English translation *Hitler* (New York, 1974).

43. Saul Friedländer, *Kitsch und Tod* (Munich, 1984), p. 28, English translation *Reflections on Nazism: an Essay on Kitsch and Death* (New York, 1984).

44. Günther Kaufmann, *Das kommende Deutschland* (Berlin, 1940), quoted in Hans Christian Brandenburg, *Die Geschichte der HJ* (Köln, 1968), p. 227.

45. *Illustrierter Film-Kurier* (Berlin), no. 1920, 1933.

46. *Film und revolutionäre Arbeiterbewegung in Deutschland 1918–1932*, 2 vols. (Berlin [GDR], 1975), vol. 2, p. 107.

47. Gottfried Korff, "Rote Fahnen und Tableaux Vivants: zum Symbolverständnis der deutschen Arbeiterbewegung im 19. Jahrhundert" in Albrecht Lehmann, ed., *Studien zur Arbeiterbewegung* (Münster, 1984), (Beiträge zur Volkskultur in Nordwestdeutschland, 44), pp. 103–40; quoted text is on p. 104.

48. Friedrich Wendel, *Die rote Fahne: ein Entwurf ihrer Geschichte als Beitrag zur deutschen Flaggenfrage* (Berlin, 1925?), p. 7.

49. Gottfried Korff, "Rote Fahnen und Tableaux Vivants," p. 114.

50. Ibid., p. 117.

51. Gerhard Schumann in *Die Lieder vom Reich* (Munich, 1935), p. 34.

52. Hannsjoachim Wolfgang Koch, *Geschichte der Hitlerjugend*, p. 80.

53. Baldur von Schirach in *Völkische Musikerziehung* (Berlin, 1938), pp. 146–8.

54. *Renzo Vespignani über den Faschismus*, ed. by Arbeitsgruppe Ausstellungsübernahme der Neuen Gesellschaft für Bildende Kunst and the Kunstamt Kreuzberg (Berlin, 1976), p. 131.

55. Peter Dohms, *Flugschriften in Gestapo-Akten: Nachweis und Analyse der Flugschriften in den Gestapo-Akten des Hauptstaatsarchivs Düsseldorf* (Siegburg, 1977), (Veröffentlichungen der Staatlichen Archive des Landes Nordrhein-Westfalen. Reihe: Quellen und Forschungen, 3), pp. 552f.

56. Paul Virilio, *Krieg und Kino: Logistik der Wahrnehmung* (Munich, 1986), p. 186, English translation *War and Cinema: the Logistics of Perception* (New York, 1989).

57. "In Treue fest—der Verein und seine Fahne," film report by Ursula Scheider. Ed.: Karl J. Joeressen. Broadcast by the ZDF, 23 July 1982.

58. Ernesto Grassi, ed., *Ohne Haß und ohne Fahne: Kriegsgedichte des 20. Jahrhundert* (Reinbek bei Hamburg, 1959).

59. "Diagonal," a program broadcast on Austrian Radio's channel 1, 5 March 1988.

✛ 2 ✛

THE FLAG IN FEATURE FILMS

The Flag in Historical Feature Films

Man in the abstract has a need for larger-than-life monuments, in proportion to his feelings and actions, even when he is made to look very small and very pitiful by comparison. As in centuries past, he needs a pedestal on which to fashion himself. Monuments are not built on flat surfaces. To make them look more imposing, they are elevated over the heads of those who pass by them.

Fritz Lang[1]

As we will see below from the many examples of Nazi documentaries, *Kulturfilme*, and newsreels, the swastika flag was not an empty symbol. Rather, it breathed life into events and created memorable images. It indicated the degree of emotional fervor that was intended. It was like wallpaper that is used to set a mood.

Flags had aesthetic appeal, but only to the extent they did not become mere works of art, and only when, beyond any dramaturgical effects, they were the focus of attention. Flags, of course, were also used time and again as symbols in feature films. In those instances, they fulfilled a dramatic rather than a decorative function. They helped to transform dramatic scenes into national myths and make historical figures into almost superhuman shapers of destiny. The historical subject matter of films directed after the beginning of the war by Veit Harlan, Karl Ritter, Wolfgang Liebeneiner, and Arthur Maria Rabenalt seemed to dictate this approach, because war, "being the most profound challenge to the emotions" (Alexander Kluge), called for the use of clever techniques to compensate for shattered hopes, especially as the military situation moved ever closer to catastrophe.

Credible portrayals of historical analogies to Hitler became increasingly necessary as the military situation deteriorated. Aside from Bismarck, the Iron Chancellor, the historical figure most often used was Frederick the Great. In films he was "made up," to the very depths of his soul, to conform to the image of Hitler. Cheered by millions, the leader was never allowed to become a mere mortal. Nor was the victor ever permitted to become a loser. "[Filmmakers] would first draw an analogy to the present on the basis of a distorted depiction of Frederick's Prussia, projecting the features that typified Hitler and the Nazi state back to the past. In drawing various individual parallels, they sought to persuade viewers to extend the analogy to everything else. They forced audiences to accept the perfect congruity between Frederick's Prussia and the Nazi state, between the Prussian leader and the "Führer." Filmmakers felt that audiences would automatically ascribe to the new state all the achievements, successes, and values connected with Frederick's Prussia. They credited the values of a state that had met the test of history to a state that had yet to prove itself. The analogy went as follows: a man who acts like Frederick the Great will rise to the same heights as Prussia did in the past."[2] In other words, every time a new film about Frederick appeared, Hitler appropriated a little more of the Prussian king's legacy.

Das Flötenkonzert von Sanssouci
(The Flute Concert of Sanssouci, 1930)

My aim was to achieve feats of eternal glory. I never gave a damn about those idiots in the field.

Frederick II on 22 October 1776

In this film, the same "menuet galant" that lends a certain musical spice to the masked ball that is being held in the splendid palace of Count Heinrich von Brühl, ruling minister of Electoral Saxony, is also the code word to gain entry to a meeting at which a plot is being hatched against Frederick in one of the back rooms of world history, in the very same palace. The conspirators have not, however, counted on the cunning of the wily Prussian king. For his part, Frederick is secretly mobilizing for a preventive strike against the Saxons, Austrians, Russians, and French which he hopes will totally surprise his enemies. While calmly playing his transverse flute for an audience of illustrious guests at Sanssouci,

his baroque summer palace, he nonchalantly reads a note on his
music stand that contains the following bad news: "The Allied
powers will be fully armed within four weeks. They will attack
simultaneously from France, Austria, Russia, and Saxony."
Between two movements of the sonata, the king issues a terse
order to General Seydlitz, prompting one of the guests to remark
euphorically: "History will take note of this concert."

Military action follows directly on the heels of the musical per-
formance. After walking down the 315-foot-long hall of a wing in
the palace and meditating deeply, the king informs his adjutant of
his decision: "Send declarations of war immediately to the
embassies of Austria and France." Then turning to his generals, he
outdoes even himself: "Contrary to every rule of war I will attack
an enemy five times stronger than myself. I must do this or all will
be lost. The glory of my country and the welfare of my people bid
me to act or they will follow me to my grave." Viewed in hind-
sight, these cinematic phrases will become maxims of Nazi perversity. Knowledge that is of immediate relevance will be
communicated by means of contrived historical causality.

"Old Fritz" (as the Prussians called Frederick the Great) strides
solemnly down the colonnaded terrace of Sanssouci to review his
fusiliers. (Even before the Nazi regime came to power, Otto
Gebühr's portrayal of Frederick had become an unintentional caricature.) Following the review, Frederick's "Longfellows," his
Potsdam Grenadier Guards who were made over into a body of
giants, none under six feet tall and not a few approaching seven
feet, file past the monarch, their Prussian standards blowing stiffly
in the breeze as they parade to the strains of the Hohenfriedberg
March, a not-so-subtle reminder of the victory that is yet to be
won over the Austrians and Saxons on 4 June 1745 in Lower Silesia during the Second Silesian War. The march-past of the gleaming white Prussian standards appears all the more beautiful as
they are illuminated by the light of a haunting gray dawn and
blown by a wind machine to form an emotion-charged backdrop,
with heroic overtones that caused spectators' hearts to race.

By 1942 Goebbels realized that it was becoming increasingly
necessary "to possess what the great Prussian monarch Frederick
always considered the decisive factor in waging a victorious war:
a heart of steel to weather the storms of time." These were the
final dramatic words of Joseph Goebbels's speech on the fourth
anniversary of Austria's Anschluss with Germany, delivered on 15
March 1942 in the main hall of the South Station in Linz.[3] He

decided to use the figure of Old Fritz, the king who had triumphed over fate, as a call to arms and a source of inspiration during the harsh winter of the 1942 campaign in Russia. *Das Flötenkonzert* ..., produced in 1930, and other successful films about Frederick were re-released to combat defeatism, for "... we live in a time when we need the spirit of Frederick the Great. We will only master the problems facing us when we exert ourselves to the utmost. If we do overcome them, they will only bolster our endurance. Here as elsewhere Nietzsche's aphorism proves true that what does not kill us makes us stronger."[4]

Gustav Ucicky, the director of such chauvinistic films as *Das Flötenkonzert von Sanssouci* (1930), *York* (1931), and *Morgenrot* (Dawn, 1932–33), helped pave the way for Nazi ideology. The extreme nationalist films he subsequently churned out, for example, *Flüchtlinge* (Refugees, 1933), *Das Mädchen Johanna* (The Maiden Joan, 1935), and *Heimkehr* (Homecoming, 1941), predestined the former ad man to become one of the most aggressive propagandists in the Third Reich.

The first filmmaker to be inspired by the theme of "Old Fritz the musician" was Oskar Messter, who produced a 98-foot film in 1898 titled *Fridericus Rex beim Flötenspiel* (Fridericus Rex Playing the Flute). Many variations on this theme followed in later years. Messter's effort represents the successful launching of Frederick the Great's posthumous career as a movie star. The mistaken notion that "the stability of the throne rests on poetry" comes from Napoleon's opponent Gneisenau.

Der große König (The Great King, 1942)

> *In the past few weeks a film titled* Der große König *has been playing in the movie theaters of the Reich. Basically, the film deals with the difficult trials and historic tribulations that Frederick II experienced during a critical phase of the Seven Years' War, before leading his forces to final victory over his enemies.*
>
> Goebbels, 19 April 1942[5]

The flag occasionally epitomized Destiny in period films dealing with Prussia's various wars, one example being Veit Harlan's *Der große König*. Harlan used the historical element in the film to create a source of knowledge for Hitler's generals. Set in the period of the Seven Years' War, the film brought Old Fritz, the military genius, out of the cellar of Sanssouci to serve as Hitler's precursor, the aim being to link the idea of the Führer and the figure of the great king. Goebbels subsequently found astounding "parallels with the present in the words uttered by the great king, in the psychological crises he went through together with his people as they fought and suffered."[6]

The prologue to *Der große König* states that the film adheres "strictly to the facts of history" and then goes on to say that the bulk of the film depicts the agonies of the Seven Years' War, during which Frederick's great character was put to the test. "The most important statements of the king have been taken from his own writings." In other words, Ufa films don't lie! "All that matters in historical films is whether the 'big picture' has been correctly presented. To be successful, historical films must deal exclusively with events and personalities that are familiar to people today and with which they can empathize or that interest them and that they consider important."[7]

During the fade-in, the Prussian king's standard seems to fill the screen. The name "Kunersdorf," the traumatic reminder of a lost battle, is projected onto the standard. Stooped, his back to the camera, the old king delivers a monologue to his commanders before the beginning of the battle, a monologue that also addresses the conditions obtaining in the third year of Hitler's war: "We live in an age that will decide everything and will change the face of Europe. Before decisions are taken, we will be obliged to withstand frightful encounters with fortune [*sic*]. But afterwards the sky will turn bright and cheery. Regardless of how many enemies I have, I trust in the justice of my cause and the laudable courage of my troops—from my field marshals to the rawest recruit. The army will attack!" Standard-bearers rush forward toward Kunersdorf in advance of Prussian Army troops marching three to four abreast. The enemy enters the field without any standards.

After the battle against the Austrians and Russians was lost at Kunersdorf [on 12 August 1759], the Bernburg regiment attempts to escape to Brandenburg. "At least we still have our standard," says standard-bearer Niehoff, seeking to console himself as he retires from the field with the soiled colors tucked beneath his belt. The collective symbol of the regiment had not fallen into enemy hands. When the standard-bearer pauses to take a breather, he pulls the colors out from under his great coat and holds it up to the camera for the fade-over. The actress Kristina Söderbaum is then shown holding the standard in her hands, using the cloth to make bandages: "Yes, the standard almost cost you your life ..." And: "So long as we have our standard, all is not lost."

Cameraman Bruno Mondi used standard-bearer Niehoff's limp piece of cloth for another dissolve: "They can't start without us." The sacred standard, still pressed under Niehoff's arm as he rides in a one-horse cart, suddenly begins to flutter in all its glory. And then we hear, "Take the colors down!" as Frederick castigates the Bernburgers and orders them to remove their stripes and rosettes and, most serious of all, never again to bear the standard. "The drummer will never again be allowed to lead the regiment and direct its movements on the march. Henceforth, a crosscut piece of wood suspended over a drum will set the pace and announce to the whole world 'Here come men who prefer life to victory.'" At that moment, Count Bernburg, sitting on horseback, puts a bullet through his noble temple in full view of his troops. The dead count and, by implication, the shame and humiliation are covered over by a dissolve of the Prussian flag. "He abandoned life, just as he abandoned the battlefield" is the king's laconic comment.

Under the command of Colonel Rochow (Otto Wernicke) the Bernburgers finally attack and defeat the enemy. Once again the white standard with the black eagle of Prussia flutters at the head of the regiment. Even after the standard-bearer's best friend, Sergeant Paul Treskow (Gustav Fröhlich) dies at his side and Niehoff experiences a brief feeling of exasperation, he charges ahead with the standard blowing in the wind. "Stick your bayonet between the enemy's ribs. In three days we'll march into Korbach as victors—or die in the attempt," Old Fritz exhorts his men. After all, "a good cry is half the battle," wrote Shaw.[8] When the regiment reassembles after their victory at Torgau, Colonel Rochow reports with evident emotion: "The victorious standards, Your Majesty. The ancient standards of Prussia." The final apotheosis shows the Prussian flag waving proudly in the wind, filling the screen like a full sail—the symbol of Prussia's glory. The filmmaker projected this symbol, with its promise of victory, onto Hitler's flag in order to generate a feeling of hope among the audience.

This combination of flags is a reminder of similar configurations that appeared during the film industry's 1942 production year and that were designed to radiate confidence in the regime's ability to resolve victoriously the crisis on the eastern front. In the end, the small group of individuals who made up the elite of Nazi film directors found themselves and their heroic historical epics stranded in an artistic no-man's land.

Goebbels used the techniques of propaganda to force Old Fritz and Hitler—two totally antithetical figures—into a symbiosis that would be accepted by the politically naive. On the one hand, there was the prince destined by an accident of birth to occupy the highest position in the land, and on the other, the painter manqué and corporal Adolf Hitler who was catapulted to power through a campaign of propaganda. Whereas Frederick was an exponent of the French Enlightenment and French philosophy, a free thinker, a Freemason, sensitive to the arts and highly educated, what characterized the autodidact Hitler was his opposition to the ideas that inspired the Enlightenment and Freemasonry and his contempt for humanistic ideals. And, in contrast to Frederick, Hitler was devoid of any aesthetic sensibilities. In the course of the war, however, it was possible to discern certain similarities in their monomaniacal personalities: their harshness and brutality to their own troops and the enemy, their reversals of fortune in war, their miscalculations regarding the enemy's strategy, and, above all, their contempt for death.

*

Hitler always had Anton Graff's oil painting of Frederick the Great hanging above the desk in his bunker. Heinz Guderian, Chief of the General Staff, quoted him as saying that he, Hitler, always derived new strength from the portrait "when bad news threatens to crush my spirit."[9] When it came to his military idol's defeats, Hitler consoled himself by noting that Frederick II had gone down in the annals of Prussian history as Prussia's greatest king in spite of Kunersdorf and Leuthen.

Apotheoses of the Flag in Feature Films

> Our flag is fluttering before us.
> Our flag is the new age,
> And the flag leads us into eternity!
> Yes, the flag means more than death!

Baldur von Schirach

The refrain of the Hitler Youth's battle song resounded like a revivalist hymn: "Forward! The young are oblivious to danger!" Rising to number one on the Hitler Youth's "hit parade," the song became the leitmotif of the first original Nazi propaganda film made after Hitler came to power. Ufa had dedicated *Hitlerjunge Quex* to the Führer's devoted young followers. Produced in 1933 by Hans Steinhoff, the film was set in Berlin. The subtitle of *Hitlerjunge Quex* was "a film about young people's spirit of sacrifice." Transforming the so-called "time of struggle" (*Kampfzeit*) and the young martyr Quex (Herbert Norkus in real life) into legends, the film sought to make young moviegoers more susceptible to the lure of Nazism. Matinee idols who had been box office hits *before* 1933 (e.g., Berta Drews, Heinrich George, and Hermann Speelmans) were enlisted to give respectability to the Nazi ideology depicted in this film based on real-life events.

The main purpose of *Hitlerjunge Quex* was to fill the minds of the young with Nazi ideas, especially young people growing up in households in which attitudes had not changed quickly enough in favor of the Nazis. Dependent on the loyalty of the masses, the regime hoped to win over parents by exploiting their more impressionable sons and daughters. The regime presupposed that young people would be susceptible to values such as comradeship, courage, and idealism.

The dramatic turning point in this the first film made under official Nazi Party sponsorship is introduced in an atmosphere charged with emotion. Heini Völker is an apprentice in a small printer's shop in Berlin. Later in the film he earns the honorable nickname "Quex"[10] from his Hitler Youth friends. He is fourteen years old and the son of an unemployed proletarian who has become a Communist because of his bitterness toward society. The film's director has Heini go on a hike in the woods with Communists. Disgusted by the promiscuity and dissoluteness of the young Communists, who are portrayed in the film as noisy and unkempt, Heini manages to slip away in the dark and comes upon a company of Hitler Youth.[11] Hearing them sing their battle song, "Forward! Forward!", he is mesmerized and starts tapping his foot to the rhythm of the song.

In the novel by Karl Aloys Schenzinger on which the film is based, the author describes Heini watching the sacred fellowship of the Hitler Youth as they celebrate the summer solstice: "He wanted to join in the singing, but his voice failed him. This was German soil, a German forest, these were German boys, and he realized that he was an outsider, alone, helpless, that he did not know where to direct his overpowering emotions."[12]

Standing on an embankment, Heini Völker gazes at the disciplined brown-shirted youths. A long shot shows them lined up rank and file, solemnly hoisting their flag. The film uses picture and sound to link Heini's longing for security, a surrogate father, and comradeship to the attitude toward life exemplified by this idealized community of young people. The blazing campfire and fluttering flags at the center of the group give the cinematic scene an emotional appeal. He would like to be part of the group and is prepared, in the spirit of the battle song, to "march for Hitler, freedom, and bread through night and through need with the flag of youth."

Next morning, with the melody still echoing in his head and having committed the lyrics to memory, he quietly hums the song while standing in the bleak family kitchen: "Our flag is fluttering before us." In an adjacent room, Heini's father hears him singing, explodes, and starts to sing the *Internationale*, forcing little Heini to repeat each line after him: "Arise, you wretched of the earth ..."

After Heini's mother commits suicide, the Hitler Youth becomes his surrogate mother. But Heini, who in the meantime has become the devoted Hitler Youth Quex, is soon to meet his fate. Alone and unprotected, he distributes Nazi flyers in the "Red" Beussel-Kiez section of Berlin when Communist "cutthroats," sheltered by the darkness, surround him on the grounds of an amusement park and stab him repeatedly. When his Hitler Youth friends arrive the next morning and find him dying, the bright eyes of the martyr are transfigured as they look past earthly friends and upward to heaven. Then as his comrades hold him in their arms and with a happy smile on his face, Heini whispers haltingly: "*Unsere ... Fahne ... flattert ... uns ... voran.*"

The following passage from a speech by the Nazi poet E. W. Möller on the murdered Hitler Youth Herbert Norkus (Hitler Youth Quex in the film) illustrates the powerful symbolism of uniforms, colors, and flags: "Herbert Norkus was murdered while wearing a white shirt. When the shirt was examined later, however, the blood had turned brown. So the boy was wearing a brown shirt after all when he died. How unbelievably marvelous for such a thing to happen!"[13]

As if this were not enough, the director Hans Steinhoff takes the film to a final ecstatic apotheosis. As Heini lies dying, a vision grows within him of an army of brown-shirted Hitler Youth and behind them the swastika which gradually changes into a monumental emblem of salvation engulfing the entire screen. In a series of dissolves, the marching columns, flags, and the dead Quex, with the sound track taking up the Hitler Youth's marching song, merge into a single heroic image. The masterly use of fade-overs and editing heighten the mythical effect of this vision of a collective identity, which was supposed to leap from the screen to the audience below and capture the psyche of the spectators. The doctrine of salvation through the sacrifice of one's life was linked to the flag in an effort to provide the Nazi movement with the requisite energy to achieve its goals.

> The brave young soldier died a hero's death. He died for a cause he believed in, for his comrades, the flag he so dearly loved, and above all for his Führer. Now other young Germans are once again hoisting the flag consecrated by the blood of one of their finest.[14]

The journal *Kinematograph* published the following article under the title "The Flag Is the New Age":[15] "The movement is off to a running start. The spirit that lives in the young is manifest in the ranks of youth on the march. The flags rustle in the wind. The song 'Unsere Fahne ist die neue Zeit' resounds ..." And: "*Hitlerjunge Quex* is a German film that was not produced with the idea of making money, but rather with genuine feeling and profound sensitivity. It is a trumpet call to Germany's young people and thus to the future of Germany."

Having lulled the audience into a sense of security, Schirach's flag-song is juxtaposed in *Hitlerjunge Quex* to the less beguiling melodies of the *Internationale* and the *Marseillaise*. The film creates the impression that after being played time and again, the battle song about the flag "gave direction to young people bound together by a common destiny," and that as early as 1931, the year depicted in the film, it was making young people happy. In fact, the Nazi bard Baldur von Schirach had written the song especially for the film. *Hitlerjunge Quex* was a personal, poetic, and political expression of devotion to the Führer who, in the words of Schirach, "aimed for the stars but was still a down-to-earth person like you and me."

The flag followed in the wake of the marching song and was supposed to lead the way to a glorious future. At the same time, it was a symbol of faith and hope that young people could easily understand. Riding a wave of popular enthusiasm, the flag was supposed to lead to the goals embodied in the alliterative slogan "For Führer, Folk, and Fatherland." Ironically, though, the first propaganda film produced in the Third Reich already anticipated its demise. "The movie starts off in the style of the Soviet montage films, only to end in an apotheosis of martyrdom engulfed in a flood of music and flags." Karsten Witte comes to the conclusion that *Hitlerjunge Quex* anticipates what was implied in the much-publicized longing to die a heroic death: "Every enterprise carries the seeds of its own destruction."

This was Baldur von Schirach's vision: "Where once the little Hitler Youth fell, there now stands a youth movement that includes one and a half million fighters, each one of whom believes in the spirit of sacrifice and comradeship.... We will fight on in his unwavering spirit."[16]

The *Quex* film had set the standard for what Nietzsche in a different (bourgeois) context called a "dual perspective" (*doppelte Optik*), which in this instance referred to a dual artistic and National Socialist perspective that enabled filmmakers to capture and hold an audience's attention. Reflecting on the psychological effect of the techniques used in *Hitlerjunge Quex*, Dr. Goebbels wrote that "when art and character are combined and a lofty idealism avails itself of the most vital and modern cinematic means of expression, German film art has a nearly unbeatable advantage over the rest of the world."[17]

The two other Party-sponsored feature films produced that same year—*SA-Mann Brand* (1933), directed by Franz Seitz, and *Hans Westmar* (1933), directed by Franz Wenzler—likewise depicted self-sacrifice in images that were both horrifying and beautiful at the same time. "I go now to the Führer," the dying Hitler Youth Erich Lohner whispers to his friend Fritz Brand in *SA-Mann Brand*.

Brand pledges "at the poor lad's deathbed that his young blood, having been spilled for the great cause of Germany, will be avenged." Even the Communists listen to Hitler's "passionately patriotic" speeches "with fists clenched and a sense of the enormous sacred wave" pouring out of the loudspeaker, for he is speaking directly to the "hearts of the German people." Finally, "National Socialist Germany has triumphed. The Storm Troops march, and Storm Trooper Brand stands tall and proud in their ranks. A thousand voices resound with a thunderous 'Hold high the banner, the Storm Troops march with calm and steady pace...' There is great rejoicing everywhere in Germany. A new era is dawning ... Germany has awakened."[18]

Franz Wenzler's feature-length film *Hans Westmar* (1933), subtitled *One of Many—the Fate of a German in 1929*, tells the story of Horst Wessel, the "most glorious blood-witness to Germany's liberation movement." The film was "so true to history" that even the captured "Communist posters, flags, banners, etc., were the 'real McCoy.'"[19] Faithful to the book on which it was based, Hanns

Ewers's *Horst Wessel*, the film conveyed the last thoughts of the murdered Hans Westmar alias Horst Wessel in the one word that stood for the whole ideology—"Germany ..." As the young warrior's soul leaves his body, it marches with the Flag into Eternity. The workers' clenched fists open symbolically in the Hitler salute. Then there are the echoes coming from the funeral oration for Hans Westmar: "Die Fahne hoch! That is, the flag will rise from the dead to new and glowing life and together with his [Hans Westmar's] ghost, risen from the grave, enter into us and march in spirit in our ranks, when we one day seize power [to fashion] the glorious and magnificent new Reich." The funeral procession includes actual footage of the historic torchlight parade of the SA through the Brandenburg Gate on 30 January 1933.

Taking place on a cold and windy day in March, the cemetery scene in Hanns Heinz Ewers's book also ends on a religious note: "And hearts were filled with a feeling that it—the body lying there—was not dead at all; that like us he was alive, living in our midst"—Yes: "Comrades killed by Red Front and Reaction in spirit keep their place."[20] The literary form shared by the three films was the allegory, and it was used to embody the Nazi ideology in mythic structures. The final apotheoses in all three were examples of the semiotics of film as reflected in Nazi hagiography. They contained not only modifications of the allegorical mode; they also represented practical attempts to transform the tenets of the ideology into goals and to make people aware of them through the use of graphic imagery.

In the figure of the prototypical young Nazi, audiences would derive a feeling for the kind of moral strength that would soon dwindle in importance under Hitler's regime. Quex, for example, served as the dramaturgical motif in a documentary style of representation that was designed to add a touch of realism to fictionalized events.

Background material on the "martyr" that had initially been drawn from the so-called "time of struggle" was not considered of sufficiently high caliber to reflect the true stature of the hero. Consequently, Goebbels ordered the immediate postponement of the picture's premiere, scheduled for 9 October 1933, so that it could be revised accordingly. The reason given was "that the film does justice neither to the figure of Horst Wessel, because the inadequacy of the portrayal detracts from his heroic life, nor to the National Socialist movement which is today the pillar of the state.

In that sense [the film] threatens the vital interests of the state and the German people."[21]

Der Rebell (The Rebel, 1932) anticipated the Nazis' ritualized cult of death. This is clearly reflected in Joseph Goebbels's remark that the film would leave a lasting impression on "even non-National Socialists." According to Luis Trenker, Hitler saw *Der Rebell* four times and each time with new enthusiasm. "Besides," mentioned the Führer, "the film is now playing at the Luitpold Cinemas in Munich." Trenker was greatly surprised that the Führer was so well informed. He himself did not know it."[22] The manner in which the three triumphant final scenes were prepared for the Nazi psyche in early political films such as *Hitlerjunge Quex*, *Hans Westmar*, and *SA-Mann Brand* follows the pattern of film symbolism laid down in Luis Trenker and Kurt Bernhardt's *Der Rebell*. Sepp Allgeier, who was later to become Leni Riefenstahl's chief cameraman, used this "mountain film about [the struggle for] freedom" to perfect the skills he had acquired in his so-called pre-fascist works. In this lavish national epic about the Tyrol's revolt against the Napoleonic occupation army, French soldiers execute the revolutionary student Severin Anderlan (Luis Trenker) and two of his comrades in the courtyard of the fortress at Kufstein "for rebelling and organizing gangs." As martyrs, they die standing up, with the pathos and personae of heroes but without any expressions of suffering that might be viewed as iconographic allusions to the crucifixion.

"But they can't murder the will of these dying men! And all those who sacrificed themselves for freedom will appear, their shades marching in an endless column. With flags waving, they will march toward a new day, toward the future."[23] Indeed, this was no natural death, for after the initial shock the student-hero rises from the dead and with undiminished patriotic ardor picks up the white flag emblazoned with the Red Eagle (which was not there before the execution). As if by magic, the two Tyrolean peasants who had been shot along with "the rebel" also rise up. A veritable army of Severin's peasant freedom fighters ascend above the billowing flags that proliferate miraculously among the menacing clouds above. The living and the dead are shown floating away on clouds into the ether, guided by a myriad of flags to the eternal light.

The devoutly religious Trenker probably borrowed this metaphor from the field of art. A flag emblazoned with the sign of the cross to enhance the pathos of the Resurrection was often used in Christian iconography as a symbol of victory over death.

The Proletarian Feature Film

There must no longer be any classes. We work too, with our heads,
and our place is next to our brother, who works with his hands.

Hans Westmar, in *Hans Westmar*, 1933

The Nazis knew well how to exploit the traditional values
reflected in the genealogy of the flag and how to reinterpret them
for their own purposes. In judging the aesthetics of *Hitlerjunge
Quex*, even non-German writers agree that it is a well-made
motion picture in the finest tradition of German proletarian films,
including those of the silent film era, such as Piel Jutzi's *Mutter
Krausens Fahrt ins Glück* (1929), G. W. Pabst's *Die Dreigroschenoper*
(The Threepenny Opera, 1931), and Slatan Dudow's *Kuhle Wampe*
(1932). In his essay "The Banner of the Proletarian Cult,"[24] V. Polianskij postulates that proletarian art, in contrast to that of the
moribund bourgeoisie, stressed content over form. In addition to
the three films mentioned above, his thesis applies to most other
proletarian pictures as well.

G. W. Pabst's pessimistic anti-war film *Westfront 1918* (The
Western Front 1918, 1930) and *Kameradschaft* (Comradeship, 1931),
his paean to international workers' solidarity, argue in favor of
this thesis. Committed to opposing reactionary and chauvinistic
trends in the cinema and to promoting the progressive left, Pabst,
together with Erwin Piscator and Heinrich Mann, founded the
Volksverbund für Filmkunst (National Association for Film Art) in
1930, with an eye to representing society realistically, as it really
was. Except for three actors, the entire cast of *Kameradschaft* was
made up of nonprofessional performers recruited directly from
the mines. The film was based on an actual French mining disaster that took place in 1906 in Courrières, near the German border.
German miners had come to the aid of their French comrades. In
the movie, Pabst heightened the significance of the story by making it take place shortly "after Versailles." The film begins with a
newsreel-like report on the brutal working conditions in the mining district and an actual introduction to the cramped living quar-
ters of the proletariat. The film's message, reinforced by its
realism, is that if working class solidarity can overcome borders,
there is also hope for eliminating borders between nations.

Following this "miraculous event," spokesmen for the two
miners' groups meet in the open air on the border separating the

two countries and extol the fraternity between the two peoples. In the concluding scene, Pabst inserted a biting epilogue. A German and a French official, separated by a new iron fence in the shafts, exchange protocols ratifying the re-establishment of the frontier: "The strictly symmetrical gestures of both officials satirize the victory of bureaucratic wisdom."[25]

The subject of these films was the 6.5 million unemployed workers of the Weimar period who were living in conditions of poverty and social deprivation. Like Piel Jutzi in *Mutter Krausens Fahrt ins Glück* (1929), leftist movie producers did not condemn individual proletarians who committed criminal acts as a result of their economic situation. Rather, they blamed the "environment" in which proletarians were forced to live—run-down housing and the poverty of the slums. Heinrich Zille, who helped inspire Jutzi to produce the film, hit the nail on the head when he wrote that "you can kill someone as easily by where you house them as you can with an ax." The state was identified as the murderer. Director Jutzi shot a closeup of an ominous official summons with the great seal of Prussia on it. He then faded over to the frightening outline of the German eagle on Mother Krause's wall clock.

In the Weimar republic these films were considered politically and artistically progressive. The power of their visuals corresponded to the vigor of their attempt to arouse public feeling. Clearly siding with the proletarians, these films intended to awaken their class consciousness by portraying their hardships in the starkest possible terms. Their common denominator was the unconcealed sympathy they had for the proletarian milieu and its human inhabitants.

Erwin Piscator's motion picture *Der Aufstand der Fischer von St. Barbara* (Revolt of the Fishermen of St. Barbara, 1934), filmed in Soviet Russia, was a latecomer, but, given its style and its message, it can be considered part of the proletarian film genre. The picture was based on the novel of the same name by Anna Seghers.

By studying the aesthetics of film, we can show how the Nazis tried to weaken the left by appropriating some of its ideas and stylistic techniques. The Nazis would change plots, but maintain a similar structure. For instance, the Nazis replaced the red flag with the swastika flag as the "colorful sign visible over long distances" (Tucholsky) that signaled the dawn of a new era. They made a promise—which they superficially kept—that workers would be allowed under the new banner of solidarity to continue identifying with one another and their class as they had done before. "So where do I belong? I belong with my friends, from my own class," says Heini Völker's father, the unemployed Communist played not unsympathetically by the well-known actor Heinrich George. Using films such as *Quex*, Nazi propagandists hoped to facilitate the integration of the senior Herr Völker's impoverished comrades into the National Socialist movement. And by promising that "everyone has to have a job and bread," Storm Trooper Brand made himself a champion of the unemployed workers of the left. However, this classless new class of National Socialists did not end the class system as such; it simply put an end to proletarian class consciousness as symbolized by the red flag. The color red of the socialist movement would eventually be transmuted into the red of National Socialism, made brighter still by the white solar disk with the swastika in the middle symbolizing strength and the future. At the same time, the swastika represented the demise of the red star of the Soviets which the Nazis regarded as a proletarian fetish.

After 1933 overtly ideological Nazi feature films with columns of marching Hitler Youth or Storm Troopers were no longer produced. The Propaganda Ministry was afraid that showing a lot of brown uniforms on the screen might be counterproductive. Goebbels used *SA-Mann Brand* (1933) to illustrate his criticism of motion pictures that adhered too rigidly to Nazi ideology: "We don't want to see our Storm Troopers marching across the screen or the stage. They're supposed to march in the streets."[26] After all, he wrote, the National Socialist regime "never ordered anybody to make films about the SA. On the contrary... it considers too many such films a threat."[27] Of the approximately 1,150 feature films produced in Nazi Germany, five percent at most were explicitly propaganda films, and of these the majority were either historical films or war movies. This does not mean, however, that other feature-length films did not serve the needs of propaganda. The propaganda was simply more subtle. Stylistically instructive in this regard is the most successful of all Nazi films Borsody's *Wunschkonzert* (Request Concert, 1940), as well as Liebeneiner's *Ich klage an* (I Accuse, 1941) and, in the latter stages of the war, important films by Harlan such as *Opfergang* (Sacrifice, 1944) and *Kolberg* (1945). In each film love stories were used to capture the audience's attention. The background against which these apparently innocuous stories unfolded was a war of conquest (*Wunschkonzert*), euthanasia (*Ich klage an*), and a "seemingly" pointless example of last-ditch resistance to invasion, i.e., the idea of "holding out to the last" (*Kolberg*). Harlan tried to persuade his viewers that the decision to go to war or "to eliminate life that is no longer worth living," i.e., to interfere with people's personal happiness, was actually made by those most directly affected by those decisions, that is, by the particular figure in the film with whom the audience was supposed to identify.

Perhaps the best indicator of the subtle effectiveness of Nazi propaganda films is the fact that for the past several years, down to the present, a Munich cinema has shown them every Sunday, hyping them as smash hits and effectively marketing them under the series title "Stars That Never Die." *Opfergang* is promoted as "one of Veit Harlan's best and most beautiful color films." Johannes Meyer's *Männerwirtschaft* (The Odd Couple, 1941) is "a hilarious film about love that will make you forget all your cares" —which, of course, was precisely the point during the war. Apparently, the ideology that was insinuated into the film is no more distracting today than it was then.

Notes

1. Fritz Lang, quoted in E. Beyfuss and A. Kosowsky, eds., *Das Kulturfilmbuch* (Berlin, 1924), p. 31.

2. Helmut Regel, "Historische Stoffe als Propagandaträger" in *Der Spielfilm in Dritten Reich: Dokumentation des 1. Arbeitsseminars der Westdeutschen Kurzfilmtage Oberhausen*. Leitung: Hilmar Hoffmann, Manfred Dammeyer, Will Wehling (Oberhausen, 1966).

3. Helmut Heiber, ed., *Goebbels Reden*, vol. 2, p. 111.

4. Louis Lochner, ed., *Goebbels Tagebücher aus den Jahren 1942–43, mit anderen Dokumenten* (Zürich, 1948), English translation *The Goebbels Diaries, 1942–1943* (New York, 1948).

5. Joseph Goebbels on 19 April 1942 at a ceremony on the eve of Hitler's fifty-third birthday, quoted in Helmut Heiber, ed., *Goebbels Reden*, vol. 2, p. 112.

6. Ibid., p. 114.

7. Fritz Hippler, *Betrachtungen zum Filmschaffen* (Berlin, 1942), p. 79.

8. George Bernard Shaw, *Man and Superman* (Cambridge, Mass., 1903), act III (Don Juan in Hell).

9. Heinz Guderian, *Erinnerungen eines Soldaten* (Neckargemünd, 1960), English translation *Panzer Leader* (London, 1955).

10. The name is short for *Quecksilber* or quicksilver, i.e., mercury, and alludes to Heini's quick wit and sprightliness.

11. The August 1937 issue, no. 1070, of the Party's secret "Report on Germany" was obliged to note that "promiscuity … being a fact" in the Hitler Youth, resulted in sexual permissiveness. A man by the name of Grünberger reported that during the 8th Party congress in Nuremberg about 900 BDM girls had become pregnant.

12. Gerd Albrecht, comp., *Arbeitsmaterialien zum nationalsozialistischen Propagandafilm Hitlerjunge Quex* (Frankfurt am Main, 1983), p. 20.

13. E. W. Möller quoted in Joseph Wulf, *Literatur und Dichtung im Dritten Reich.* (Reinbek bei Hamburg, 1966), p. 243.

14. *Illustrierter Film-Kurier* (Berlin), vol. 15, 1933.

15. "Die Fahne ist die neue Zeit," in *Kinematograph* (Berlin), 12 September 1933.

16. Oskar Kalbus, *Vom Werden deutscher Filmkunst*, pt 2: Der Tonfilm (Altona-Bahrenfeld, 1935), pp. 121f.

17. Joseph Goebbels in a letter to Ufa Director E. H. Corell (25 September 1933) in Joseph Goebbels, *Der Angriff: Aufsätze aus der Kampfzeit* (Munich, 1935).

18. *Illustrierter Film-Kurier* (Berlin), vol. 15, no. 1975, 1933.

19. *llustrierter Film-Kurier* (Berlin), vol. 15, no. 2034, 1933.

20. Hanns Heinz Ewers, *Horst Wessel: ein deutsches Schicksal* (Stuttgart, 1933).

21. Curt Belling, *Der Film in Staat und Partei* (Berlin, 1936), p. 70.

22. Joseph Wulf, *Theater und Film im Dritten Reich* (Gütersloh, 1964), p. 335.

23. *llustrierter Film-Kurier* (Berlin), vol. 14, no. 1890, 1932.

24. Valerian Polianskij, "Das Banner des Proletkult," *Ästhetik und Kommunikation* (Hamburg), vol. 2, no. 5/6, February 1972, pp. 85f.

25. Siegfried Kracauer, *From Caligari to Hitler: A Psychological History of the German Film* (London, 1947), p. 240.

26. Joseph Goebbels in a speech delivered on 19 May 1933, quoted in Gerd Albrecht, comp., *Arbeitsmaterialien zum nationalsozialistischen Propagandafilm Hitlerjunge Quex*, p. 442.

27. *Kinematograph* (Berlin), 11 October 1933.

✢ 3 ✢

REASONS FOR THE RISE
OF HITLER

Excursus on the Origins of National Socialism

Thus, as Nietzsche said, the gentlest part of our nature must become the toughest. We must rise above ourselves, onward and upward, until our stars are below us.

Joseph Goebbels[1]

Some fifty years after the collapse of the Nazi reign of terror, we are still grappling with the question of how a Stalingrad, a Coventry, or an Auschwitz could happen. The so-called *Historikerstreit* or "historians' debate" raged in Germany in the 1980s. The debate was triggered by the May 1986 Römerberg Colloquium in Frankfurt am Main[2] and Jürgen Habermas's rejoinder to the theories advanced by Ernst Nolte, Michael Stürmer, and Andreas Hillgruber, which he titled *Eine Art Schadensabwicklung* (A Kind of Settling of Damages).[3] The way in which conservative historians have tried to deny the uniqueness of these calamities highlights Germany's continuing search for a bearable past.

The direction in which this kind of "high-wire balancing act between creating meaning from the past and de-mythologizing" (Michael Stürmer) is headed is obvious—namely, to step out of Hitler's shadow and disencumber today's Germany of the "burden" of the crimes committed by the Nazis, including the systematic murder of six million European Jews under National Socialism.

In his 1963 book *Faschismus in seiner Epoche*[4] Ernst Nolte argued that the rise of fascist movements, including National Socialism, should be understood as a counterrevolution by bourgeois liberalism against the "threat of Bolshevism." His theory of fascism as the "reaction to a threat" misled him ultimately to become an apologist for the Holocaust. In a 1986 essay titled *Zwischen Mythos und Revisionismus* (Between Myth and Revisionism), Nolte espoused the incredible theory that the September 1939 declaration by Chaim Weizmann (President of the Jewish World Congress) that the Jews were in a state of war with Germany amounted to a "declaration of war" against the Nazis and therefore "entitled" Hitler to segregate Jews as prisoners of war and to deport them. In fact, the date September 1939 itself is an utter canard, for it obscures the fact that the declaration was made four years after the promulgation of the Nuremberg racial laws, nearly one year after the pogrom of November 1938, and immediately after the introduction of the Yellow Star of David as a badge to mark Jews as "subhumans."

From this point it was but a short step to the following conclusion: "The *so-called* [emphasis added by the author] annihilation of the Jews during the Third Reich was a reaction to or a distorted imitation of [other acts of state terrorism], but it was not a unique event nor the first act of its kind." What strikes us here is the way in which Nolte has subliminally accepted the same reasons advanced by the Nazis themselves and then refurbished and reused them, e.g., the "justification" for taking action against the Jews, the Holocaust as a "reaction" to a "threat," to an "Asiatic deed."[5] Arguments once repressed have resurfaced in covert form, but are nonetheless effective.

As Horst-Eberhard Richter has written, "The most important omission on the part of both victors and vanquished was (and is) not to have understood the phenomenon of Nazism as merely the radical consequence of a universal temptation to which we are all prone. Hitler was unique. Auschwitz was unique. But the Germans under Hitler who submitted to his inhumane regime were no different from their offspring today, and they, in their turn, share these predispositions with many other nationalities."[6]

It is not easy or pleasant, of course, for Germans to live with their past. However, the intent of this kind of historical interpretation is to deny *responsibility* (but not *guilt*) for what happened in German history and—this is the important point—to refuse to learn any lessons from it. In actual fact, though, it is virtually impossible to become a disinterested party to this history—least of all by engaging in the kind of interpretive gymnastics illustrated above. For history continues to affect us through our contact with the people who participated in it. They inevitably pass on their experiences and modes of thinking to succeeding generations. Consequently, the starting point for coming to grips with and learning from the recent past (*Vergangenheitsbewältigung*) has to be anchored in the present, not in a reinterpretation of the past. Horst-Eberhard Richter has described the psychodynamic mechanisms involved in this process.

This in no sense diminishes the uniqueness of the Nazis' crimes. They live on as grave warnings and reminders of events unique in history, which is why Richter is correct in saying that these singularly horrible memories offer Germans a special opportunity. It is important for the younger generation "to use the example of their parents and grandparents to recognize their own potential for setting off in dangerous directions."[7] Thus, National Socialism will not become some "exotic exception." Instead, it will be a "didactic drama" about what human beings are capable of.

This approach does more justice to history than the formulaic cliché "empathetic understanding" (*Verstehen*) that lies behind the attempts at explanation undertaken by Nolte et al. Not long ago, Dolf Sternberger vehemently rejected Nolte's attempt "to make Auschwitz comprehensible." "In fact, the sadistic atrocities subsumed under the name 'Auschwitz' are totally incomprehensible; all one can do is report them. Even if it could be shown that the plan for the 'Final Solution of the Jewish Question' had been hatched in Hitler's brain as some kind of response to earlier ('more original') atrocities committed by the Bolsheviks, this still would not make the execution of the plan, namely the actuality of industrialized mass murder, one whit more comprehensible. At most, new light would be shed on the twisted minds of those who carried out the crimes.... If it is true that the purpose of scholarship is understanding, then one would have to conclude that scholarship is unfit to contribute to our knowledge of the 'Auschwitz' phenomenon" (Dolf Sternberger, "Unverstehbar" ["Incomprehensible"], *Frankfurter Allgemeine Zeitung*, 6 April 1988).

There is, of course, another problem in conducting research on the history of fascism over and above the dilemma posed by psychological and moral determinism, i.e., the complex nature of the fascist phenomenon which, in its outward manifestations and at the time of its birth, sought to embrace every sphere of life. The result is that the various theories on the origins and role of fascism differ not only because of their different ideological premises and methodologies, but also with regard to the aspects of the subject they emphasize, that is, with regard to the characteristics that a particular school of thought considers the decisive factors in the development of fascist ideologies and regimes.

Theories about fascism existed well before fascism came to power in Germany, for example, the Marxist analysis of Italian fascism by August Thalheimer (1930),[8] and the studies by Hermann Heller and Theodor Geiger. The attempts at explanation reflect the various forms assumed by the subject under study. Georgi Dimitroff (1935) described the "class character of fascism,"[9] Reinhard Optiz saw fascism as the "dictatorship of monopoly capital,"[10] which sought to standardize society while prosecuting or proscribing any efforts to oppose its monopoly. Besides these Marxist theories there are a number of writers who have focused their studies of National Socialism on the person of Adolf Hitler, primarily Joachim C. Fest,[11] John Toland,[12] and Friedrich Heer.[13] Several sociopsychological theories concentrate on the mechanisms and phenomena that occur below the surface of political and economic events. Wilhelm Reich[14] and Klaus Theweleit[15] investigated the writings and pronouncements of the fascists themselves, studying them to discover the underlying psychological mechanisms that would explain the effect of historical, social, and political developments on the *individual* and the reasons for the mass appeal of Hitler and his movement. Finally, in a broader context, the history of enlightened industrial society was seen to be moving in the direction of standardization [or "mass culture"], self-alienation, and the worship of modern technology (Adorno/Horkheimer, [16] Ralf Dahrendorf).[17]

Each of the above-mentioned theories illuminates specific aspects of the complex issue of National Socialism, and in principle they are not mutually exclusive, though their methods probably are to some degree. So for those who have to live with the past and who seek an explanation of (not absolution from) pre-1945 history, some of the ideas and explanations advanced by these divergent theories can be extremely useful in helping to understand conditions before and during the Nazi dictatorship. As Saul Friedländer writes, National Socialism is "in its singularity, as in its general aspects, the result of a large number of social, economic, and political factors, of the coming to a head of frequently analyzed ideological currents, and of the meeting of the most archaic myths and the most modern means of terror."[18]

Within the context of this study of the National Socialist view and depiction of reality as reflected in the documentaries and newsreels produced by the Nazi propaganda machine, we are interested primarily in the history of the psychological and social conditions that made fascism possible. Therefore, we must deal with questions such as the following: Why did so many people find fascism attractive? What kind of people willingly allowed themselves to be mesmerized and carried away by the behavior and self-portrayal of Nazis in these documentaries and newsreels? What did Nazism appeal to *within* these individuals? Fascism's allure was not based primarily on rational grounds. Rather, it was triggered by external phenomena that struck a chord within each individual—songs, forests of flags, parades, the cult of the body beautiful, symbols of fire, etc., which is why we are chiefly concerned with the aesthetics of fascism. Ultimately, its appeal had religious implications that are revealed in the Nazis' own strategic plans. To quote directly from Hitler:

> The broad masses of a people consist neither of professors nor of diplomats. The scantiness of the abstract knowledge they possess directs their sentiments more to the world of feeling.... Their emotional attitude at the same time conditions their extraordinary stability. Faith is harder to shake than knowledge, love succumbs less to change than respect, hate is more enduring than aversion, and the impetus to the mightiest upheavals on this earth consisted less in a scientific knowledge dominating the masses than in a fanaticism which inspired them and sometimes in a hysteria which drove them forward.[19]

Hitler decided in favor of a secularized, surrogate nationalist-religious self-image that culminated in his pronouncement: "I awakened the masses."

It is now easier to determine which segments of the population regarded Hitler as their redeemer and believed fanatically in a national *Götterdämmerung*. For a long time National Socialism was considered an "ideology of the middle class,"[20] though even then the term "middle class" (*Mittelstand*) raised many problems. Today it is more generally accepted that the NSDAP, by the early 1930s, had become a *Volkspartei*, i.e., it attracted voters from all sections of the population—middle class, upper class, and even working class, though the last remained underrepresented.[21]

After the onset of the Depression, white-collar workers were hard hit by the Weimar republic's lack of social security since they had virtually no unions to represent their interests, making their slide down the social ladder that much bumpier if they lost their jobs. In an essay titled "The White-Collar Worker" (*Die Angestellten*)

Siegfried Kracauer explained their susceptibility to fascism by showing how this group of salaried workers, which began to emerge in Germany in the early twentieth century and continued to evolve through the 1920s and 1930s, was unable to develop a sense of class consciousness and create organizations to represent its interests.[22] However, those who ascribe the effectiveness of the Nazi propaganda machine during the 1920s and early 1930s solely to its promise to eliminate unemployment and social grievances clearly miss the point. A Nazi election announcement dating from 1932 described Hitler not only as "the last hope" of those "who have lost everything—house and home, savings, livelihood, the strength to work," but also, with nationalist and religious over-tones, as the "shining beacon of all those who dream of a future for Germany," "who believe in Germany's resurrection."[23]

Ralf Dahrendorf and others have underscored the myth of the leader, i.e., the idea of a Führer who would lead the Germans through a "storm of steel" to a twilight of the gods. This was the aspect of utopian nationalism he viewed as a "brutal break with tradition and a strong push toward modernity."[24] Hitler had promised to achieve secular, nationalist transcendence by means of an exhilarating revolution that would institutionalize the idea that only "might makes right." What we now call a seizure of power or a takeover of power was always referred to by the Nazis as a "revolution," a revolution that was to encompass every aspect of life. To lay the groundwork for this revolution, the Nazis por-trayed social conditions in the Weimar republic as miserable and the republic's political standing in the world as hopeless. The fact that the Nazis recruited so many of their voters from the bour-geois conservative and reactionary parties (mainly the DNVP), while the Catholic parties (Zentrum and BVP) and the parties of the left were less affected until 1932,[25] showed just how quickly the National Socialists succeeded in mobilizing the hopes and fears of the lower middle class—hopes and fears that were trig-gered in equal measure by the Weimar republic's failed social poli-cies, the defeat of Germany in World War I, and the "diktat of Versailles." Last but not least, Hitler used the media to turn a cli-mate of instability into something approaching an atmosphere of revolutionary change in the name of a dynamic, racially "pure" Germany purged of the power of "Jewish" high finance and cleansed of Marxism.

Except for the Nazis, the left—at the other end of the political spectrum—represented the only utopian movement that was both future-oriented and able to communicate its hopes and desires to the masses in an increasingly radicalized society. It is one of history's tragedies that the forces of the left were too half-hearted and too late in establishing a united front.

In his two-volume psychoanalysis of fascist male fantasies titled *Männerphantasien*,[26] Klaus Theweleit describes the reasons for the deep-seated desire of men to exhibit their power, to lose themselves in combat, to get off "the liberating shot," a desire that blocked out their conscious minds if not everything that made them individual human beings. In examining men's fantasies Theweleit used auto-biographies and diaries of World War I veterans who later became members of the Freikorps. The way in which these men—and it was, of course, almost exclusively men who determined Nazi ideology and strategy—depicted their wartime experiences in retrospect is, in my opinion, inadequately described by the term "sexual repression," used by Wilhelm Reich in his *Massenpsychologie des Faschismus* to pinpoint the source of fascist power fantasies. Indeed, the Nazis considered these Freikorpsmen the epitome of the individual combatant who came to symbolize the role played by the heroic individual in the struggle of the fascist community. Films such as *Hitlerjunge Quex*, *SA-Mann Brand*, and *Hans Westmar* communicated this heroic ideal to millions of moviegoers.

Theweleit shows that these fighters were not examples of the neurotic repression of sexual desires lived out in fantasies glorifying war. Rather, he writes, they exhibited signs of the so-called "basic fault"[27] which prevented them from ever developing a viable ego capable of coping with life, i.e., an individual personality.

Theweleit cites the repressive education of children in the Wilhelmine era as the cause of this "basic fault." For the total destruction of these men's individuality he blames the war that robbed them and the rest of their generation of their youth. These men had become fixated on the war to the exclusion of everything else, and when it came to a less than glorious end, they lost the only thing that had given meaning to their lives. In their memoirs they fantasized about having been a bulwark against "red floods," "rifle-women" (*Flintenweiber*), "oceans of slime, dirt, and pulp." For them, battle was an "inner experience" (Ernst Jünger). They internalized it. In this sense, they became the avant-garde of the Nazi attitude toward life and models for all those who wished to lead Germany to power and glory, all those who were incapable of doing anything else—assuming we can give credence to this psychological explanation.

It would be unfair to extrapolate to the other members of the generation of World War I in Germany the psychological mechanisms that were supposedly operating in the psyche of the Freikorpsmen. On the other hand, the Freikorpsmen certainly represented one of the idealistic images of Nazi ideology and would soon become role models for the millions of German men and boys who related to the experience of war through books, pamphlets, and films glorifying these protofascist warriors.

Depersonalization left its mark on every aspect of the subsequent Nazi aesthetic: combat, power, the exaltation of death, the great phallic hero standing alone amid the tumult of battle. In idealizing the archetypal soldier, it made the idea of fulfillment through battle and absorption into the mass part of these men's deepest desires—men who were empty shells without the masses they had led as conquering heroes but that had shamelessly abandoned them in course of the First World War.

"Finally, there is ecstasy—a state of mind granted not only to the holy man, to great writers and great lovers, but also to the great in spirit. Ecstasy is an intoxication beyond all intoxications, a release that bursts all bonds ... Man in ecstasy becomes a violent storm, a raging sea, roaring thunder. He merges with the cosmos, racing toward death's dark gates like a bullet toward its target. And should the waves crash purple above him, he will be long past all consciousness of movement or transition; he will be a wave gliding back into the flowing sea."[28] Jünger celebrates war as a sexual experience. In another part of the book he writes: "Blood whirled through our brains and pulsated through our veins, as if anticipating a long-awaited night of love—but this night would be more passionate and more furious."[29] However, war is also a cultural experience. Here Ernst Jünger is describing the old social Darwinist assumptions: the cultural superiority of the victor, the oneness of victory, power, and culture. Jünger's entire book *Der Kampf als inneres Erlebnis* (Battle as Inner Experience) is animated by the glorification of battle and uses the same style throughout.

Once again Ernst Jünger and once again *Der Kampf als inneres Erlebnis*: "Regardless of how great a culture is, if men's nerves fail, it is nothing more than a giant with feet of clay. And the more massive its structures, the more horrible the collapse ... therefore it is the sacred duty of the highest culture to have the most powerful battalions."[30] In other words, culture in all its aspects is synonymous with having the best military forces. Here at last it is perfectly clear that fascism had another dimension, one that affected the individual much more directly and profoundly than the mere promise to eliminate unemployment and rectify other social ills. The aestheticization of politics—that is, the total integration of the individual into mass organizations, military, and paramilitary groups—had taken possession of all spheres of public life. The "most powerful battalions" had become the "highest culture."

The Nazis had another name for the totalist or totalitarian aesthetic; they called it propaganda. It is practically impossible today to imagine the impact of this propaganda without a knowledge of how history had prepared the masses to respond to it. In the 1920s the attitudes of an entire generation had been formed by the traumatic experience of having "pointlessly" risked their lives in war and then having a "humiliating" peace foisted upon them. The feeling of pointlessness recurred after World War II, but in this case people assessed the war quite differently. The surrender was not considered a "humiliation"; in fact, at least a majority felt it to be a liberation.

This radically different assessment is one of the many reasons that the feeling of meaninglessness after 1945 did not develop a dynamic similar to that of the 1920s. The East German film *Die Russen kommen* (The Russians Are Coming, 1968/87), directed by Heiner Carow, shows the last days of World War II through the eyes of the 16-year old Hitler Youth Günter and how his hopes and values are shattered overnight. However, since the idea of limiting the film's perspective to that of a young fascist hero (a first time for a Defa[31] picture) was apparently a bit too radical for the GDR, since in 1968 the country was trying to come to terms with the past, the film was consigned to the archives and was not premiered until 1987. Entire sequences from Veit Harlan's Nazi propaganda film *Kolberg* were edited in so as to emphasize the drama surrounding the battle for the fortress town of Kolberg— the sacrifices made by the townspeople, their ability to hold out to the end, and above all the fact that the decision was taken by a civilian militia rather than the regular military. In *Die Russen kommen* the young people of the village see *Kolberg* at the local cinema, and their reactions reflect the various functions of propaganda films: to divert people's attention from the daily experience of war (a soldier on leave and a young woman use the time in the theater for a bit of hanky-panky); to motivate them to carry on the war and be ready to die. The faces of the younger Hitler Youth are aglow after the Kolbergers finally repel the French attack on the town's fort.

"Until now it seems as though the fascists have been consulted too little about fascism, while those who claim to understand it have been consulted too much." Though there is a good deal of truth in this the starting point of Klaus Theweleit's study, it does not mean that National Socialism should be tied primarily to the person of Adolf Hitler. On the contrary, by personalizing the system in this way one lays oneself open to the suspicion of succumbing to the spell of the Hitler myth, as is the case of Joachim Fest's documentary *Hitler—eine Karriere* (Hitler: the Whole Story, 1977). Rather, the point is to analyze the psychological and social conditions of the people who fell under the Führer's spell, who burst into tears when they saw the documentaries and newsreels in those days, who enthusiastically shouted "Heil" thousands upon thousands of times.

In order to generate this kind of enthusiasm millions of times over, the Nazis put every available medium and means of communication at the service of their propaganda machine. Still, it is worth emphasizing with regard not only to the success but also to the form and content of Nazi propaganda that Goebbels mainly used the most modern, cutting-edge means of mass communication, i.e., radio and, most powerful and effective of all, film.

In *Dialektik der Aufklärung*, Adorno and Horkheimer note that "the step from the telephone to the radio has clearly distinguished the roles. The former still allowed the subscriber to play the role of subject, and was liberal. The latter is democratic: it turns all participants into listeners and authoritatively subjects them to broadcast programs which are all exactly the same."[32] However, as they go on to bolster their argument, they draw most of their examples from the most avant-garde technology in the field of art—film. Adorno and Horkheimer are not opposed to the technological advances in film production and the creation of fantasy, but to the use to which they are put in standardizing the production of thoughts and ideas. Published in 1944 and deeply affected by the phenomenon of fascism, the book sees the cause of the "self-destructiveness of the Enlightenment"[33] in the totalitarian *Gleichschaltung* of the expression of ideas by means of industrial technology.

Helmut Färber analyzes the unique opportunity of the film medium to influence the masses: "In film, reality, imagery, and the commercial-like use of imagery become one, creating a second-rate reality. Even images that are inherently incongruous can be, as it were, forced into a relationship. In this sense, film is directly related to demagoguery."[33] Béla Balázs points to another aspect of film's effectiveness as a tool of propaganda: "The way in which a director arranges a shot reflects his attitude toward a subject—his affection, his hatred, his pathos, or his mockery. Hence the propagandistic power of the film medium. For the director does not have to prove his point of view; he leaves it up to us to absorb it visually."[35]

The eye of the camera and montage—two devices available to the filmmaker—help the viewer to accept film as reality. Irresistibly, they draw the moviegoer into their version of reality, based on laws established in authoritarian fashion by the director. There is no escape. In this respect, though, film is no more than a reflection and a function of the modern industrialized world that gave birth to it, a world that negates the individual, as the Nazi documentary shows us in such exemplary and cynical fashion. Film epitomized and perfected the one factor that formed the basis of the entire Nazi movement and that, in a much broader sense than is connoted by the term today, embraced every area and aspect of life—propaganda.

Notes

1. Joseph Goebbels, "Der totale Krieg" in Joseph Goebbels, *Der steile Aufstieg* (Munich, 1944), p. 128.

2. Cf. Hilmar Hoffmann, ed., *Gegen den Versuch, Vergangenheit zu verbiegen* [with essays by Martin Broszat, Gordon Craig, Jürgen Habermas, Hans Mommsen et al.] (Frankfurt am Main, 1987). See also Charles S. Maier, *The Unmasterable Past* (Cambridge, Mass., 1988); Richard J. Evans, *In Hitler's Shadow* (New York, 1989); Peter Baldwin, ed., *Reworking the Past* (Boston, 1990).

3. Jürgen Habermas, "Eine Art Schadensabwicklung" in *Die Zeit* (Hamburg), vol. 29, 11 July 1986, p. 40.

4. Ernst Nolte, *Faschismus in seiner Epoche* (Munich, 1963), English translation *Three Faces of Fascism* (New York, 1965).

5. Ernst Nolte in *Frankfurter Allgemeine Zeitung* , 6 June 1986.

6. Horst-Eberhard Richter, *Leben statt machen* (Hamburg, 1987), p. 110; cf.: Hilmar Hoffmann, "Zukunft ist wieder denkbar" in *Frankfurter Rundschau* , 21 May 1988.

7. Horst-Eberhard Richter, *Leben statt machen*, p. 141.

8. "Über den Faschismus" in *Gegen den Strom*, Organ der KPD, Berlin (Opposition), 1930; now in Abendroth, Wolfgang, comp., *Faschismus und Kapitalismus*, 2nd ed. (Frankfurt am Main, 1967).

9. Georgi Dimitrov, *Arbeiterklasse gegen Faschismus* (Moscow, 1935; Mannheim, 1975).

10. Reinhard Opitz, "Über die Entstehung und Verhinderung von Faschismus," *Das Argument* (Berlin), no. 87, 1974.

11. Joachim C. Fest, *Hitler*.

12. John Toland, *Adolf Hitler* (New York, 1976).

13. Friedrich Heer, *Der Glaube des Adolf Hitler: Anatomie einer politischen Religiosität* (Munich, 1968).

14. Wilhelm Reich, *Massenpsychologie des Faschismus* (Copenhagen, 1933; Cologne, 1971), English translation *Mass Psychology of Fascism* (New York, 1970).

15. Klaus Theweleit, *Männerphantasien*, 2 vols. (Frankfurt am Main, 1977–78), English translation *Male Fantasies*, 2 vols. (Minneapolis, Minn., 1987–89).

16. Theodor W. Adorno and Max Horkheimer, *Dialektik der Aufklärung* (Frankfurt am Main, 1969; 1987), English translation *Dialectic of Enlightenment* (New York, 1944; 1972).

17. Ralf Dahrendorf, *Gesellschaft und Demokratie in Deutschland* (Munich, 1965), English translation *Society and Democracy in Germany* (New York, 1967).

18. Saul Friedländer, *Kitsch und Tod* (Munich, 1984), p. 118, English translation *Reflections on Nazism: an Essay on Kitsch and Death* (New York, 1984).

19. Adolf Hitler, *Mein Kampf*, p. 371, English translation *Mein Kampf* (Boston, 1943).

20. Seymour Martin Lipset, *Soziologie der Demokratie* (Neuwied, 1962), English original *Political Man: The Social Bases of Politics* (New York, 1960).

21. See, e.g., Thomas Childers, *The Nazi Voter* (Chapel Hill, 1983); Richard F. Hamilton, *Who Voted For Hitler?* (Princeton, 1982); Detlev Mühlberger, *Hitler's Followers* (London, 1991); Michael Kater, *The Nazi Party* (Cambridge, Mass., 1983). The extent of blue-collar Nazification before 1933 has remained controversial. See, e.g., Conan Fischer, ed., *The Rise of National Socialism and the Working Classes in Weimar Germany* (forthcoming).

22. Siegfried Kracauer, *Die Angestellten* (Frankfurt am Main, 1930).

23. Walter Hofer, ed., *Der Nationalsozialismus: Dokumente 1933–1945* (Frankfurt am Main, 1957), p. 24.

24. Ralf Dahrendorf, *Gesellschaft und Demokratie in Deutschland*, p. 442. See also Ian Kershaw, *Der Hitler-Mythos* (Stuttgart, 1980), English translation *The "Hitler Myth": Image and Reality in the Third Reich* (Oxford, 1987).

25. See the studies cited in note 21 above. [DNVP stands for Deutschnationale Volkspartei or German National People's Party, Zentrum for the Catholic Center Party, and BVP for the Bayerische Volkspartie or Bavarian People's Party.—Transl.]

26. Klaus Theweleit, *Männerphantasien*.

27. Ibid., vol. 1, pp. 212–3.

28. Ernst Jünger, *Der Kampf als inneres Erlebnis* (Berlin, 1922), p. 53.

29. Ibid., p. 12.

30. Ibid., p. 37.

31. [Defa was the acronym for Deutsche-Film-AG, the name of the GDR's film company—Transl.]

32. Theodor W. Adorno and Max Horkheimer, *Dialektik der Aufklärung*, p. 109.

33. Ibid., p. 1.

34. Helmut Färber, *Baukunst und Film: aus der Geschichte des Sehens* (Munich, 1977).

35. Béla Balázs, *Schriften zum Film*, 2 vols. (Frankfurt am Main, 1972), vol. 2: *Der Geist des Films: Artikel und Aufsätze 1926–1931*, p. 73.

✛ 4 ✛

FILM PROPAGANDA IN THE THIRD REICH

History of Propaganda

The most striking success of a revolution based on a philosophy of life will always have been achieved when the new philosophy of life as far as possible has been taught to all men and, if necessary, later forced upon them ...

Adolf Hitler[1]

The Nazis will always have a place in the annals of mass deceit and inciting hatred. No one will dispute their right to this claim to fame. In fact, it seems perfectly justifiable to characterize the National Socialist movement as a "propaganda movement." "We must inspire propaganda to proceed at an active, modern pace, and we must endow it with life and breath," was Joseph Goebbels's recommendation in a lecture delivered at Nuremberg on 16 September 1935 to the Gau and Kreis propaganda leaders of the movement. Unlike any other politician before or since, Hitler, from the time he began his political activity, had very definite ideas regarding the effectiveness and the methods of modern mass propaganda.

Even when the Nazi movement was made up of nothing more than a bunch of stragglers and numbered only several dozen members, its rallies and recruitment meetings clearly differed from those of other political splinter groups. Like a clever advertising executive, Hitler had effectively planned a strategy for marketing his product, namely himself, never confusing propaganda with sales promotion. A uniform set of party symbols, a party newspaper (which was founded very early in the history of the movement), and later a Nazified eclectic mass culture were all part of the strategy. The most important component, though, was the perfectly stage-managed public appearances of the Führer, which Hitler had a flair for transforming into gigantic circus-like mass rallies. Unlike his political adversaries, Hitler did not travel across the country by car or rail. He preferred to use a plane and descend from the clouds like some mythical savior to the waiting crowds of Germans below. Since the Nazis' mania for theatrical effects and the way in which they staged their spectacular shows are already well known, the following brief comments should suffice.

Even though they considered "propaganda" the actual objective of their policy (the content of which was more often than not of very low quality) and perfected the art during their period of rule, the Nazis were not the inventors of the concept. Consequently, a few remarks on the history of propaganda are warranted in order to provide an overview of the historical material that Hitler so unscrupulously appropriated and twisted for his own purposes.

Initially, the term propaganda had meaning only within the context of the Roman Catholic church, where it originated as part of the Counter Reformation. During the reign of Pope Gregory XV, the cardinals of the Roman Curia set up the *Sacra Congregatio de Propaganda Fide* (the Congregation for the Propagation of the Faith), the chief purpose of which was to combat Lutheranism in Germany. Founded in 1622, it became both famous and infamous as the Counter Reformation's main institution for training missionaries to spread the Catholic faith around the globe.

During the French revolution of 1830, conspiratorial groups secularized the ecclesiastical term, calling their international campaigns "*La Propaganda.*" The extreme left were the first to "propagandize" their various causes.

Proponents of revolutionary activism in Russia imported the concept of propaganda from France, along with the idea of agitation. The anarchist Sergei G. Nechayev introduced the term into the vocabulary of Russian anarchism with the activist slogan "taking propaganda to the people" (1869). Coauthor of a work titled *Revolutionary Catechism*, Nechayev was later vehemently criticized by Marx and Engels. He died after being imprisoned for ten years in Peter Paul Fortress in St. Petersburg. Dostoyevsky, himself an adherent of "utopian socialism," immortalized S. G. Nechayev by basing the character Pyotr Stepanovich Verkhovensky on the famous anarchist in his *Possessed*, sometimes translated as *Demons*.

In 1903 Lenin ridiculed the competition to generate relevant ideas for the purposes of indoctrination with his often-quoted ironic remark that propaganda disseminates a lot of ideas to the few, while agitation spreads a few ideas to the many. Be that as it may, Lenin's CPSU (Communist Party of the Soviet Union) was the first organized mass movement to use propaganda as an instrument and a weapon to mobilize an entire nation. Radio and the press were not the only media forced to pound the programs of totalitarianism into the hearts and minds of the masses. The state used literature, film, the fine arts, and even music as tools in the campaign to protect the revolution from an unbridled individualism that could threaten the state's *raison d'être*. However, it was not until 1932 that Stalin established socialist realism as the only officially approved school of art within the Communist empire. Henceforth, the depiction of social reality could be used only to emphasize the positive accomplishments of socialism as the supreme principle of the new reality. At the same time, the party decreed that the "new man" was to be made the exemplary Soviet hero of this new society. Any deviation from the general line of the party's officially established virtues was denounced as formalism or decadent bourgeois art—and not just verbally. Repression, denial of permission to work, and persecution were the responses to any attempts at producing art on one's own.

Hitler pursued his plans to subordinate the press, the cinema, and the arts to the purposes of Nazi propaganda with similar uncompromising vigor, albeit in a different direction with regard to subject matter. In his case, others had already laid the "groundwork" for him in Germany. In a letter to the War Ministry dated 4 July 1917, General Erich Ludendorff had made the connection between "propaganda" and the subject of this book—"film." Given the universal hatred of Germany provoked by American film propaganda and with a view to the "further course of the war … German film propaganda must make a special effort to clarify the German point of view."

In fact, we see a worldwide and extremely effective film propaganda campaign waged during World War I by the powers arrayed against Germany. From the outset of the war, Prime Minister Asquith continued the age-old British tradition of using propaganda as a weapon. Interestingly, in 1826 Foreign Secretary George Canning made a prescient statement in a speech to the Lower House of Parliament in which he foresaw that if His Majesty's government went to war over Portugal, his country "could not avoid seeing ranked under her banners all the restless and dissatisfied of any nation with which she might come in conflict."[2] In 1914 Asquith immediately set up an Office of Propaganda that came directly under the War Cabinet. Among his advisors was Lord Northcliffe, who for twenty years, until 1928, was Britain's press baron. As temporary director of propaganda in enemy countries under Lloyd George, he was able to expand his influence. Northcliffe fired the first shot in the journalistic world war by publishing in his various newspapers a horrific vision of "child-molesting beasts." He celebrated the Allies' sustained propaganda barrage as the third factor—aside from the land war and the war at sea—in deciding the outcome of the conflict: "The most ordinary pictures could become rabble-rousing propaganda when combined with captions that were in common use at the time, e.g., under a photograph of German soldiers, the words 'And then hordes of the Kaiser's child-murderers arrived.'"[3]

Charlie Chaplin's film *Shoulder Arms* (1918), which Kurt Tucholsky called a "perfect satire of the military," was the story of Charlie's dream about capturing the Kaiser. While it was generally condemned as vile enemy propaganda, Tucholsky, on the other hand, pleaded: "This brilliant film should be shown in darkest Germany. Cross the Rhine, Chaplin, cross the Rhine."[4] The most obviously unrestrained of all Allied propaganda films, *The Kaiser —Beast of Berlin*, was advertised in a correspondingly hostile manner: "Keep your guns in your pocket and don't shoot at the screen next Friday, because that's the day we're showing *The Beast of Berlin*." There was no absolute difference in quality between the inflammatory propaganda produced by the Allies and that turned out by Imperial Germany in the First World War. Even French Premier Aristide Briand set up an office of propaganda (*Maison de la Presse*) in October 1915, which Georges Clemenceau raised to a secretariat for propaganda toward the end of the war.

Under Woodrow Wilson, who had been elected president on a platform to keep America out of the war, influential industrialists like Andrew Carnegie and Henry Ford gave their initial financial support to pacifist films such as *Intolerance* (1916), directed by D. W. Griffith, and *Civilization* (1916), directed by Thomas Ince. Director James Stuart Blackton signaled a 180-degree change in attitude with his *The Battle Cry of Peace* (1916), the first nationalistic dramatic feature film. When America entered the war on 5 April 1917, the Committee on Public Information took over responsibility for the organization of U.S. film propaganda. Wartime U.S. propaganda newsreels were distributed by Pathé and Hearst and were seen in more than twenty thousand European movie theaters. George Creel, who supervised film propaganda in his capacity as director of the U.S. Film Division, summarized his achievements with a measure of self-satisfaction: "In our battle for public opinion in foreign countries, we overcame the obstacle of a hostile press in almost every case through our use of film to inform and advertise."[5] War propaganda is only successful when the soil has been prepared well in advance. Aldous Huxley wrote that "political and religious propaganda is effective, it would seem, only upon those who are already partly or entirely convinced of its truth."[6]

Since the subject matter of propaganda films was often dreary and did not have great entertainment value, Hollywood, being more interested in profit than politics, soon returned to producing schmaltzy melodramas after the end of the First World War. The interest in business to the exclusion of everything else helps explain the fact that America produced hardly one film from 1933 to the beginning of the Second World War that dealt with the subject of Nazism. On the contrary, high-quality Nazi documentaries such as Leni Riefenstahl's *Olympia* (1938) and glorifications of war like Fritz Hippler's *Sieg im Westen* (Victory in the West, late 1940) packed movie theaters in America right up to the beginning of World War II. "Cheer up, America—the show will go on" assured an MGM slogan.

In his war memoirs, published in 1919, Ludendorff confirmed the fact that enemy propaganda was one of the causes of the widespread defeatism inside Germany: "Blockade and propaganda began gradually to undermine our fighting spirit ... Before the enemy propaganda we were like a rabbit before a snake ... The propagandists were clever in understanding the effects of such phrases as 'a peace without victors or vanquished' (*Verständigungsfrieden*, or peace of understanding), 'post-war disarmament,' 'league of nations,' and so on, on the German people."[7] Even Hitler acknowledged that he ultimately "learned enormously" from "the amazing skill and truly brilliant calculation of enemy war propaganda."

As early as 1910 Ludwig Klitzsch, the publisher of the *Leipziger Illustrierte Zeitung*, had recommended a "nationalist political advertising campaign" to counteract "the encirclement policy of future enemy powers by using similar means of propaganda." Klitzsch invited the captains of German industry to the Adlon Hotel in Berlin to alert them to "the great effectiveness of film propaganda as used by our economic competitors" and to suggest launching a series of counteroffensives. Germany, he said, must not allow itself to be pushed into a corner in the world market. France had ostensibly spread anti-German "hate" films in Egypt in 1909 "in order to acquire renown not only as the inventor of the motion picture but as the inventor of the 'hate' film as well."

But it was not until the middle of the war in 1916 that Klitzsch was able to persuade the Supreme Command and the Foreign Office by arguing that the British government had allocated the equivalent of 80 million marks solely for the purpose of producing "hate" films for its anti-German propaganda campaign in Latin America.[8] To counter this effort, the German government, with the support of other interested parties, founded Deulig, a film company that through appropriate documentary films was to publicize the fatherland at home and abroad. The *Deutsche Lichtspiel-Gesellschaft* (German Motion Picture Company) assumed the task of producing and distributing propaganda films until General Ludendorff, ever the omnipotent commander, decided to put film production under his authority. At the beginning of 1917, there followed the establishment in Berlin of Bufa (*das Königliche Bild-und Filmamt* [Royal Picture and Film Office]), set up purely as a government agency. Within a short time kiosks carried film posters proclaiming "The heroic exploits of our incomparable soldiers"; "Kaiser Wilhelm in the midst of enemy fire"; "Our soldiers parade proudly past the Supreme War Lord in their field-gray uniforms."

Ludendorff, the Quartermaster-General, was now in charge of another, different kind of ordnance—film. In order for film "not to lose its enormous importance as a means of political and military influence, " it is "absolutely necessary for the successful prosecution of the war that film be used with utmost vigor wherever Germany is still able to exercise its influence." In retrospect, this order, issued in 1917 by the Chief of the Army General Staff, may be considered the charter that actually established Ufa (*Universum-Film-AG*) in December of that same year.

On 5 February 1917 Bufa commissioned the Imperator-Film-Gesellschaft to produce an official propaganda film titled *Die Schuldigen des Weltkrieges* (Those Responsible for the World War). The notes shown below, on which it was to be based, illustrate the Royal Picture and Film Office's naiveté regarding effective counterpropaganda:

1. The instigators of the worldwide conflagration;
2. Who fanned the flames? (Sir Edward Grey sitting behind his desk);
3. Who added fuel to the fire? ((Clemenceau, the fanatic revanchist);
4. Who volunteered to be their accomplice? (Sazonov, the lackey of the Entente);
5. Who was the butcher of Sarajevo? (Cinoci [sic], the minister of war and purloiner of millions);
6. The gang of murderers and arsonists;
7. Who ravaged and despoiled East Prussia? (Nikolayevich, the murdering Cossack);
8. Who wanted German children to go without milk and German mothers to go without bread (Asquith, who planned to starve us to death);
9. Who allied himself with savage tribes on every continent? (Poincaré, England's loyal servant and Grey's co-conspirator);
10. Who ordered German doctors, nurses, officers, and men to be tortured, murdered, mutilated? (Delcassé, King Edward's minion);
11. Who is deceiving and swindling the whole world? (Briand, the windbag of the "grande nation");
12. Who is responsible for the *Baralong* incident and *King Steffen* [sic] [possibly the *Stephano*, a British steamer sunk by the British themselves—Transl.]? Who is spoiling for a fight to the finish? (Lloyd George, England's Satan);
13. Who is Europe's biggest hypocrite? (Bratianu the two-faced);
14. Who violated his pledge to the Triple Alliance? (Sonnino, the most mendacious among this gang of thieves);
15. Who is going to prosecute them? (Hindenburg).

Evidently, the project to produce *Die Schuldigen des Weltkrieges* never came to fruition.

While the war was still in progress, Ludendorff prepared to centralize filmmaking, with an eye "to having a more systematic and stronger influence on the great mass of the people in the interests of the state by using general standardized themes." A certain Major Alexander Grau, a press specialist in the War Ministry, was detailed to carry out Ludendorff's orders. Ludendorff showed his true colors when he founded the "Tannenberg League" in 1926. It described itself as a militant *Kampfbund* (Fighting League) directed against so-called "supranational powers" such as Jews, Freemasons, Marxists, and Jesuits. With its stock of shares amounting to about 25 million marks, of which the Reich took over one-third, Ufa was set up as a virtual film cartel without any competition. Messter-Filmgesellschaft, P. Davidson's Film-Union, and the motion picture companies controlled by Nordisk merged to form the new Ufa enterprise. The official mission of Ufa was nothing less than to advertise Germany's greatness. "[Government directives] asked not only for unambiguous screen propaganda, but also for films that would give people in foreign countries a picture of German culture ..."[9]

The new consortium's first report, published on 10 October 1918, reflects the spirit one would expect of an enterprise that was born as a result of the war: "In close collaboration with Lieutenant Colonel von Haeften of the military department of the Foreign Office, Major Grau of the Royal War Ministry, Privy Councillor Walter of the Reich Treasury, and under the guidance of Herr von Stauß of the Deutsche Bank, and with the direct participation of the Prince Donnersmarck Foundation, the negotiations to effect a merger in the film industry were expanded. On the one hand, the merger represented a vigorous and promising enterprise, and on the other it offered assurances that important questions in the areas of German propaganda and German cultural and popular education would be resolved in the spirit of the Imperial government. The private-sector program was aimed at creating a concern in which the most important activities of the film industry, i.e., production, distribution, and screening, would be adequately represented."[10]

Even at this time Ufa was already a quasi-governmental operation. Consequently, it was not difficult for the Nazis "to induce [this oligopoly of different companies] to cooperate by offering specific economic incentives and autarkic protective measures and, after they had assumed power, gradually to transform it into a monopoly subservient to their regime."[11] So far, though, the Germans, in the words of Gottlieb Hermes, would not consider making movies "like the Belgians, who defame our army and its supreme commanders, or like the French." Instead, after the peace treaty was signed, the naive Germans turned out movies "that were heavily weighed down by didacticism, statistics, and other methods associated with academe ... and that now, as at the time they were produced, would have little or no prospect of finding acceptance abroad."[12] Hence, there was a determination quickly to reverse the defensiveness reflected in the German cinema's underdeveloped chauvinism and, with the help of Ufa and the inclusion of nationalist themes, go over to the offensive on a worldwide scale.

The German *Kulturfilm* industry owed its rapid rise after World War I to two men: Emil Georg von Stauß, president of the Deutsche Bank, who successfully gave it the financial wherewithal through his bank's acquisition of the shares held by the Reich and Nordisk, and the above-mentioned Alexander Grau, who was responsible for conceptualizing the plan.

Alfred Hugenberg, leader of the nationalist conservative party from 1928 and cofounder of the so-called Harzburg Front, which briefly assembled all the right-wing enemies of the Weimar Republic in October 1931, soon appeared on the scene to help pave the way for the development of the cinema into a tool for propaganda. A cold, calculating profiteer who made a fortune out of the inflation of the 1920s, Hugenberg bought up dozens of provincial newspapers, including the much-read *Berliner Lokal-Anzeiger*. With the acquisition of the huge Scherl Verlag and with his news agency, Hugenberg soon controlled the largest media empire that had ever existed in Germany. After buying the Deulig film company and the bankrupt Ufa (1927), he also used the film medium to advance his reactionary views. The media mogul was therefore able to conduct an unrestrained campaign against the Weimar republic and Stresemann, the Locarno Pact and the League of Nations, internationalism, liberalism, socialism, and pacifism.

Hugenberg's nationalistic weekly newsreels spread anachronistic and chauvinistic ideas about German supremacy. They were originally designed as contributions to help the Kaiser regain his throne. After the attempt failed, Hugenberg exploited them with greater success to push Hitler's *völkisch* ideas. Using his cartel-like empire to manipulate public opinion, Hugenberg ultimately helped Hitler to achieve power. He had hoped, as a consequence, to realize his long-range personal and political goals with Hitler's help. But Hitler's gratitude to Hugenberg was short-lived. Less than six months after Hitler appointed Hugenberg Minister of Economics in his first coalition cabinet after being named chancellor, he used massive pressure to force the conservative press baron to resign his post on 26 June 1933. Hugenberg's resignation led to the dissolution of his party, the National People's Party (DNVP), a day later.

This short excursus does not seek to portray Nazi propaganda as a lineal heir to Catholic or even Stalinist propaganda. The only direct line was the one that led from Ludendorff to Hitler. What it does intend to show is that the Nazis did not originate the idea of propaganda. At the same time, however, it is impossible to explain Nazi propaganda's attempt to have a profound influence on ideas and attitudes—"while disengaging the critical faculties (*unter Ausschaltung des Denkens*)" (Hitler)—without referring to its ideological origins, the roots of which lie mainly in the nineteenth century. Here we will outline some of the theories of mass psychology on which Hitler and his henchmen based their efforts to bring the mind of the masses into line (*gleichrichten*) and standardize their thinking, theories that they also used to give a "scientific" underpinning to the staged spectacles that were both contemptuous and destructive of human life and individuality.

In his psychology of crowds, the French social psychologist Gustave Le Bon (1841–1931) developed a pseudoscientific, elitist, and cynical theory of man that became the basis for his rejection of democracy and socialism. It also became the foundation for demagogues whose efforts were aimed at using—or more properly, abusing—human beings and the truth. "Mass psychology" is a variant of the nineteenth century conservative theory of revolution. In his *Psychologie des Foules*, published in 1895, Le Bon used the following characteristics to identify individuals whose personality has been submerged in a crowd and whom he contemptuously termed "primitive people":

> Disappearance of the conscious personality, predominance of the unconscious personality, the turning by means of suggestion and contagion of feelings and ideas in an identical direction, the tendency to immediately transform the suggested ideas into acts.... He is no longer himself, but has become an automaton who has ceased to be guided by his will. Moreover, by the mere fact that he forms part of an organized crowd, a man descends several rungs on the ladder of civilization.[13]

The individuals who have been reduced to the level of "automatons" and whose sentiments and ideas coincide with those of all others in the crowd become ready targets of propaganda. Even though Le Bon considered crowds, as a matter of principle, destructive, he also recognized their "heroic" function, which made them important to the Nazis: "It is crowds rather than isolated individuals that may be induced to run the risk of death to secure the triumph of a creed or an idea, that may be fired with enthusiasm for glory and honor, that are led—almost without bread and without arms, as in the age of the Crusades—to deliver the tomb of Christ from the infidel, or as in 1793, to defend the fatherland."[14] In his chapter titled "The Leaders of Crowds and Their Means of Persuasion," Le Bon described the malleability of crowds as though he were establishing a set of guidelines for future fascists.

The most influential successor to Le Bon, the enemy of democracy, was the Spanish cultural philosopher Ortega y Gasset. His most popular work, *La Rebelión de las Masas*, published in 1930 and still popular today, represents a noteworthy variation on the theory of mass psychology. According to Ortega y Gasset, the negative qualities of the masses are not limited to them alone; they apply to the individual as well. This individual, whom he calls "mass man," only serves to enhance the superior individual's sense of his own superiority. Ortega's definition of the masses concludes with the kind of imperious language that is difficult to imagine writing today: "The mass is all that which sets no value on itself—good or ill—based on specific grounds, but which feels itself 'just like everybody,' and nevertheless is not concerned about it; is, in fact, quite happy to feel as one with everybody else."

In his theory of the group leader, published in 1921, Sigmund Freud anticipated the emergence of the masses who would eventually be manipulated by a dictator. The gist of his theory is that the members of a group are bound by libidinal ties to identify with a leader who then uses those ties to become, as it were, the group's "superego."

In his *Doktor Faustus* (1947) Thomas Mann introduces through indirection an influential exponent of an overbearing elitism. Clearly, the ideas he represents are those of the French socialist Georges Sorel (1847–1922) and are meant to induce the illustrious group of gentlemen conversationalists, gathered in the postrevolutionary Munich of 1919, into good-humoredly approving the scrapping of truth, science, and reason. Mann has his chronicler Serenus Zeitblom recall this intellectual soirée with a sinking feeling in the pit of his stomach. Following the experience of Hitlerism, Mann takes Georges Sorel's theory on the positive role of myth and violence—a theory which is said to have had a powerful influence on Mussolini—and uses it to to make the following point:

> ... that in this age of the masses parliamentary discussion must prove entirely inadequate for the shaping of political decisions; that in its stead the masses would have in the future to be provided with mythical fictions, devised like primitive battle-cries, to release and activate political energies. This was in fact the crass and flaming prophecy of the book: that popular myths or rather those proper for the masses would become the vehicles of political action—fables, insane visions, chimeras—which needed to have nothing to do with truth or reason or science in order to be creative,

to determine the course of life and history, and thus to prove them-selves dynamic realities."[15]

Conditions for the Rise of Hitler

The first task of propaganda is to win people for subsequent organiza-tion; the first task of organization is to win men for the continuation of propaganda. The second task of propaganda is the disruption of the existing state of affairs and the permeation of this state of affairs with the new doctrine, while the second task of organization must be the struggle for power, thus to achieve the final success of the doctrine.

Adolf Hitler[16]

A number of the works cited above laid the intellectual founda-tions and helped pave the way for Hitler and his propaganda machine. But ultimately it was contemporary political and social factors that allowed these destructive seeds to fall on fertile soil. How could such unimpressive surrogate ideals, such high-sound-ing but empty formulations, and such immoral theories possibly prove themselves "dynamic realities" (Thomas Mann)?

In researching the question of what might have induced broad segments of a nation of seventy million people to follow a politi-cal pied piper like Hitler, Adorno based his essay *Aufarbeitung der Vergangenheit* (Working Up the Past) on American studies in the field of social psychology. According to these studies, the psycho-logical makeup (*Charakterstruktur*) of voters, that is, of groups, is defined in relation to factors such as power or powerlessness, rigidity or flexibility, conventionalism, conformism, lack of self-determination, and, ultimately, "the general lack of ability to learn through experience." Adorno concludes that groups are fond of identifying with power *per se* and, what is more, do so "regardless of the particular nature [of that power]." Basically, Adorno believes that most people have poorly developed egos, and in their attempt to bolster them, they need to identify existentially with and have the protection of large groups. Adorno's interpre-tation follows Sigmund Freud's line of argument.

There is no need to go into the details of these kinds of socio-psychological interpretations. What we are ultimately interested in knowing is what kinds of people in what kinds of actual situa-tions and with what kinds of outlooks were impelled to join the

Nazi movement—not simply to escape material hardship, but to find a way out of what Georg Simmel, in describing conditions after 1900, called "the crisis of the soul." Already in 1932, Theodor Geiger had analyzed the social makeup of Hitler's supporters. The social crisis that developed toward the end of the Weimar republic as a result of unemployment and the Depression played into Hitler's hands and helped him to give people a sense that the Nazis would take care of and protect them from "society's natural disasters": "[The Party] tightened the knots of the social [safety] net to catch everything (and everybody) and insure protection against the universal fear of falling through the mesh and slipping into poverty."

Hitler and the groups close to him clearly understood how to create the impression that only the radical forces that he represented and that were determined to change the system could, in fact, turn the catastrophic economic and social situation around for the better. They claimed that under Hitler the kind of devastating inflation that took place from 1922 to 1923 would not recur. Using every means of propaganda at his disposal, Hitler communicated to people the hope that under his rule fascism would become totalist and thus better able to solve all of society's problems. [Fascist] totalism, he said, would prove to be a good and beneficial solution—not to mention the correct one.

The propagandists sought to justify their shrill and effective appeal to injured national pride and historical instincts by pointing to what Hitler called the "shameful *diktat* of Versailles." Indeed, the peace treaty of 1918 forced Germany to suffer considerable losses of territory. Alsace Lorraine, taken after the Franco-Prussian War, was returned to France. The Saar coal region remained under French administration until 1935, the Rhineland demilitarized until 1936. East Prussia was separated from the rest of Germany by a wide strip of territory running through West Prussia to Poland. The German Baltic port of Danzig was transformed into an internationalized free city under the League of Nations. Large parts of Upper Silesia were lost to the reconstituted Polish state. Finally, the occupation of the Ruhr by French and Belgian troops remained a thorn in the side of national pride, with painful long-term effects.

In addition to the veterans of World War I and the army of six million unemployed, the Nazis drew their massive social strength from the ranks of the *déclassé* lower middle class and a large segment of the upwardly mobile "new middle class," the so-called white collar proletariat (*Stehkragenproletariat*).

Aside from the terrorism that had already begun, Hitler owed his electoral success in 1933 to the multitudes of voters who felt totally confused by the overwhelming number of parties and party platforms that were a result of the use of proportional representation in elections to the Reichstag. In addition, he garnered the votes of anybody who was disgruntled over Germany's battered international reputation. Hitler admitted that Germany was positively panting for order during these momentous days of decision. Parliamentarism seemed to have reached the point of absurdity when in 1932 just thirteen meetings of the Reichstag were deemed necessary and the legislature had in effect been abolished as a result of the frequent use of presidential emergency decrees (*Notverordnungen*). The Nazis promised to lead the masses out of this vale of woe. Moreover, Hitler understood how to capitalize on the bankruptcy of other parties.

Alexander and Margarete Mitscherlich refer to the "interdependencies" that played an important part in the whirlpool effect of the mass media campaign to mislead and that furthered the notion of "the helpless man in the street being passively swept along." The Mitscherlich's are correct in recognizing that consideration of the problem should begin, not with the period of catastrophe, but "with the state of untroubled harmony that previously existed between people and dictator." Broad segments of the German population were, after all, very much in favor of a leadership "that ... succeeded in combining typical Teutonic ideals with national self-esteem. It gave people the chance to embody their self-importance in a uniform. Authorities, visibly organized in ranks and hierarchies, suddenly appeared in profusion before the eyes of 'fellow Germans' long disillusioned by 'party squabbles.' The readiness and promptness of our Germanic obedience was duly tested, and an almost unbounded will to show ourselves worthy of the Führer's hopes spread quickly."[17]

The Nazis promised to set an example and undertake punitive expeditions against the "initiators" of the ever-present crises in people's personal lives, i.e., against Bolsheviks, Marxists, and capitalists—the three collective enemies of the people—and, above all, against the Jews, again and again, against the Jews. Anti-Semitism became the centerpiece of National Socialist propaganda, and the Nazis used any occasion to stir the flames of hatred against the Jews.

By airing similar themes in the press, on radio, in films and public speeches, the Nazis fulfilled what Adorno called the "collective power fantasies" of people who were powerless as individuals and "considered themselves somebody only in terms of a powerful collectivity." This is why the stab-in-the-back legend, as Hitler adapted it for propaganda purposes, fell on such fertile soil, especially in view of the fact that it was linked to the promise of revenge. The Nazis were determined to generate a new national self-confidence in which every individual would share. The national humiliation of Versailles would be erased; the all-corrupting influence of the Jews eliminated, along with the initiators of corruption themselves; the class warfare stirred up by capitalists and communists would end; the working class, threatened by a decline in its social status, and the notoriously disgruntled lower middle class would be absorbed into a new egalitarian German national-racial community (*Volksgemeinschaft*).

However, since it was not as easy to do away with capitalism as it was to get rid of communists—at least for the time being—capitalists were enlisted to work for the national cause. The Nazis considered they had done their socialist duty by establishing the German Labor Front (Deutsche Arbeitsfront or DAF), which supported the government, and by setting up a classless national community. Therefore, they had no need to interfere with private ownership or "creative Aryan capital."

Nationalist sentiment, once inflamed, called for a red flag to give it cohesion, a flag "with a big swastika for the little man" (Bertolt Brecht). With its *völkisch* ideology and its various organizations, the Nazi Party was able to "combine symbols that were effective in persuading the masses and revolutionary in style with a doctrine that masked the reactionary class structure of German society. Uniforms and ranks, medals and decorations were used for the purpose of integrating people and opening up opportunities for 'individuals to rise' in the newly created militarized hierarchy.... Thus numerous opportunities were created to promote and satisfy individual ambitions without threatening private property rights."[18]

Along with the new social hierarchy, there also existed a new hierarchy of mutually dependent fascist virtues that served as the foundation of the new state: loyalty, honor, comradeship, obedience, willingness to make sacrifices, fighting spirit, bravery. The Nazis used these martial values to legitimize their efforts to exterminate anyone who opposed their fascist scale of values.

In bringing together the various virtues designed to stabilize Nazi power, Saul Friedländer sees a "singular expression of a flow of ideas, emotions, and phantasms" that are kept separate in all other modern Western societies. National Socialism, he writes, "in its singularity, as in its general aspects, is the result of a large number of social, economic, and political factors, of the coming to a head of frequently analyzed ideological currents, and of the meeting of the most archaic myths and the most modern means of terror."[19]

The Nazis allowed their followers to work off their pent-up or stirred-up aggressions, unhindered and with impunity, against anyone deemed by Hitler to be a "representative of the system" (the Weimar republic) and therefore fair game. Jews suffered the most in this regard. Hitler had, in his own words, "fanaticized the masses" in order to make them a tool of his policy. The masses were to be "swept along" by the emotional appeal of the movement.

The Ministry for Popular Enlightenment and Propaganda

Only after the simplest ideas are repeated thousands of times will the masses finally remember them.

Adolf Hitler[20]

Hitler's bequest to *his* people—a bequest fraught with grave consequences—was one of total submissiveness, as evidenced by the enthusiasm of the masses for certain aspects of his destructive utopia and their acquiescence in his vague promises. To replace the previous state of confusion, the Nazis prescribed a set of political "convictions" and their own code of ethics for the masses. Since National Socialism was incapable of developing a coherent ideology of its own, the Nazis proceeded to plunder other ideologies and create surrogate religions by means of a kind of aggressive anti-ideology, the purpose of which was to maintain the new social order and keep themselves in power. In essence, there was no ideology to propagandize. Propaganda was a substitute for ideology. Propaganda itself was the message, down to and including school textbooks. On 11 March 1933, six weeks after the so-called *Machtergreifung* or "seizure of power," the Nazis set up the "Ministry for Popular Enlightenment and Propaganda." On 13 March Joseph Goebbels was named to head the ministry and was sworn in the following day. A decree issued by President von Hindenburg that same day outlined the mission of the new ministry whose very name was a perversion of the concept of enlightenment. "The Ministry for Enlightenment and Propaganda has been established for the purpose of enlightening and propagandizing the people with regard to the policies of the Reich government and the national reconstruction of the German fatherland."

The supreme demagogue of the ministry announced the programmatic objectives of total mass persuasion: "The great initiatives must come from here. There are two ways to make a revolution. You can blast your enemy with machine guns until he acknowledges the superiority of those holding the machine guns. That is the easy way. Or you can transform the nation through a revolution of the spirit, and instead of destroying your enemy, win him over. We National Socialists have taken the latter approach and will continue to do so. The noblest goal of this ministry is to win the entire nation over to the new state." *Gleichschaltung* or bringing everyone into line was now the chief task of the newly created ministry, and Bernhard Rust, a Reich Commissioner in the Prussian Culture Ministry, was quite frank when he described the process on 12 May 1933: "Our [policy of] *Gleichschaltung* means that the new German view of the world (*Weltanschauung*), simply by dint of the fact that it has the force of law, takes precedence over any other view."

It soon became patently clear that *Gleichschaltung* was simply a euphemism for annihilation. Those who resisted being brought into line were forced to back down. In fact, radio had become so thoroughly attuned to the Nazi world-view within just a matter of a few weeks that even Dr. Goebbels felt obliged the following year to reprimand broadcasters for their "vigorous politicization." Apparently, zealous party members had gone overboard in trying to achieve their goals.

A short time later, the cinema, the theater, the press, and every other branch of journalistic, artistic, and scientific activity subordinated itself to the dictates of propaganda. What had now come to fruition was perfectly consistent with what Hitler had formulated in *Mein Kampf* in 1925. Although two million copies of the book were in circulation in 1933 (one of the most bought and least read books in Germany), even those few who were familiar with its contents evidently did not take seriously the consequences of Hitler's hateful and cynical theories. In *Mein Kampf* Hitler had plainly anticipated the role of propaganda in a National Socialist state. The form and content of propaganda "must be geared to the broad mass." Therefore, "all propaganda must be popular and its intellectual level must be adjusted to the most limited intelligence among those it is addressed to. Consequently, the greater the mass it is intended to reach, the lower its purely intellectual level will have to be."[21] Hitler's cynical estimation of the intellectual level of the people who applauded his actions was outstripped by reality and in that sense confirmed the "correctness" of his view that propaganda "must be measured exclusively by the effect of its successes." The first Reichstag elections in the one-party state on 12 November 1933 confirmed the Nazis' calculations and gave them 92 percent of the vote: "The battle has been fought and victory achieved. Just yesterday on Sunday the flags and banners were waving … to invite every German to do his duty, and today they wave as beacons of jubilation and victory."[22]

By the same token, however, propaganda revealed the "intellectual level" of those like Goebbels and Rosenberg who "marketed" ideology using every device at their disposal and in a way that was unsurpassed in its lack of moral scruples. In his book *Blut und Ehre* (Blood and Honor), Rosenberg came to the conclusion that in comparison with the other arts "film, because of its capacity to affect primarily the emotions and the poetic [side of man], i.e., nonintellectuals, has a particularly forceful and enduring impact on the psychology of the masses and in propaganda."[23]

For Goebbels, too, the first commandment of the cinema was "not to practice psychology, but to tell a story through pictures."[24] He tried to downplay Hitler's actions by calling them "a process for developing an opinion" (*Willensbildung*). In actuality, of course, Hitler's actions were based on a well thought-out plan whose aim was to create total dependence and subordination. In Hitler's own words: "All effective propaganda must be limited to a very few points and must harp on these in slogans until the last member of the public understands what you want him to understand by your slogan."[25]

The "very few points" enunciated in 1933 differed from the arguments advanced during Hitler's wars of conquest. Likewise, the arguments brought forward during the middle period of Hitler's regime differed from those advanced during its final phase, when the Nazi rulers "put them to use as slogans" in the disintegrating Third Reich. During the first six years of the regime, in other words, until Hitler's attack on Poland, the intent of the Nazis' propaganda slogans was to anesthetize the Germans ideologically, that is, to instill into the national consciousness the dubious criteria formulated to prove the innate superiority of the Germans over other races, criteria that were proclaimed as new national virtues. Propaganda formulas accessible to all Germans gave birth to clever catch phrases that were used to arouse the "masses' most basic instincts" (Goebbels).

Scientifically untenable claims and elitist ideas regarding "racial purity," and "Aryan blood" were put forward to highlight the Nazis' negative image of Jews and to warn the Germans of the mortal national danger posed by "subhumans."

The Nazis took control of the arts by imposing their own National Socialist ideals and dictating which artists were to be the object of public adulation. They laid the groundwork for the takeover by juxtaposing so-called "degenerate art" and Nazi-approved "*völkisch* culture." Hitler was "absolutely" convinced that all culture was "almost exclusively the creative product of the Aryan."[26] Verbal montages such as "German culture," "the German national community," "German youth," "the German woman," "German blood," etc., implicitly belittled anything that was not German. Only Germans were endowed with the most noble virtues, e.g., cleanliness, discipline, courage, the spirit of sacrifice, loyalty, honor. "Loyalty is my honor" ("*Meine Ehre heißt Treue*") was the motto inscribed on the belt buckle of every SS man. The thousand-year Reich was to be made up of men imbued with these sorts of hyped virtues. The Nazis generated catchy metaphors to prepare the nation for Hitler's wars of conquest, to justify them as legitimate acts of defense, and to mobilize the army of fellow-travelers for the purpose of achieving "final victory." Hans Grimm's novel *Volk ohne Raum* (Nation Without Space)[27] offered arguments to justify the conquest of territories in Eastern Europe. The "shameful *diktat* of Versailles" was used to legitimize the invasion of France. "What could you do with the Versailles peace treaty?" Hitler asked rhetorically. His answer: "[The treaty's] boundless repressiveness and shameless demands [have produced] the greatest propaganda weapon for rousing the nation's dormant spirit of survival."

To make the German masses aware of the need for launching a preventive war against the "plutocracies" that were controlled by "the enemies of the people," the Nazis conjured up the horror scenario of a "conspiracy between World Jewry and Freemasonry directed against Hitler's Germany." In order to maximize the use of the film medium in the coming war, Goebbels in 1940 put the four existing newsreel companies (Ufa, Tobis, Deulig, and Fox) under the control of his ministry and merged them to form a single war newsreel, the *Deutsche Wochenschau*. "News policy is a weapon of war in wartime. It is used to wage war, not to provide information," Goebbels noted in his diary.

As the fortunes of war began to turn against Hitler after the defeat at Stalingrad in 1943, Goebbels's propaganda and prevarication machine constantly ground out new slogans about the need to "hold out" against all odds (*Durchhalten*), which he convincingly "authenticated" with the aid of "film documents." Newsreel propaganda reveled in the outpourings of hate about "German soldiers horribly mutilated by Soviet beasts" and "women raped by eastern subhumans," as it sought to mobilize the last reserves in the homeland against Germany's mortal enemy. These "documents," which were never described more specifically, were important in maintaining the will to endure. The propagandists wanted every German man to see his own mother, wife, or sister, and every German woman to see her own husband, son, brother, or father in the figure of the dead fellow German projected on the screen. This kind of atrocity propaganda was not the least of the reasons that Hitler was able to prolong the war until May 1945.

When Germans greeted or saluted each other, they did so in the name of the Führer ("Heil Hitler"); and when they died, they were prepared to die with his name on their lips. Virtually every officer trainee in the trenches carried a copy of Hölderlin's novel *Hyperion* in his knapsack and could quote the line in which the famous poet glorified sacrificing one's life for one's country: "Now heralds of victory descend: the battle is ours. Live on high, O Fatherland. And count not the dead! For you, Beloved, not one too many has fallen!" In his Christmas Eve radio address on 24 December 1942, Goebbels sought to mitigate the idea of dying on the battlefield by showing that Hölderlin's words reflected "[one of the] harsh but courageous lessons of war, a lesson that offers comfort and strength, only in a loftier sense."

Propagandists had prepared the road to destruction so well, disguising it as a kind of *Götterdämmerung*, that soldiers on the front line and the party faithful on the home front proceeded down it with a mixture of fatalism and fanaticism. Using the example of songs such as *"Volk ans Gewehr"* ("People: To Arms"), which he considered fascist exhortations, Theodor Adorno concluded that feelings hoisted up "to an irrational enthusiasm for death" could be drilled into people mechanically.[28] For propaganda purposes the Nazis denied the fact that taking pleasure in one's own destruction, i.e, the longing for death, was an inherent part of fascism. The Nazis harked back to the traditions of archaic cults as they developed their own special self-promoting rituals and ceremonial style in an effort to create meaning from the past (*Sinngebung*), capture the soul of the Germans, and stir their emotions. Ritual and style were combined with an eye to "mind-raping" the masses. One example of the kind of mass demonstration designed to capture the emotions was the quasi-religious ceremony solemnly performed to the accompaniment of men bearing standards and waving banners: the ritual of the "blood flag." It proceeded as follows: first, a song about the flag; then a poem about the flag; a pledge to the flag; a march-past of flags; finally, the consecration of rows of flags and standards as Hitler solemnly touched the new flags with the old "blood flag," culminating in the singing of the Horst Wessel song by all those present ("Hold high the flag …"). Many of the symbolic forms of expression used in Nazi ideology, especially in the case of Himmler's SS, were geared to tribal-Germanic customs and to masquerading as ancient Germans. Leni Riefenstahl developed a cinematic aesthetic of Nazi iconography out of this melange of pagan mythology and magic symbols. The Germans were prohibited from using their reason in formulating their thoughts; instead, they were to use their emotions.

Totalitarian propaganda also took possession of the deepest recesses of the subconscious. The ideal Nazi would never indulge in formulating his own arguments or critical judgments. He internalized prepackaged role models and standardized beliefs and acted in uncompromising conformity with them. According to Hermann Glaser, the real aim of propaganda was to "erase people's identity and individuality." People were to be manipulated "like a bundle of reflexes on the basis of their instincts, urges, and 'gut feelings.' Nazi propagandists felt that they were operating the control panel of the human psyche."[29] Propaganda, however, does not create a new transcendence; it merely substitutes for transcendence. In order successfully to mislead the "national psyche," Goebbels had developed an efficient aesthetic that he imposed on the audio-visual media, an aesthetic that worked subliminally. The documentary film seemed particularly well suited for this purpose. Since it used authentic-looking pictures, it was the genre that could most persuasively represent lies as truth. The Nazis had realized that "the best way to tell lies is to use facts," Hans Richter noted in "Der politische Film."

Since Nazism was not an intellectual but rather a "spiritual movement, one cannot comprehend it intellectually (*mit Argumenten*)." In fact, the intellect was of value only to the extent that the movement increased in size as a result of using the intellect (Wilhelm Stapel). The goal of mass persuasion was to conceal the vacuousness of all those things that had been made an official part of the political landscape (*politische Heimat*) and which were included under the broad heading of "the movement." This goal was to be reached primarily through the use of the visual media and the arts, and Leni Riefenstahl exploited them to develop the prototype of her aesthetic in *Triumph des Willens* (1934). Whether masquerading as art or as artfully arranged slices of reality, "the movement" was intent on expanding its influence. Goebbels believed that only spectaculars that met these criteria deserved the distinction marks (*Prädikate*) "artistically valuable" or "educational." Long before, Leo Tolstoy knew that the influence of art—which he termed its "infectiousness"—was not simply "a sure sign of art, but the degree of infectiousness is also the sole measure of excellence in art."

According to Goebbels, the cinema was "one of the most modern means of mass persuasion" and therefore "could not be left to its own devices" (Goebbels, 9 February 1934). These principles led Goebbels to pronounce his infamous credo: "We are not one of those secretive types with a silly childish fear of words like 'propaganda' and 'overtly political' (*Tendenz*) (Goebbels, 5 November 1939). In 1933 the Nazi film propagandist Hans Traub defined "pro-active propaganda" as the "intentional application of overtly political means to achieve a political end, to make a [particular] ideology (*Gesinnung*) a goal."[30]

Goebbels, like Hitler, was fond of displaying his interest in the cinema. He demonstrated this during an evening function, held fourteen days after his appointment as propaganda minister, to which he had invited the *Filmwelt* or the top representatives of the German cinema. These included the *Dachorganisation filmschaffender Künstler Deutschlands* or DACHO, the industry's official trade union, the *Reichsverband deutscher Filmtheaterbesitzer*, the cinema owners' association, and the *Spitzenorganisationen der Filmwirtschaft* or SPIO, the industry's main professional representative body. That evening Goebbels praised himself as a man "who had always had a close relationship to the German film." In fact, he was "an inveterate film addict." Of course, he also issued a clear warning: "Should the cinema develop in a dangerous direction, the state has a duty to intervene and take matters in hand."

Several years earlier, in 1930, Goebbels's thugs demonstrated what the propaganda minister meant by "intervening and taking matters in hand" when, in December, they disrupted the Berlin premiere of Lewis Milestone's movie version of *All Quiet on the Western Front*. The city's reactionary chief of police prohibited the film from being shown because of the threat to public safety. That same year Carl von Ossietzky objected in the journal *Weltbühne* to the banning of the film in "the obscure censorship office" and wrote: "Against the National Socialist rabble party we have only one logic: the heavy knout; to tame them, we have only one doctrine: *A un corsaire—corsaire et demi!*"[31] With its realistic battle scenes, Milestone's film was even more persuasive than G. W. Pabst's German anti-war move *Westfront 1918*—made the same year—in demythologizing war.

All Quiet on the Western Front was a cinematic plea for pacifism. It told of the experiences of seven German boys as they matured from students avid for the glory of war to weary war veterans who learned that war was no more than a living hell, by which time only one of them was still alive. Erich Maria Remarque's novel exposed the stab-in-the-back legend propagated by Hindenburg and Ludendorff for the lie that it was. What had disgusted Goebbels, the "clubfooted psychopath" (Ossietzky), about the book was magnified many times over through the film's relentless realism.

Immediately after Hitler became chancellor, Goebbels banned Fritz Lang's film *Das Testament des Dr. Mabuse* (The Last Will of Dr. Mabuse, 1932/33), an eerie allegory of the strife-torn political conditions in contemporary Weimar Germany. The analogy between the paranoid Führer and the psychopathic demagogue Dr. Mabuse appeared much too obvious to the Nazis. (The censorship office that enabled the Nazis to ban the film had been established during the Weimar republic as part of the Reich Cinema Law passed by the National Assembly on 12 May 1920.)

Shortly before banning *Dr. Mabuse*, Goebbels, in a speech to representatives of the German film industry, had praised *Die Nibelungen* (The Nibelungs, 1922/24), another movie by the same director, as a model of cinematic art. Goebbels went on to mention that *Die Nibelungen* was one of the films that "made a lasting impression on me." "In this instance the story projected on the screen has not been separated from what's happening today; it is so modern, contemporary, and up-to-date that it would even move those who are fighting for the National Socialist movement." As for the reaction to Goebbels's speech by those who were there, the journal *Die Filmwoche* reported: "Thunderous applause for the Reich Minister rang out from all those present. The members of the party who were in attendance broke into a rendition of the Horst Wessel song, and the assembled filmmakers rose to their feet and listened."

Joseph Goebbels did not try to win Hitler's confidence in the efficiency of his propaganda machine simply by making bellicose speeches. He also used more concrete means, such as the passing of legislation. On 14 July 1933, for example, he enacted a "law establishing an interim film chamber." This allowed him, among other things, to cancel all of Ufa's contracts with its Jewish staff members and with Jewish artists and be under no obligation to give them notice. "No individual, be he at the top or on the bottom, has the right to use his personal freedom at the expense of the nation's freedom. This applies to the creative artist as well." So said Goebbels on 15 November 1933 at the opening of the Reich Chamber of Culture. Ten weeks later Goebbels did not mince words when he addressed members of the specialty advisory council on film (*Reichsfachschaft Film*). He was convinced, he said, "that film was one of the most modern and far-reaching means for influencing the public that has ever existed."

As promised, the Nazis did not leave the film medium to its own devices. Applying direct and indirect censorship to every detail of form and content, the Nazis eventually created the kind of film that Goebbels envisaged in 1934: "We intend to give film a German face." "May the bright flame of enthusiasm never expire," Goebbels proclaimed to the hundred thousand faithful at the 1934 Nuremberg Party congress. "It is this flame alone that gives brightness and warmth to the creative art of modern political propaganda."

In 1942 a giant holding company, *Ufa-Film-GmbH* (Ufa Film Corporation), assumed control of the entire German film industry and its foreign subsidiaries, creating a truly state-owned enterprise. The following example will show the constantly increasing importance that propaganda strategists accorded to the film medium. On 30 January 1945, the day of its premiere in Berlin, a print of Veit Harlan's epic *Kolberg* was flown into the beleaguered fortress of La Rochelle to lift the morale of the defenders and encourage them to hold out to the bitter end.

The Youth Film Hours of the Hitler Youth

Remember, whenever you see the flag waving, it isn't some inconse-
quential piece of cloth. Remember, that behind this flag stands the will
of millions of people bound to Germany in loyalty, bravery, and fervent
love. You must remain inseparably bound to this flag, in good times
and bad. You must defend it when it is attacked and, if need be, cover it
with your young bodies when you die, just as your comrades did in the
Great War and during [the Party's] time of struggle in decades past.

Baldur von Schirach, during the dedication of the Hitler Youth's
Bann[32] flags in the Potsdam Garrison Church on 24 January 1934

"These young people are learning nothing other than to think German, to act German, and after these boys have come into our organizations at age ten and gotten their first breath of fresh air there,
they move four years later from the *Jungvolk* to the Hitler Youth,
where we keep them for another four years, by which time the last
thing we want to do is hand them back to the old originators of
our [social] classes and estates [*Stände*], so [we] take them immediately into the Party, into the Labor Front, into the SA or the SS,
into the NSKK and so forth. And after they have been there for
two years or a year and a half and they still have not become true
National Socialists, we put them in the Labor Service and drill
them for six or seven months—all under one symbol, the German
spade. And any class-consciousness or pride in one's social position still remaining after six or seven months will be taken over for
further treatment by the *Wehrmacht* for two years, and when they
come back after two, three, or four years *then we take them back*
immediately into the SA, SS, and so on to prevent any relapse, and they
will never again be free for the rest of their lives" (Adolf Hitler).[33]

The German Youth Movement expanded its activities during
the late 1920s against the somber background of a republic scorned
as chaotic and deliberately destabilized as a result of the proliferation of political parties. The majority of the disillusioned young
people searching for absolute beauty and the innocence of nature
came from the middle class. Their motivations for joining youth
movements such as the *Wandervögel* [literally, wandering or migratory birds—Transl.] were more emotional than rational. They were
seeking an affective substitute for the freedom that had been
denied them. More and more of them viewed the world from a
perspective informed with the romantic values of the past. They

discovered their own world huddled around the bonfires of summer solstice celebrations or in camping out, reading Stefan George and Rainer Maria Rilke, singing the songs of the *Bündische Jugend* (The German Youth Movement), reciting archaic texts from the hoary past, and enjoying the fellowship of like-minded comrades, occasionally homosexual ones as well. Many of them expounded "a pantheistic love of nature and mystical love of the fatherland."[34]

Characteristically, the preface to the *Zupfgeigenhansl* [the *Zupfgeige* being a dialect term for the guitar or mandolin—Transl.], a compilation of folksongs popular during the Weimar period, began as follows: "And because we are the disinherited, because at our stage of life we feel more strongly within ourselves the spur and desire to achieve total harmony with mankind, folksongs are a balm and a comfort for us, indispensable and irreplaceable treasures."[35]

The Nazis cleverly exploited and turned to Hitler's advantage the latent desire of this generation for a different way of life and their longing to be independent of their parents. They took the conglomeration of unfulfilled wishes and forged them into an ideology of adolescence that ultimately found organizational expression in the Hitler Youth.

The ten- to fourteen-year-olds, or *Pimpfe*, were the most impressionable age group throughout the entire period of Nazi rule. Since they were naive, they were easy prey for the new movement. The Nazis captured the hearts of these children with catchy slogans borrowed from the fascist catechism. They mixed the vocabulary of Prussian militarism with the program of the *Bündische Jugend to* produce a new way of thinking that would strike a chord with young people. Given the alternatives offered by the Nazis, young people felt that they could dispense with religious instruction and the values it imparted. The Nazis channeled the natural enthusiasm and naive trust of youth into areas where they could generate activities and expend their pent-up energies while at the same time feeling that they were members of a winning team. The inflation in the number of badges of honor and winners' medals took place against this psychological backdrop. The Hitler Youth developed a dazzling variety of programs to meet young people's need for comradeship and to satisfy their desire to make sacrifices. Scouting games, cross-country expeditions, team sports, camps, summer solstice celebrations, and sun worship sparked the enthusiasm of the young, an enthusiasm that carried over to a higher cause that was shrouded in romantic mysticism. Their symbol was the swastika flag. Under the heading "War Games 'Round the HY Banner," *Deulig* newsreel no. 275 of 7 April 1937 provides a graphic example of the utter seriousness with which the Hitler Youth regarded this quasi-religious relic. In the tormented Weimar republic, many middle- and working-class young people were attracted to some of the important components of *völkisch* thought adopted by the Nazis—secularized myths and tribal-Germanic rituals—viewing them as glamorous alternatives to the values, attitudes, folkways, etc., through which they had earlier become integrated into German society. The new beliefs seemed more natural to them "than traditional Christian values which were, admittedly, derivatives [of these more ancient religions]."[36]

In analyzing this psychological phenomenon, however, it is impossible "to find any specifically fascist element ... The special character [of this phenomenon] lies not in its individual components, but in their configuration." In the preface to *Inszenierung der Macht*[37] a number of factors are credited with fostering a climate in which "individuals were exempted from any social liability for their actions because they had voluntarily become part of a system (*Gefüge*)." Given their new sense of community, adolescents felt powerful, destined to fulfill a higher purpose. Two factors—"a sensuality akin to happiness and successful collective change"— facilitated their integration into the movement and their conversion into its most faithful followers. Evening get-togethers (*Heimabende*)[38] and school lessons alone, however, were not sufficient to instill the Nazi ideology and the determination to "struggle for survival as a group." To accomplish this, other means were called for.

Nazi educators would have to project role models onto the movie screen and bring them to life in the minds of spectators. In other words, the experience of seeing these role models must leave an impression that could be recalled in the course of a lifelong learning process. The first party-sponsored films to accomplish this objective were *Hitlerjunge Quex* (1933), *SA-Mann Brand* (1933), and *Hans Westmar* (1933). All three propaganda figures produced effects that went beyond the aesthetic enjoyment of the film. The appearance in these films of actors who were popular before the Nazis came to power, such as Berta Drews, Heinrich George, and Hermann Speelmans, induced even non-Party members to see them. A film like *Hitlerjunge Quex* showed just how determined director Hans Steinhoff was "to continue the brief tradition of the Weimar proletarian film and use familiar things to communicate the new *Weltanschauung*."[39]

By the end of that same year, the task of disseminating Party propaganda was assigned exclusively to the *Kulturfilm*, the documentary, and the newsreel. Goebbels believed that authentic pictures of the "new reality" would be better able to persuade audiences than would feature films. Whereas the purpose of a short subject would be to monopolize people's thoughts, the sole task of the feature-length film in the future would be to offer people "lively entertainment" so as to assure the Führer that his people would always be in a good mood. It soon became obvious that adolescents greatly preferred short subjects and Riefenstahl documentaries to so-called "serious films."

Goebbels's film propagandists derived some of their insights from a dissertation written in 1933, stating that "the majority of young people even then liked natural, pure, and unaffected films that reflected the spirit of the nation more than so-called 'love stories' or run-of-the-mill movies.... The responses of young people clearly showed that youth was becoming enthusiastic about qualities such as beauty, strength, naturalness, and heroism.... In general, young people are attracted to anything that is fast-paced, exciting, or sensational, which reflects the growing need to be active and seek new experiences that is characteristic of this age group."[40]

To exploit in demagogic fashion an aesthetic medium like film, Goebbels needed young people who were susceptible to every type of kitschy, "beautiful" fiction. How could a means of indoctrination such as film be made accessible to young people on a regular basis? Since the short subjects and documentaries that were included in the weekly movie bills were not very popular with the viewing public, special screenings were organized for the Hitler Youth in which entire groups, not just individual boys and girls, would be brought together to see films. The journal *Der deutsche Film* stated in its December 1937 issue that only when a "strong sense of community" has been established could film truly become a vital experience, that is, "only when the audience thinks homogeneously, when—how should one put it—it shares the same view of the world; and when a film is shown, its point of view mirrors that of the community." Film gives expression to the forces that go to form a community, but only "when the [idea of] a community has already been planted in viewers' minds and only when film acts to enhance that community, i.e., when it has an ideological message to communicate. We believe the 'Youth Film Hours' (*Jugendfilmstunden*) of the Hitler Youth do both."

The grandiose premiere of the Youth Film Hour took place in Cologne on 20 April 1934, the Führer's birthday. The Film Hours were not subsidized by the state; the government expected them to be self-supporting. At 20 pfennigs per show the price of a ticket was low, the return on investment in terms of fellowship high. Fanfares, drumrolls, the singing of the Horst Wessel song, and the reading of stirring Nazi poems were some of the elements that helped create a quasi-religious atmosphere, which for many became a substitute for church services. When a film "is provided with a framework in keeping with its contents, its impact is enhanced and its feeling for what is genuine, valuable, and beautiful is roused, especially by reference to things outside itself."[41] Performances such as these completely satisfied the need for "affirmation and self-validation" (Habermas). The Hitler Youth's march to the theater in close-order formation under the swastika flag "was a very special prelude to any visit to a Hitler Youth Film Hour and gave it a very special flavor." "After being seated, the young demonstrated the unique power of the Youth Film Hour to build a community as they sang the songs that play such an important part in the Hitler Youth, since they were born out of these young people's spirit of nationalism (*aus dem volkbewußten Geiste*)."[42] "You belong to the Führer, too!" was the slogan on a poster with an index finger pointing at a *Jungmädel*, a subdivision of the *Bund Deutscher Mädel* (League of German Girls) for girls ten to fourteen.

With the promulgation of the Youth Service Law (*Jugenddienstpflicht*) on 1 December 1936, Hitler imposed the state's control over most young people, including almost all boys and girls between the ages of ten and eighteen. Of the total number of 8.87 million youths born between 1921 and 1931, 8.7 million were obliged, beginning in 1939, to become members of Nazi youth organizations, for "the future of the German people depends on its young people." The preamble to the law stated that all young Germans "must therefore be prepared [to fulfill] their future obligations," specifically:

§1. All German young people are to be included in the Hitler Youth.

§2. Except for the parental home and the school, all German young people are to be educated physically, spiritually, and morally in the spirit of National Socialism for service to the nation and the national community.

§3. The responsibility for educating all German young people in the Hitler Youth is assigned to the Reich Youth Leader of the NSDAP. He is thereby the Youth Leader of the German Reich. He occupies the position of a Supreme Reich Authority with headquarters in Berlin and is directly responsible to the Führer and Reich Chancellor.

§4. The Führer and Reich Chancellor will issue the requisite decrees and regulations for enforcing and amending this law.

Berlin, 1 December 1936
The Führer and Reich Chancellor
Adolf Hitler
State Secretary and Head of the Reich Chancellery
Dr. Lammers

Even before membership became compulsory, the Hitler Youth and its subdivisions enjoyed great popularity. From the end of 1932 to the end of 1934, membership in the Hitler Youth rose from 107,956 boys to 3.577 million; membership in the League of German Girls during the same period increased from 24,000 to 1.334 million.[43]

During the initial year of the Youth Film Hours in 1934, attendance was approximately 300,000, even though the Hitler Youth had launched them in just a few big cities. During the 1938/39 season, the number of attendees had grown to over 2.5 million; the number of performances was 4,885 that season. Later, almost all of the 5,275 cinemas in Germany with an average seating capacity of more 750 made their facilities available for Youth Film Hours every month. Goebbels's success statistics of 29 September 1940 counted a total of 9,411,318 young attendees at 19,694 Youth Film Hours from 1934 to 1940 "within the framework of the Winter Aid campaigns" alone. The highest attendance figure was during the 1942/43 season when 11.2 million young people visited 45,290 performances.[44]

In rural areas where, in contrast to the cities, there were virtually no cultural diversions, not even a cinema, the Youth Film Hours that were held in school houses, inns, and church halls were much appreciated sources of entertainment. In the 1942/43 season alone there were approximately 18,250 performances attended by nearly 2.5 million Hitler Youth and BDM girls in areas without cinemas, while in cities with cinemas there were 24,100 screenings with 8,355,000 attendees during the same period.

In 1942/43, 1,500 mobile film units traveled around the countryside to spread the Führer's word. A secret *Sicherheitsdienst* (Security Service) report[45] dated 3 April 1941 informed "higher authorities" that these film presentations were particularly popular in rural areas where there were no cinemas, since they were often the only source of entertainment and information. German cinema owners were obliged "on the basis of a directive from the Reich Film Chamber to make their theaters available once a month on Sunday or, as local conditions require, twice monthly, for the purpose of holding Youth Film Hours."[46]

Though attendance at the Sunday performances was not mandatory, whenever a Hitler Youth *Stammführer* or a BDM *Ring-führerin* invited their charges to see films such as *Das große Eis* (*Kulturfilm* documentary about Prof. Alfred Wegener's expedition to Greenland, 1936), *Nanga Parbat* (documentary about a German mountaineering expedition to the Western Himalayas, 1936), *Triumph des Willens* (Triumph of the Will, 1935), *Fest der Jugend* (Festival of Youth) or *Fest der Schönheit* (Festival of Beauty, 1938), *Hitlers 50. Geburtstag* (Hitler's 50th Birthday, 1939), *Feldzug in Polen* (Campaign in Poland, 1939) or *Sieg im Westen* (Victory in the West, 1941), young people turned up in droves, occupying every seat in the house.

Of course, feature films such as *Fridericus Rex* (1936), *Der große König* (The Great King, 1942), *Bismarck* (1940), and *Die Entlassung* (The Dismissal, 1942) were also shown, for as Hitler said, "our educational system lacked the art of picking a few names out of the historical development of our people and making them the common property of the whole German nation, thus through like knowledge and like enthusiasm tying a uniform, uniting bond around the entire nation.... They were not able to raise what was glorious for the nation in the various subjects of instruction above the level of objective presentation, and fire the national pride by such gleaming examples."[47]

The Nazis were skilled in persuading people that the dreary, mythless era represented by the "bourgeois," "Marxist," "Jewified" Weimar republic was in urgent need of bright shining role models who would lead the way to the "light." It was an era that called for "Luther types" (as Rosenberg termed the purveyors of myth) "to lift people's hearts in this chaos ... [and] deliberately remagnetize them."[48]

Great scientists, inventors, and artists as well were portrayed in films such as *Robert Koch: der Bekämpfer des Todes* (1939), *Friedrich Schiller* (1940), *Friedemann Bach* (1940/41), *Andreas Schlüter* (1942), and *Diesel* (1942), for "an inventor must not only seem great as an inventor, but must seem even greater as a national comrade. Our admiration of every great deed must be bathed in pride that its fortunate performer is a member of our own people. From all the

innumerable great names of German history, the greatest must be
picked out and introduced to the youth so persistently that they
become pillars of an unshakable national sentiment."[49]

Beginning in the 1940s, anti-Semitism had an important part to
play in the Youth Film Hours. Films like *Der ewige Jude* (The Eternal Jew, 1940), *Jud Süss* (Jew Süss, 1940), *Leinen aus Irland* (Irish
Linen, 1939), and *Die Rothschilds* (The Rothschilds, 1940) sought to
create an aura of historical authenticity. In the words of Hitler,
"the crown of the folkish state's entire work of education and
training must be to burn the racial sense and racial feeling into the
instinct and the intellect, the heart and brain of the young
entrusted to it. No boy and no girl must leave school without having been led to an ultimate realization of the necessity and essence
of blood purity."[50]

The war gave rise to a series of combat spectaculars and war
hero films, all characterized by a bellicose chauvinism. They
ranged from *Stukas* (1941) through *U-Boote westwärts* (U-Boats
Westwards, 1941) and *Kampfgeschwader Lützow* (Battle Squadron
Lützow, 1941) to the epic *Kolberg*, which premiered in March 1945
to bolster the population's endurance in the face of overwhelming
odds. With regard to young people, the purpose of these films was
to help render them fit for military service and inspire them with
the courage to die, to prepare them psychologically to sacrifice
their lives.

Even before war broke out—in fact, from the inception of the
Nazi regime—films considered pacifist or "effeminate" were
strictly taboo for the Hitler Youth. "Healthy young people, concerned about their fitness for military service and the defense of
their [nation's] borders, young people educated in this spirit, are
immune to the effects of pacifist war movies. Indeed, this whole
question is only of historical interest for us Germans, since,
because of their wholehearted commitment and unambiguous
portrayals, the nationally minded films of the new Germany deal
with the issue of their psychological impact in a much more
straightforward way than the films of the past, especially since
they are confronted with young people who are more [than ever]
of one mind and one will."[51]

The subordination of the Hitler Youth to the dictates of "total
war" was not so much a matter of collecting woolens for the winter on the eastern front, scrap metal for the latest battle, or potato
beetles for the purpose of saving crops. Rather, it meant sending
entire high school classes to help man anti-aircraft batteries during

air raids. And it culminated in the creation on 24 June 1943 of the 12th SS Panzer Division, the Hitler Youth Division of the Waffen-SS, for the final battle in France. Ten thousand sixteen-year-old youths were sent to their death in the desperate German counter-offensives on 6 July and 4 September near Caen and Yvoir de Meuse. By the time Field Marshal von Rundstedt lamented, "It's a crying shame that these trusting young people are being slaughtered in such hopeless circumstances," the situation was already beyond help.

The *Pimpfe*, the youngest members of the Hitler Youth, were never shown this "storm of steel" during Youth Film Hours. Instead, they heard newsreel commentaries such as the following: "In one sector of the front we see the Hitler Youth Division of the Waffen-SS engaged in combat ... as they advance, they pass burning American tanks. German tanks roll onward" (July 1944). What the newsreel commentator did not say was that they were rolling toward certain death. Before that happened, though, they knocked out twenty-eight Canadian tanks. A British tank commander recalled that they sprang at Allied tanks "like wolves, until we were forced to kill them against our will."[52]

On orders from the Reich Youth Leader dated 27 February 1945, even younger boys, armed with *Panzerfäuste* [a primitive weapon modeled on the American "bazooka"—Transl.] and anti-tank mines, were pushed into the final battle—a battle that was lost even before it had been fought—in order to serve their hero Adolf Hitler to the last day of the war "with love for and loyalty to the Führer and our flag," as the Hitler Youth pledge commanded. The war movies shown during the Youth Film Hours were not the least of the reasons they were willing to make the ultimate sacrifice.

When Goebbels spoke on German radio to the young people of the Reich at the opening of the 1942/43 Youth Film Hours on 25 October 1942, he said nothing regarding the subject of film; however, he had a great deal to say about the heroic ethos of German boys in the war. The Propaganda Minister was intoxicated by a recent visit of "some thirty Hitler Youth between the ages of ten and seventeen ... who were without exception [decorated] with the Iron Cross or the War Service Cross." Two of the boys had each shot down a British fighter plane and "had been decorated with the same medals awarded to soldiers at the front." Because of their "service to the nation," they had grown "several inches in terms of morale."[53] Who among the boys listening to Goebbels's speech in a movie theater as it was broadcast that Sunday would not also liked to have grown "several inches"?

After the war, Bernhard Wicki used the motion picture camera with brutal effectiveness in his film *Die Brücke* (The Bridge, 1959) to examine the misguided heroism and idealism of "Hitler's children" and the horrible absurdity of sacrificing young lives as Germany's defenses crumbled. He showed schoolboys throwing themselves in the path of advancing American tanks, only to die pointlessly two days before the end of the war.[54]

"Nazism never gave people ... anything but power. You still have to ask why it was, if this regime was nothing but a bloody dictatorship, that on 3 May 1945 there were still Germans who fought to the last drop of blood—whether these people didn't have some form of emotional attachment to power."[55]

Goebbels recalled a valiant Hitler Youth who was still breathing as he was pulled out of a burning tank: "Unconscious for most of three days, no word of complaint ever crossed his lips; and then as he gave up the ghost, he whispered a greeting to the Führer. If Schopenhauer's dictum is correct that you can judge a man in part by how he dies, this boy was ... a real man."[56]

Just four weeks after the Battle of Stalingrad, Goebbels assigned the Youth Film Hours the mission of making "real men" out of the Hitler Youth (at least as Hitler understood the concept) and showing films that would prepare them for sacrificing their young lives on the battlefield like their movie heroes. The kitschy romanticization of warfare expressed in songs and poems lent emotional support to the Film Hours as they celebrated heroic sacrifice. The poem below is representative of their quality:

> Now let the flags wave
> against the great red sky of morning
> lighting our way to victory
> or burning us to death!
>
> Even if we fall in battle,
> our state will stand like a mighty cathedral!
> A nation takes in hundreds of harvests
> and sows many hundreds of times.
>
> Look at us, Germany, death in battle
> is the least we can offer you!
> Should the grim reaper cut down our ranks,
> we will become the seeds of the future!
>
> Hans Baumann

Whenever a Youth Film Hour was held, the newsreel for that week was also shown. To Goebbels, newsreels were "make-believe reality." Especially during the war, weekly newsreels fulfilled a special function in the propagation of Hitler's war aims. In 1941 Goebbels noted in his diary that "the newsreel is the best means we have for leading the people."[57] Newsreels were made more effective by skillfully combining them with appropriate feature films, "cinematic epics of German heroism" (Goebbels) that would ensure a continuing supply of "heroes." The party newspaper *Das Reich*,[58] of 8 June 1941, devoted a lead article to the subject of film as a propaganda medium in wartime. Among other things, it stated that "the newsreel reports on the Polish campaign gave individuals for the first time the exciting sensation of being placed in the middle of events as they were unfolding. As a result of this experience with newsreels, audiences began to practice an unconscious but very effective film policy that they no doubt pursued most energetically during the summer of 1940. In terms of content, technique, and effectiveness, these films were very closely related to the newsreel." The films referred to were features such as *Kopf hoch, Johannes* (Chin Up, John, 1941), *Wunschkonzert* (Request Concert, 1940), *Feinde* (Enemies, 1940), *Kampfgeschwader Lützow* (Battle Squadron Lützow, 1941), *Stukas* (1941), and *U-Boote westwärts* (U-Boats Westwards, 1941). More important than the inclusion of documentary footage in these features was the fact that the newsreel had "clearly" become "their leavening agent. Like [the newsreel] these films put the moviegoer directly within the experiential vicinity of events ... There are scenes that plainly show the close connection of this film genre to the newsreel."

Since the German people had become spoiled as a result of hearing nothing but announcements of victory, Goebbels had to be extremely careful not to squander the trust built up through the newsreels by fabricating victories when there were nothing but defeats to report ("enemy" radio stations, of course, kept German listeners updated with regard to the military situation). Consequently, Goebbels concealed huge retreats from the public by shifting the news to reports of "victories" achieved by combat patrols, U-boats, and individual airplane and tank crews. The cumulative effect of these minor triumphs created the impression of a massive "forward defense" punctuated by occasional "tactical retreats" and efforts to "straighten the front," that is, by relatively positive events. However, to the very last, the film propagandists never went so far as to show German soldiers dying on the screen;

that was strictly taboo. As Nietzsche said, "art exists so that the bow won't break." In the case of the film medium, the art was in what was omitted.

However, since young people "also [have] a right to laugh, the Youth Film Hours feature comedies as well." According to film journalist Hans Joachim Sachsze, "National Socialist youth education is not oriented in an angry, violent, or rigid way to any particular ideological concept of 'heroism.' Rather, the Hitler Youth recognizes the need of young people to relax and lead healthy lives."[59]

Among the comedies produced during the war, the following were shown during Youth Film Hours: Arthur Maria Rabenalt's *Weißer Flieder* (White Lilac, 1939), Kurt Hoffmann's *Quax, der Bruchpilot* (Quax the Crash Pilot, 1941), Helmut Käutner's *Kleider machen Leute* (Clothes Make the Man, 1940) and *Wir machen Musik* (We Make Music, 1942), Helmut Weiß and Heinrich Spoerl's *Die Feuerzangenbowle* (Hot Wine Punch, 1944), Heinz Rühmann's *Sophienlund* (1943), and Willi Forst's *Wiener Blut* (Vienna Life). "In addition to getting a spiritual uplift and boost, [young people must be able] to relax from the harsh daily grind of wartime when they go to see a movie " (Goebbels).

The government conducted periodic surveys to determine the popularity of films and gauge the extent of young people's interest in political events and subjects, with the aim of increasing the effectiveness of state-sponsored film productions. In responding to the question "Which movies did you like best?" young people came out unequivocally in favor of the following films, which the press had also given top marks for both style *and* content. They are listed in descending numerical order based on number of votes received: *Der große König* (The Great King, 1942), *Bismarck* (1940), *Die Entlassung* (The Dismissal, 1942), *Friedrich Schiller* (1940), *Heimkehr* (Homecoming, 1941), *Ohm Krüger* (Uncle Krüger, 1941), ... *reitet für Deutschland* (Riding for Germany, 1941), *Andreas Schlüter* (1942), *Stukas* (1941), *Kadetten* (Cadets, 1941), *Diesel* (1942), *Wunschkonzert* (Request Concert, 1940), and *Kampfgeschwader Lützow* (Battle Squadron Lützow, 1941). Way down on the list, by the way, came the anti-Semitic *Jud Süss* (Jew Süss, 1940), which received 92 votes, as compared to 1,115 for *Der große König*.[60]

Propaganda films, of course, were shown not only at Youth Film Hours. They were also screened wherever school-age young people gathered on a daily basis, namely, in classrooms and school auditoriums, where they may have been received with even greater enthusiasm. Even during the Weimar period there were enterprising urban and regional educational picture centers (*Stadt-bildstellen, Landesbildstellen*) that had both a well-diversified assortment of films and portable 16 mm projectors so that they could present films in any classroom, in any university seminar room, or at any evening social function. Bernhard Rust, who was appointed Reich Minister for Science, Education, and Public Instruction on 30 April 1934, was interested in using audio-visual aids primarily to educate students in the spirit of militarism, German nationalism, and anti-Semitism: "We need a new Aryan generation ... or we will forfeit the future."

In order to win the future, Nazi ideological training would have to begin in childhood. The schools would be responsible for the total adaptation of the individual to the new politically regimented society. The inculcation of political attitudes "would take place before and during the time when young people are trying hardest to come to terms with their own identity and individuality, i.e., puberty."[61]

On 26 June 1934 Bernhard Rust issued a directive to introduce political films into schools for the purpose of education: "The National Socialist state asks the schools of Germany to assume new and important responsibilities. To carry them out they must avail themselves of every educational and technical aid. Educational films are among the most important aids. Only the new state was able fully to overcome the psychological inhibitions to the use of the technological achievements of film, and it is determined to enlist the film medium in the service of its *Weltanschauung*. This must take place primarily in the schools and, moreover, as an integral part of classroom instruction."

In 1943 the regional educational picture centers had thirty-seven centers throughout Germany and were optimally placed to distribute their propaganda films. The regional centers were further subdivided into urban and rural districts numbering 1,242, ensuring the delivery of films to any desired target group. Moreover, by 1936 the Propaganda Ministry had 32 Regional Party Film Centers (*Gaufilmstellen*), 771 District Party Film Centers (*Kreisfilmstellen*), and 22,357 smaller party film centers (*Ortsgruppenfilmstellen*).[62]

Reichshauptstellenleiter der NSDAP Curt Belling, one of the Party's official spokesmen on film matters, reported in the *Film-Kurier* of 31 December 1936 in an article titled "Film and the Party": "Over three hundred mobile cinemas, fitted out with the most modern equipment, travel around the country every day, and wherever they appear hundreds of Germans gather to share the experience of participating in the great political events of our day through film. In this way, it was possible to bring the issues of our times in a lively format to the twenty-five million people who live outside the large population centers and away from the major traffic routes."[63]

Letter from an Old Soldier on the Siegfried Line to His Sixteen-Year-Old Son

Come on, comrades, come on! When at the end of this war, on the day of our great victory, the Führer looks around, may he see beside his armies the shining banners of his Hitler Youth.

Refrain of the Hitler Youth war service song from the documentary *Junges Europa II* [Young Europe II, 1942], directed by Alfred Weidenmann

"I'm so proud of you, my boy! You've become the standard-bearer of your *Jungbann*. No other news from you could make me happier than this. I am grateful to Providence for allowing me, an old soldier, to fulfill my destiny so proudly. When I was about the same age you are today, my son, I was allowed to march off to the Great War. I was permitted to join the wall of bodies ringing the Fatherland, a wall that was sunk deep into enemy soil, braving every hailstorm of iron and every hurricane of fire, defending the homeland, for days, weeks, months, years. Then suddenly it was all over. We had to return home and were derided for all our sacrifices. Our flags were torn down, the flags in which all we ever saw was the homeland. We were forced to feed these sacred pieces of cloth to the flames to prevent them from being desecrated. We returned to a topsy-turvy world, one that they called a world of peace, but was nothing more than a total humiliation. Many of us who for four years withstood every hell of this worldwide conflagration were shattered by feelings of revulsion and contempt. Many clenched their teeth and managed to pick up the pieces of their lives. Some like me were compelled to set out again, to the Baltics, Upper Silesia … You know the stations of my life as a soldier, my son.

"But while we mourned, feared, despaired, and defended ourselves, there arose from our midst, from the army of unknown soldiers who had passed through all the horrors of war, one man: the Führer.

"... *In the midst of the doubters and the hopeless* he hoisted *a flag,* a *new flag* with *the old sacred colors and symbols, the flag of a united Reich and a united people.* With a few loyal followers rallied around him, he marched off to do battle on behalf of a great and distant ideal.

"Around the time you were born, my boy, *the first casualties* consecrated *this flag with their blood.* There were sixteen of them; they were *the first to give their lives because they believed in this flag.*

"In a dogged, infinitely arduous struggle fraught with sacrifice, the Führer won his people over. And he built the Reich, the great, strong, eternal Reich. He became the Führer and father of all Germans.

"*The flag of this Reich* now *waves,* and *no power on earth can pull it down. Driven into the heart of every German, its staff stands unshakable*—in men and women, old people and children—*an entire nation bearing the standard.*

"While we wait for the enemy here on the Siegfried Line, my thoughts turn back to the homeland. And they are different from what they were twenty-five years ago; they are tranquil, more joyful, certain of victory. Pure of heart and with strong hands, my boy, carry *the flag of the Jungbann* in front of the thousands upon thousands of your young comrades. *Only the best, the strongest, the bravest, the most valiant shall be standard-bearers!* This you know.

"In this spirit, greetings from

Your Father, February 1940."[64]

Notes

1. Adolf Hitler, *Mein Kampf,* p. 654.
2. Wolf Schneider, *Wörter machen Leute: Magie und Macht der Sprache* (Hamburg, 1982), p. 121.
3. Hans Traub, ed., *Die Ufa: ein Beitrag zur Entwicklung des deutschen Filmschaffens* (Berlin 1943), p. 26.
4. Kurt Tucholsky, "Chaplin in Kopenhagen" in *Die Weltbühne* (Berlin), 7 June 1927 (under the pseudonym Peter Panter); in Kurt Tucholsky, *Gesammelte Werke.,* vol. 5 (Reinbek bei Hamburg, 1975), p. 226.
5. Hans Traub, ed., *Die Ufa,* p. 29.

6. Quoted in Richard Taylor, *Film Propaganda: Soviet Russia and Nazi Germany* (London, 1979), p. 22.

7. Erich Ludendorff, *Meine Kriegerinnerungen* (Berlin, 1919), pp. 285f., English translation *Ludendorff's Own Story, August 1914–November 1918*, 2 vols. (New York, 1920); *My War Memories, 1914–1918*, 2 vols. (New York, 1920).

8. Oskar Kalbus, *Pioniere des Kulturfilms* (Karlsruhe, 1956), pp. 18f.

9. Siegfried Kracauer, *Von Caligari bis Hitler*, p. 26.

10. Hans Traub, ed., *Die Ufa*, p. 35.

11. Jürgen Spiker, *Film und Kapital* (Berlin, 1975), p. 34.

12. Gottlieb Hermes, "Politische Auslandsfilme" in Heinrich Pfeiffer, ed., *Das deutsche Lichtbildbuch* (Berlin, 1924), p. 35.

13. Gustave Le Bon, *Psychologie der Massen* (Leipzig, 1908), pp. 18f., English translation *The Crowd* (New York, 1896).

14. Ibid., p. 20.

15. Thomas Mann, *Doktor Faustus* (Stockholm, 1947), English translation *Doctor Faustus* (New York, 1948).

16. Adolf Hitler, *Mein Kampf*, vol. 2, p. 11.

17. Alexander and Margarete Mitscherlich, *Die Unfähigkeit zu trauern: Grundlagen des kollektiven Verhaltens* (Munich, 1967), English translation *The Inability to Mourn: Principles of Collective Behavior* (New York, 1978).

18. Iring Fetscher, *Kunst im Dritten Reich* (Frankfurt am Main, 1974), p. 8.

19. Saul Friedländer, *Kitsch und Tod*, p. 118.

20. Adolf Hitler, *Mein Kampf*, vol.1, p. 6.

21. Ibid., p. 197.

22. *Licht-Bild-Bühne* (Berlin), 13 November 1933.

23. Alfred Rosenberg, *Blut und Ehre* (Munich, 1940), p. 214.

24. *Film-Kurier* (Berlin), 29 March 1933.

25. Adolf Hitler, *Mein Kampf*, p. 198.

26. Ibid., p. 317.

27. Hans Grimm, *Volk ohne Raum* (Leipzig, 1926).

28. Theodor Adorno, *Einleitung in die Musiksoziologie* (Reinbek bei Hamburg, 1968), p. 60, English translation *Introduction to the Sociology of Music* (New York, 1989).

29. Hermann Glaser, *Das dritte Reich* (Freiburg, 1961), p. 54.

30. Hans Traub, *Der Film als politisches Machtmittel* (Munich, 1933), p. 26.

31. Quoted in Peter Gay, *Die Republik der Außenseiter*, pp. 107f., English original *Weimar Culture: The Outsider as Insider* (New York, 1968).

32. [The Hitler Youth was divided regionally into six *Obergebiete*, each containing six *Gebiete* and a maximum of eight. Each *Gebiet*, depending on size, contained several HY *Banne*. By 1943 there were 42 *Gebiete* and 223 *Banne.*—Transl.]

33. Adolf Hitler in a speech on 4 December in Reichenberg, quoted in *Völkischer Beobachter* (Munich), 4 December 1938.

34. Peter Gay, *Die Republik der Außenseiter*, pp. 107f.

35. Quoted in Werner Kindt, comp., *Grundschriften der deutschen Jugendbewegung* (Düsseldorf, 1963), p. 66 (Preface by Hans Breuer to the 10th ed. of the *Zupfgeigenhansl*).

36. Götz von Olenhusen, *Jugendreich, Gottesreich, Deutsches Reich* (Cologne, 1987) (Archiv der deutschen Judgendbewegung, 2), p. 8.

37. F. Wagner and G. Linke, eds., *Die Inszenierung der Macht: ästhetische Faszination im Faschismus* (Berlin, 1987).

38. [*Heimabende* were obligatory Hitler Youth meetings held during the evening hours. They consisted of a prescribed program of ideological indoctrination and activities such as singing and making things for Winter Relief (*Winterhilfswerk*). See Christian Zentner and Friedemann Bedürftig, eds., *Das grosse Lexikon des Dritten Reiches* (Munich, 1985), p. 243.—Transl.]

39. Karsten Witte, "Der Apfel und der Stamm" in *Schock und Schöpfung* (Darmstadt, 1986), p. 306.

40. Hans Joachim Sachsze, "Filmpublikum von morgen" in *Der deutsche Film* (Berlin), vol. 2, no. 6, 1937, pp. 168f.

41. Ibid., p. 199.

42. Curt Belling and Alfred Schütze, *Der Film in der Hitlerjugend* (Berlin, 1937), p. 62.

43. Arno Klönne, *Jugend im Dritten Reich* (Düsseldorf, 1982), p. 34.

44. Anneliese Ursula Sander, *Jugend und Film* (Berlin,1944) (*Das junge Deutschland*: Sonderveröffentlichung, 6), p. 72.

45. Secret report of the SD [*Sicherheitsdienst*], 3 April 1941 in: Bundesarchiv Koblenz R 58/159.

46. W. Häcker, "Der Aufstieg der Jugendfilmarbeit" in *Das junge Deutschland*, Amtliches Organ des Jugendführers des deutschen Reiches (Berlin), no. 10, 1943, p. 235.

47. Adolf Hitler, *Mein Kampf*, p. 471.

48. Alfred Rosenberg, *Der Mythus des zwanzigsten Jahrhunderts* (Munich, 1930), p. 521, English translation *The Myth of the Twentieth Century: An Evaluation of the Spiritual-Intellectual Confrontations of Our Age* (Torrance, Calif., 1982).

49. Adolf Hitler, *Mein Kampf*, pp. 473f.

50. Ibid., p. 118.

51. Alois Funk, *Film und Jugend* (Doctoral thesis, Munich University, 1934), p. 97.

52. Hannsjoachim Wolfgang Koch, *Geschichte der Hitlerjugend*, p. 173.

53. Ibid., p. 173.

54. Cf. Hilmar Hoffmann, "Die Brücke" [review of Bernhard Wicki's film] in *Rheinischer Merkur/Christ und Welt* (Bonn), no. 7, 12 February 1988.

55. Interview with Michel Foucault in *Cahier du Cinéma* (Paris), no. 251/252, July–August 1974, p. 19.

56. Joseph Goebbels, *Der steile Aufstieg*, pp. 45 and 48.

57. Diary entry by Joseph Goebbels, 23 July 1941 in: Bundesarchiv Koblenz BA NL 118.

58. *Das Reich* (Berlin), no. 23, 8 June 1941.

59. Hans Joachim Sachsze, *Filmpublikum von morgen*, p. 199.

60. Anneliese Ursula Sander, *Jugend und Film*, p. 118.

61. Kurt-Ingo Flessau, *Schule der Diktatur: Lehrpläne und Schulbücher des Nationalsozialismus* (Frankfurt am Main, 1984), p. 117.

62. Curt Belling, *Der Film in Staat und Partei* (Berlin, 1936).

63. Curt Belling, "Film und Partei" in *Film-Kurier* (Berlin), 31 December 1936.

64. Horst Kerutt and Wolfram M. Wegener, eds., *Die Fahne ist mehr als der Tod: ein deutsches Fahnenbuch* (Munich, 1943), pp. 139–41.

÷ 5 ÷

THE NONFICTIONAL GENRES OF NAZI FILM PROPAGANDA

The Cultural and Educational Film

The harmonically educated man should, as was true of Goethe, be well versed in representational as well as abstract thinking. Cultural films are therefore a culturally desirable counterweight to the excessive growth of abstract thinking and against the one-sidedness of a predominantly intellectual education.

Das Kulturfilmbuch, 1924[1]

"Aunt Ufa's" Culture

Not merely the aesthetics of the cultural film present a typically German phenomenon, but the notion of *Kulturfilm* as well. From the cellular division of an amoeba to an artistic giant such as Michelangelo, the cultural film deals with everything that is being investigated by biology and medicine, by research and technology, art and literature, ethnology and geography and incorporates it all into a more elevated way of looking at the world that is peculiar to this genre. Germany's *Kulturfilm*-makers demystify creation and cosmos. The French respectfully called the German cultural film *"film de niveau"*; the Americans spoke of "oddities." Between 1926 and 1929, the United States channeled some one hundred German cultural films in thousands of copies through its largest cinema chains.

As Rudolf Oertel put it in 1941:

Among the many gifts that the movie gave us, none seems to be more precious and exhilarating than the gaze into the miraculous world of the universe.... The immense richness of microscopic life

in a water hole, the struggle for survival, the multiplications of invisible microbes, the slow growth, blossoming, wilting of plants, the
impenetrability of the nocturnal skies, the stars, the realm of the
clouds, the light rays, the currents of energy, the circulation of the
blood, the penetrating eyes of x-rays, the physician's operating skills,
but no less so the grandiose world of modern factories ... the infinite
cosmos and the small universe of humans.... The cultural film is the
great magician who shows us secrets that even our most daring
imagination could not visualize more magnificently and colorfully.[2]

Speaking at the *"Filmforum"* in 1955, Nicholas Kaufmann, for
many years director of Ufa's cultural film division, provided a
somewhat more sober retrospective assessment of this genre's
genesis.[3] During the reign of Emperor Wilhelm II, the government
had taken a stake of twenty-five million goldmarks in the founding of Ufa on condition that a special department be established
for the production of films to instruct, enlighten, and educate the
population. Since this kind of film was controlled by the *Kul-
turpflege* department of the Reich Ministry of the Interior, it was
simply renamed Ufa "cultural department" after 1 July 1918, and
its products were thenceforth called "cultural films." In 1925, he
added, the leading association of the German film industry (SPIO)
defined this genre narrowly as a triad of educational film, scientific film, and film purely concerned with landscape.

As late as 1947, a Swiss encyclopedia offered the following
description: "Cultural film is a catch-all for all films that have cultural objectives: films on scientific research, educational films for
community colleges and universities, films about expeditions and
reportage, films to enlighten and advertise, documentaries. Cultural films in a stricter sense are shorts supporting the main program for the purposes of entertainment and education." In other
words, the term comprised a hodge-podge of diverse subgenres
on the one hand, and was used as a bracket for autonomous genres, such as documentaries, reportage films, or marketing films, on
the other.

Supported by Wilhelm Prager, Kaufmann had decisively
shaped the aesthetics of the German *Kulturfilm* with the 1925
movie *Wege zu Kraft und Schönheit* (Paths toward Power and
Beauty). As he stressed in his postwar assessment, this genre was
not invented by the Nazis. He referred to the catalogue of "supporting films suitable for screening in public cinemas" that as
early as 1919 listed eighty-seven completed cultural films and
another forty-four that were in production relating to some

twenty-one different fields. The preface to this catalogue contains the following telling passage: "The wounds that the war has inflicted can be healed only by fulfilling the cultural tasks in this world. Among them is to be found the reconstruction of instruction and of humane education that has been badly affected by the war." In 1918 there existed in Germany no less than 3,130 permanent cinemas, i.e., one movie theater per 18,000 inhabitants.

Ufa was indebted to Ulrich K. T. Schulz for the first edition of a biological *Kulturfilm*, the popular-scientific movie *Der Hirschkäfer* (The Stag Beetle, 1920/21), which, screened at the Tauentzien-Palast, inaugurated the supporting film. Having perfected the time accelerator method in cooperation with his cameraman Krien, Schulz developed the first microscopic film camera together with Zeiss, the optical engineering company, in order to reveal the "mysteries" of the microcosmos. What filmmakers were still lacking on their journey into the unknown was the telephoto lens with which to capture elusive wild animals on a forest clearing or the distant flight of exotic birds. As E. W. M. Lichtwark remembered it, in 1925 Schulz and Krien "created their first telephoto lens from an old camera. The first photo hunt for deer was successfully started."[4]

In becoming more perfected technically, the cultural film hoped to emancipate itself from the one-dimensional character of the newsreel, not merely artistically, but also thematically. In contrast to the newsreel camera that cannot reproduce more than what is seen by the human eye, the cultural film aimed to show all those things that the eye cannot see: the variety of the world beyond the visible and the secrets of nature. According to Kaufmann, the *Kulturfilm* alone offers "unique documents of life in the star-studded skies above." In order to make these discoveries, the filmmaker needed the x-ray screen, a time accelerator, slow motion cameras, telephoto and wide-angle lenses. People began to revel in the technical language of "panchromatic film" (e.g., R. Reinert's *Der geheimnisvolle Spiegel* [The Mysterious Mirror, 1928]), of "*Schlieren*" cinematography (e.g., Martin Rikli's *Unsichtbare Wolken* [Invisible Clouds, 1932]) or of "insect perspectives" as first developed in 1929 (e.g., Ulrich K. T. Schulte's *Der Ameisenstaat* [State of the Ants, 1934] which was awarded a prize at Venice a year later). Panchromatic films are films that are sensitive to all colors and the full spectral range. The "*Schlieren*" optic was an invention of A. Toepler and E. Abbe and facilitates the nuanced visibility of materials of divergent transparency, such as condensations, clouds, or gases; it also captures irregular light and pictures of moving currents.

In 1955 Kaufmann put his memories of this period before 1945 into the following words: "We had three axioms. The first was: 'The world is my domain.' This meant that there were no limits as far as the subject matter was concerned." In order to support his own de-Nazification, he enumerated innocuous cultural films with biological, natural-lyrical, and scientific topics listed in the 1941–44 catalogues, such as *Tiergarten Südamerika* (Zoological Garden of South America); *In Obedska Bara; Meerestiere in der Adria* (Marine Life in the Adriatic Sea); *Das Sinnleben der Pflanzen* (The Inner Life of the Plants); *Können Tiere denken?* (Are Animals Capable of Thinking?); *Unsichtbare Wolken* (Invisible Clouds); *Unendlicher Weltraum* (Infinite Outer Space); *Röntgenstrahlen* (X-Rays); *Radium*. These were the kinds of films in which people could develop a "truly genuine creativity" (*wurzelechtes Schöpfertum*) à la Goebbels.

These wonders of nature that could be seen ever more frequently during the war on the screens of an ever more ravaged country were designed to distract. The untouched purity of nature was juxtaposed to wartime destruction; they were a feast for eyes that had become accustomed to seeing the somber images of war.

Kaufmann's second axiom reads: "Seize hold of the fullness of life; it is interesting, if you film it properly." Accordingly, he lists (unpolitical?) strips like *Jugend im Tanz* (Dancing Youth); *Jagd unter Wasser* (Underwater Hunt); *Der Zirkus kommt* (The Circus Is Coming); and *Der Geisbub* (The Boy Shepherd).

The third Ufa axiom is set in Latin: "*Suum cuique!*" by which Kaufmann implied that each topic was to be staged in such a way as was appropriate to its essence.

On 1 July 1918, Ufa founded its own division for cultural and educational film. On the Ufa grounds in Berlin-Babelsberg, this division had several studios and equipment that was always up to date. For example, it had a fully equipped microlab that guaranteed the high standard of film on biological subjects. Movies such as *Kraftleistung der Pflanzen* (The Power of Plants); *Der Bienenstaat* (The State of the Bees); *Mysterium des Lebens* (The Mystery of Life); *Natur und Technik* (Nature and Technology); *Hochzeiten im Tierreich* (Animal Weddings); *Bunte Kriechwelt* (The Colorful World of Creepy-Crawlies); *Können Tiere denken?* (Are Animals Capable of Thinking); or *Tiergarten des Meeres* (Maritime Zoo) set, if nothing else, standards of perfection. Even in their time these films lived up to two demands that Nelson Goodman belatedly postulated in 1967: the scientific goal was insight; the aesthetic goal was satisfaction. [5]

Next to Ufa, companies like Bavaria, Tobis, Wien-Film and others also produced cultural films. Bavaria's *Germanen gegen Pharaonen* (Teutons versus Pharaohs, 1939), for example, attempted to illuminate man's early history by comparing the cultural monuments of ancient Egypt and Germany. What the objects cannot deliver in ideological terms is complemented by actors on the stage. At the time of the Nazi seizure of power, Svend Noldan's *Was ist die Welt?* (What Is the World?, 1933) attracted considerable attention. It was the story of creation in nine acts that surpassed even the high "Ufa standard" of the time. The famous physicist Max Planck is said to have been no little astonished by the technical feats and stunts of this film as a result of which Noldan succeeded in "giving visual expression" to developments "that in reality took millions of years" to evolve. Planck was convinced "that such films appeal not only to a small circle of so-called intellectuals, but could also give much to the broadest sections of the population." This all the more so because "the ordinary man is longing to fulfill his life, is longing for the opportunity to understand life and genesis that he sees around him in a deeper sense." To the music of Beethoven's *Die Himmel rühmen des Ewigen Ehre*, planet Earth recedes into space as a barely visible speck.

Since its founding in July 1918, Ernst Krieger was the director of the Ufa cultural division—"a major from the front line with many war wounds and a regimental comrade of Ufa director Grau." According to Oskar Kalbus's testimony "this old drilling-ground connection was extraordinarily important."[6] Between 1919 and 1926 Kalbus was responsible for the economic and public relations side of Ufa's cultural film division.

The department dealing with scientific films was led by two medical doctors, Curt Thomalla and Nicholas Kaufmann. They jointly produced Ufa's first medical blockbusters: *Die Geschlechtskrankheiten und ihre Folgen* (Venereal Diseases and their Consequences); *Die Pocken, ihre Gefahren und deren Bekämpfung* (Smallpox, Its Dangers and the Fight Against It); *Die weisse Seuche* (The White Epidemic); *Krüppelnot und Krüppelhilfe* (The Plight of the Invalids and How to Help Them); *Säuglingspflege* (Infant Care).

Within the first five years alone, Ufa's cultural film division produced a total of 135 films on medical and pharmaceutical subjects. However, the division soon got into financial difficulties

since these films were not box office successes and turned out to
be too sophisticated for use in schools.

In April 1919 the Central Institute for Education and Instruction
established a film archive and office for the promotion of educational and instructional films designed for schools. As the Minister for Cultural Affairs put it when speaking before the Prussian
Diet: "The Government is nonetheless of the opinion that there is
no better investment today than to sink as much money as possible into popular education, especially at the primary level. Reconstruction and the inner recovery of the national body (*Volkskörper*)
must start from within Germany's schools."

Up to the end of the inflationary period in 1923, Ufa's cultural
film division had produced over four hundred educational and
cultural films suitable for schools. Previously, the *Kulturfilm* had
been treated as a negligible quantity in schools and at best had
been deemed suitable for screening on the Kaiser's birthday or on
Sedan Day, celebrating Prussia's 1870 victory over France. Hyper-
inflation then put a temporary stop to this development. The Law
of 13 October 1923, which introduced the *Rentenmark* as the temporary currency, was designed to stabilize the German currency
system. Many smaller film companies went broke in this period.
To prevent further bankruptcies, the Reich government introduced by decree the so-called quota system: a German film was to
be made for every film imported from abroad.

The financial crisis of the cultural film coincided with a general
lull in moviegoing. An attempt was made to make a virtue out of
necessity and to nationalize the film industry. As M. Pfeiffer, a conservative Reichstag deputy, had declared as early as 1917, "The
privately owned cinema is dependent on the needs and expectations of the population. A publicly funded cinema, by contrast,
can remain impervious to changing tastes and fashions."[7] Two
years later, Fritz Tejessy, a socialist, writing in *Die Glocke*, also
demanded that all cinemas be rigorously taken into communal
public ownership, like in "Soviet Hungary." He claimed that "the
flooding [of the market] with disreputable films" had assumed
catastrophic proportions.

During the "tempestuous year of the communalization movement in 1919," the *Kulturfilm* "optimists" had envisaged a vast
array of communal cinemas, Urania theaters, church cinemas, and
cinema clubs. They dreamed of showcases that would screen nothing but cultural films and would one day generate an "enormous
demand" for such movies.[8] In his *Der Wagenlenker* (The Driver),

Willy Stuhlfeld pleaded for the nationalization of all Bavarian cinemas that he characterized as "gold mines." If nationalization or communalization never materialized, this was probably also due to the sharp protest by the powerful Ufa trust which, on 11 November 1919, conjured up the specter of "grave dangers for the continued existence of our society and hence also a threat to the Reich's stake in our company" if cinemas were communalized.

Moreover, for a long time—indeed until 1926—the development of the German cultural film was impeded by the economic repercussions of the entertainment tax decree of 9 June 1921. Suddenly, local governments pocketed between 25 and 80 percent of cinema profits as quasi-sleeping partners of the industry. In 1926, the journal *Bildwart*, with barely veiled irony, compared this "immoral" source of income to nude shows whose entertainment value was being taxed at a mere 5 percent. According to Hans Traub, Ufa during its financial year 1921/22 paid ticket sales taxes to the tune of 63 million marks, amounting to "more than the total net profit." This downward spiral was stopped only on 10 June 1926, when the Reich Council issued a decree that linked the entertainment tax to an equalization mechanism: the tax maximum was pegged at 15 percent of the gross income. Furthermore, the screening of cultural films was made attractive to cinema owners by guaranteeing them a lucrative tax reduction. The pejorative term "tax grinder," used in connection with program pictures, originates in this period.

Looking back from a Nazi perspective, Leopold Gutterer, the chairman of the Ufa supervisory board and state secretary in the Reich Propaganda Ministry, judged the reduced entertainment tax to be in line with "the essence of the [Weimar] system period": "First of all, it was based on purely material considerations; secondly, it was a half-measure; and thirdly, it achieved the opposite of what it was designed to accomplish.... This was the time when the name *Kulturfilm* became popular for films relating to nature and research—sadly in an often negative sense."[9]

After 1926 the water-hole, insect and bird films mushroomed: *Die verborgenen Wunder unserer Gewässer* (The Hidden Wonders of Our Inland Waters); *Biene Maja und ihre Abenteuer* (Bee Maya and Its Adventures), directed by Wolfram Junghans and based on Waldemar Bonsel's book; Bengt Berg's *Mit den Zugvögeln nach Afrika* (To Africa with the Migratory Birds); or Erich Waschneck's *Kampf um die Scholle* (The Struggle for the Soil). However, there are other typical subjects—art as reality of a secondary kind. In 1919

Hans Cürlis founded his Institute for Cultural Research and invoked the *Geist der Gothik* (Spirit of the Gothic) and the *Dom über der Stadt* (The Cathedral above the City). He demonstrated the otherness of the world of art—a world that is elevated above life and put on a pedestal.

Many of the hypocritical, parareligious films depicting the little pomposities of the fitness movement would today draw ridicule—films such as *Insel der Seligen* (Island of the Blessed), *Die Grazilen* (The Graceful Ones), and *Licht, Luft, Leben* (Light, Air, Life). Kurt Tucholsky reviled as having nothing to do with art those Najades who were bathing their beautiful nude bodies in Max Reinhardt's first film poem *Insel der Seligen* (1913).[10] The journal *Film und Bild* felt at least able to identify the "embodiment of an idea" in this movie. "Here this idea has been pushed to utmost perfection, and the principle of a viewing value (as the fundamental concept of the movie) has been realized to a high degree."[11]

Restrained as they were, these films were modest precursors of the Prager-Kaufmann film *Wege zu Kraft und Schönheit* (Paths to Vigor and Beauty) which, released in 1925, used the skin as the message. In 1926 Ufa alone satisfied the demand for artistic movies by producing some 90 cultural films and over 850 educational and instructional ones. Yet, however successful these films may have been from an artistic point of view, profitability left much to be desired. According to *Ufa-Dienst* of 11 January 1927, the company's cultural film division was disbanded "for reasons of reorganization." It was only when Ufa and Deulig merged in the spring of 1927 that things began to look up again.

Greatest attention and corresponding financial support was given to the scientific film and its more popular versions. By recruiting well-known scientists, the German scientific and popular-scientific movies gained broad appeal as genres that were both educational and thrilling. Even Albert Einstein, whose relativity theory—though still controversial at this time—was produced as a trilogy, praised cultural films, arguing that they provided "a valuable enrichment for city dwellers" because the visual experiences of the latter "mostly tend to be of great monotony."[12]

Films of this type, and in particular the scientific insights contained in them, also earned the German cultural film respect abroad. No less a person than G. W. Pabst put himself at the service of this genre. In 1926 and in cooperation with two pupils of Sigmund Freud, he made two films about the latter's psychoanalytical methods, titled *Das Geheimnis der Seele* (The Mystery of the

Soul). Under Pabst's direction, cameraman Guido Seeber succeeded in producing a fascinating visualization of dream images.
With the help of expressionist stylistic elements, the human soul
was given images that opened up a new dimension of film aesthetics. Three years earlier another famous director had trans-
posed a dream into images with extraordinary filmic means.
Walter Ruttmann produced Kriemhild's "dream of the falcon"
that anticipated Siegfried's death in Fritz Lang's 1923 two-part
film *Die Nibelungen* (The Nibelungs). (In the Third Reich, part one
was turned into a sound movie under the title *Siegfrieds Tod*
[Siegfried's Death], while part two was deposited in an archive.)

The year 1926 was a year of major change also in the sense that
Ruttmann's *Berlin—Symphonie einer Großstadt* (Berlin—Symphony
of a City) left the bounds of the cultural film and established the
documentary as a category *sui generis*. It also produced the style of
Neue Sachlichkeit (New Sobriety). The enthusiasm for naked reality
was inspired by the desire "to see things objectively and in their
material substance, without burdening them *a priori* with ideas."[13]
Through their Berlin symphony, Ruttmann and his coauthor and
cameraman Karl Freund created the prototype of the synchronic
film: apart from Berlin's skyline, the film captures the inner physiognomy of the hustle and bustle of a metropolis, its social con-
flicts and the human beings affected by them. Through the rhythm
of sequences that is structured like a symphony and that translates
Berlin's hectic daily life into the dynamic of a film, the viewer is
sucked into the eddy of images. The mobility of objects and an
unfettered camera by which even spaces are being shifted, produced a fascinating picture of pure movement.

Also in 1926 movie enthusiasts were captivated by two other
synchronic films with analogous dynamic elements: Berthold
Viertel's *Die Abenteuer eines Zehnmarkscheines* (The Adventures of
a Ten-Mark Bill) and Alberto Calvacanti's portrait of Paris, titled
Rien que les heures (Nothing But the Hours). Viertel's Berlin movie
was scripted by Béla Balász and produced with Karl Freund
behind the camera. A ten-mark bill provided the "red thread" by
fluttering from sequence to sequence through the "texture of life"
(Balász) within which people meet merely coincidentally. Changing kaleidoscopically on the hour, Calvacanti's movie represents a
stroll through the rhythmically charged asphalt labyrinth of Paris.

Ruttmann, Balász, and Calvacanti had all been studying the
montages in Eisenstein's *Battleship Potemkin* (1925). And yet reality
gets lost in the rapid sequence of the images. As Siegfried Kracauer

put it, "Life in its transient form, street crowds, unintended gestures and other ephemeral impressions provide the main diet of
the cinema."[14] John Grierson first used the term "documentary
film" in his 1929 movie *Drifters*, or more precisely in his critique of
Robert Flaherty's *Moana* made in 1926.

When, with the rise of right-wing nationalist parties and associations, films, too, drifted into nationalist waters, left-wing and
liberal artists and writers founded the People's Association of
Film Art in 1928. Heinrich Mann, G. W. Pabst, and Erwin Piscator
formed its presidium. They wanted to unmask the "hypocrisy" of
cultural films and newsreels. When their enthusiasm went no further than verbal actionism, film directors associated with Hans
Richter founded the German League for the Independent Film.[15]

After the Invention of Sound Film

*It is in the nature of its technology that the movie has abolished the
distance between the viewer and a world of art that is itself secluded.
There is an inexorable revolutionary tendency in the destruction of the
solemn distance of that cultic representation that surrounded the theater. The film's gaze is the closeup gaze of the participant.*

Béla Balász[16]

Just as all technological innovations were first tried out in cultural
films before they became perfected in feature films, Ufa's first
sound film experiment also was made with this genre. The movie
Gläserne Wundertiere (Transparent Miracles) was premiered on 2
August 1929 at the Universum Cinema in Berlin. This was two
years after Hollywood had declared the short film *What Price
Glory* and later *Lights of New York* (1928), the first feature film with
running dialogue, to be the beginnings of sound film. Similarly,
the first German color film was a *Kulturfilm* titled *Bunte Tierwelt*
(Colorful Animal World), which premiered in December 1931 and
fully lived up to its title. No more than a total of sixteen color features were made up to the end of World War II. Owing to the new
synchronization techniques, film also became more interesting to
political parties for the verbal transmission of propaganda than
had earlier been the case, when its agitational potential had consisted only in moving pictures.

Even before the start of sound film, Social Democrats, Communists, Conservative Nationalists, and Nazis used short

films and documentaries for the purposes of self-portrayal, publicity, campaigning, and propaganda. Thus, the Social Democrats commissioned Ernö Metzner in 1928 to make a semi-documentary, entitled *Im Anfang war das Wort* (In the Beginning Was the Word), which dealt with the consequences of Bismarck's anti-Socialist laws. In 1930 M. Harder was asked to do a social study, *Lohnbuchhalter Kremke* (Bookkeeper Kremke). The two documentaries *Bau am Staat* (Working on the State, 1929), with a speech by the Social Democrat Reich Chancellor Hermann Müller, and *Ins Dritte Reich* (Into the Third Reich) two years later were more or less limp statements in the style of manifestoes. Short cartoons, like *Was wählst Du?* (What Are You Going to Vote For?, 1927) and *Dem deutschen Volke* (To the German People, 1930), that were inspired by Social Democratic ideas, proved more attractive.

The Nazi Party had founded its own Reich Film Office as early as 1 November 1930. As early as 1925, Hitler had noted in his book *Mein Kampf* that visual images transmit information instantly, unlike the written word that requires slow reading.[17] Nazi terminology and strong visual images notwithstanding, the NSDAP evidently was more successful in this market than others, as demonstrated by films such as *Zeitprobleme. Wie der Arbeiter wohnt* (Problems of the Time. How the Worker Lives, 1931) or *Hitler über Deutschland* (Hitler over Germany, 1932). In the place of analytically sharpened criticism of the Weimar state, these movies provided straight polemics.

In 1927 the Hindenburg Committee produced *Unser Hindenburg* (Our Hindenburg), which inaugurated a repetitive series of tired films for the Field Marshal's and Reich President's glory. It marketed the hero of the Battle of Tannenberg in World War I as an image of steel that transcended the ages. This was not history writing the script, but historicizing manipulation. The German Nationalist People's Party (DNVP) tried to keep up in this competition for filmic ideas and programs by commissioning *Wohin wir treiben* (Whither We Are Drifting, 1931).

Between the invention of sound film and its use in party propaganda on the one hand, and Hitler's seizure of power in 1933 on the other, there remained little time for audiovisual productions opposing the Nazi movement. In 1932 the Communists won over Slatan Dudow to produce *Kuhle Wampe oder: Wem gehört die Welt* (Kuhle Wampe or: To Whom Does the World Belong), a feature film with artistic ambitions, which was directed less against the Nazis than against the Social Democrats, and indeed quite massively so. The film censors released *Kuhle Wampe* only after radical cuts had been made. This propaganda film, which cunningly mobilized emotions with the help of Brecht-style alienation effects and Hanns Eisler's ballads sung by Helene Weigel, represented materialist hedonism pure and simple; but it is worth seeing to this day. *Weltenwende* (The Beginning of a New World) and *Was wollen die Kommunisten?* (What Is It That the Communists Want?), both made in 1928 by Carl Junghans, by contrast offered worthy propaganda which in compilatory fashion operated with dissociative elements. Junghans denied responsibility for another 1928 Communist film, titled *Die rote Fahne* (The Red Flag), with which he had been credited. These films demonstrate nothing more than the interchangeability of parts that were in themselves homogeneous and that represented a present turned into history.

With the help of a pub owner and a number of unpaid Czech actors, Junghans had made a name for himself after shooting a social-critical film of the life of a washerwoman, titled *So ist das Leben/Takovy je zivot* (This Is What Life Is Like, 1929/30). This was a silent film with a tragic ending that sided with the downtrodden working class in an unsentimental way. In terms of film history, it must be seen as part of the brief but impressive phase of movies about the proletariat. Its artistic success was also due to the intelligent editing techniques that Junghans later perfected into a dynamic montage, when he produced a documentary about the 1936 Winter Olympics entitled *Jugend der Welt* (Youth of the World). Similarly, he refined the art of alienation à la Brecht through the use of well-positioned intermediate titles. After 1933, Junghans had to make certain concessions to avoid having to submit to the regimentation of Nazi filmmaking.

In 1932 the powerful *Stahlhelm* veterans association commissioned films like *Freiwillige vor* (Volunteers Step Forward) or *Der Stahlhelm marschiert* (The Stahlhelm Is Marching) whose images and texts came across in the staccato style of machine-gun fire; during the same year, the Hindenburg Committee produced *Einer für alle* (One Man for All). All these movies represented nothing but the noisy war cries of barbarism (*Unkultur*).

Among the unpolitical *Kulturfilm* spectacles, Svend Noldan's 1934 genesis film *Was ist die Welt?* must be seen as an important step in the evolution of the genre. Even Käthe Kollwitz confessed to having been "captivated" by it; it was, she added, as a result of this film that she had become conscious of "the enormity of the Creation" that Noldan had presented "through the eyes" to "the senses."

Even if due credit is given to Noldan's strenuous efforts that pre-date the Nazi period by three years and to the almost perfect way in which scientific knowledge was transmitted, the pompous nar-rative is nonetheless a nuisance. Against the background of Beethoven's *Die Himmel rühmen des Ewigen Ehre* the pathos of the commentary reduced science to a question of fate and faith.

For the purposes of Nazi propaganda, cultural films were of interest only to the extent that they could be "appreciated with interest by viewers of all educational and occupational back-grounds."[18] The monies that Goebbels invested in this genre—amounting to at least 30,000 marks per 10- to 15-minute film—were assumed to be paying off through popular appeal. By view-ing cultural films, everyone was to have an opportunity to "study the few laws of nature" and to "inform himself" of "what is hap-pening in the infinite realm of nature." As Fritz Hippler added in his *Betrachtungen zum Filmschaffen* what "concerns all of us directly is becoming evident all over in most varied forms: the great polar-ity of life, the law of inertia, gravity, and striving for the center, of fighting and conception, of growth and aging, of giving birth and dying, of killing and devouring. The great law, the inexorable necessity that never disappears exists everywhere and in every-thing; it is an infinite world that, its pitilessness notwithstanding, is still so beautiful."[19] Hippler saw the cultural film as a kind of healing water from which man can gain, "beyond insight and cog-nition, strength and faith to deal with his daily jobs and with the great objectives of the struggle."

Struggle in and with nature becomes one of the Nazi *Kulturfilm*'s inexhaustible themes, deemed to be "significant from a state-polit-ical point of view and valuable for popular education." Indeed, is there another subject with which to justify more easily the Social Darwinist ideology of eating and being eaten, of racist wars of extermination against what is "un-German" and "degenerate" than by reference to nature which provides a seemingly fitting analogy. It was not mentioned that calculated murder and the systematic liquidation of ethnic, religious, or social minorities is unique only to the human species. Other strategists of the Nazi cultural film, fas-cinated with power, either did not recognize this anymore, or they tried to drown it in a romantic and misconceived sentimentality.

Ufa's cultural films for the first time gave artistic expression to living nature; or to quote Georg Lukács, "the rushing water, the breeze moving through the trees, the silence of sunset and the roar of a thunderstorm as natural events are being transformed here

into art, though not, as in painting, by means of artistic values that
are taken from other worlds. Man has lost his soul, but he gains
his body instead; its grandeur and poetic power lies in the force of
his skill to overcome physical obstacles and its humor consists in
how he succumbs to them."[20]

The Popularity of the Mountaineering Film

*A sharp incline lies before us. But we believe that it can be mastered
more easily by a people that through many years of tough exercise is
trained in the tribulations of mountaineering than by a people that has
learned its mountaineering skills in the plains.... We fully appreciate
our tasks, but also our opportunities. We know what we want. But
what is even more important: we also want what we know.*

Joseph Goebbels[21]

The lyrical portrayal of the Alps reached a culmination well before
the advent of the Third Reich. The world was initiated to the
mountaineering film by Arnold Fanck. It was also he who
declared the mountain peaks to be the symbolic expressions of a
world-view and who created a new type of film that combined the
feature with the documentary. It is wonderfully easy to extend the
horizon of meaning by adopting the panoramic view from atop
the mountain. With films like *Wunder des Schneeschuhs* (The Snow-
shoe Wonder, 1920), *Der Berg des Schicksals* (Mountain of Fate,
1924), *Der heilige Berg* (The Holy Mountain, 1926), or *S.O.S. Eisberg*
(S.O.S. Iceberg, 1933), Fanck promoted the Nazis' fuzzy philosophy of nature, as did Luis Trenker. The latter, a native of the Alps,
likewise tended to make the high ascent into the glaciers' paradise
with his films *Der Kampf ums Matterhorn* (Struggle for the Matterhorn, 1928), *Der Sohn vom weissen Berge* (The Son from White
Mountain, 1930), *Berge in Flammen* (Mountains in Flames, 1931), or
Der Rebell (The Rebel, 1932).

Both giants of this genre helped Leni Riefenstahl rise from a
lowly career as a dancer to a continuous success in filmmaking.
Not only did she play the lead parts in Fanck's *Der heilige Berg* and
Trenker's *S.O.S. Eisberg* as well as *Die weisse Hölle von Piz Palu* (The
White Hell of Piz Palu, 1929); she also devoted her own talent as a
director to the cultivation of the frigid soul and to the delusion of
unadulterated beauty when in 1932 she filmed *Das blaue Licht* (The
Blue Light) in the Dolomites high above the clouds. There was no

room for the dark sides of this world in the shadowless light "at the peak of the skies" (Riefenstahl). She had to be "'on top' at all costs." In her view, the idyllic setting of the mountains à la Stifter symbolized the beautiful. Margarete Mitscherlich called it a metaphor of "the heroic, of the masculine principle that radiated eternal glamour."[22] For Riefenstahl, the mountains represented the metaphysical. However, she shared with many other contemporaries her worship of the mystical and eternal of the world of mountains. Thus, when Thomas Mann describes the cloud-covered Alps as "the experience of eternity, of nothingness and of death, a metaphysical dream ... [as something] elementary in the sense of ultimate and untamed extrahuman grandeur,"[23] he presents a wide spectrum of possible experiences. And Fanck, Trenker, and Riefenstahl then selected one particular facet that, given their tendency to mystify things from the position of their life philosophy, no longer allowed for critical distance.

Riefenstahl, after a lot of trouble with philistine party and film industry functionaries would have "loved nothing more" than to take refuge "in the mountains." But, she added naively, "unfortunately I first had to finish the film of the [1935 Nuremberg] Party rally."[24] To quote Klaus Theweleit's sarcastic assessment: "What the elevated individual, what the higher culture lacks to achieve beatific totality, to gain bodily wholeness, is a 'beneath' that it can subjugate."[25] Riefenstahl expressed this "beneath" that is to be subjugated more convincingly than anyone else before her. In Theweleit's psychoanalysis of fascism, the "beneath" is represented by the unordered chaotic world of male sexual drives. This world does not appear in Riefenstahl's movies. She—a woman—has probably been most consistent in cleansing her artistic worlds of the filth of the "beneath." Her stories are set on top of the whitest peaks; her figurative images stretch upward into the light; her gaze is that of the leader of the masses who merely notes them as well-ordered formations, linear columns, and imposing line-ups. The masses (the "beneath") are so suppressed in Riefenstahl's work that they seemingly no longer appear in it, or if they do, they appear in a highly cultivated form. They appear as nonliterary formations, as shock troops. The massive appearance of the "beneath" is so clean that it no longer presents a danger to "the man of higher culture;" on the contrary, it makes him "shudder." This is what Riefenstahl's films do to this day, though for different reasons. At his Berghof retreat near Berchtesgaden, Hitler once praised Fanck's trashy and dishonest film *Der heilige Berg*, in which Riefenstahl acted the lead part, as "the most beautiful that I have ever seen on screen."

Above all, however, it was the cultural film that invariably rose to lofty heights that, in its strenuous attempt to create a lyric of nature, mostly failed to excel artistically whenever its makers, following Ufa's *Alpen* prototype, produced in 1918 by F. Lampe, built a sublime world of its own, as can be found in *Majestät der Berge* (Majesty of the Mountains), *Bergbauern* (Highland Farmers), *Heuzug im Allgäu* (Hay Harvest in the Allgäu) or else in Hitler Youth movies like *Hitlerjugend in den Bergen* (Hitler Youth in the Mountains, 1932), *Bergsommer* (Mountain Summer, 1936), *Aus der Geschichte des Florian Geyer* (From Florian Geyer's Story, 1940), *Hochland HJ* (Highland Hitler Youth, 1941), or finally plodding war movies like *Alpenkorps im Angriff* (Alpine Corps on the Offensive, 1939), *Die Funker mit dem Edelweiss* (The Wireless Operators with the Edelweiss Flower, 1939), and *In Fels und Firn* (Rocks and Permanent Snow, 1943). These are just a few typical examples of movies in which the line between the cultural film and the documentary had been moved in favor of the latter. In the period *prior* to the Nazi film, many movies that were called *"Kulturfilm"* defy strict classification in this category.

It was only after 1933 that the documentary can be clearly defined as a one-sided propaganda device. Even the subcategories of this genre, such as art film, educational film, travel film, etc., came to be put in the service of a higher ideological mission. In those cases where the ideology cannot be explicitly discerned, it is nonetheless present in every foot of film. Accordingly paragraph 2, section 5 of the Film Law of 16 February 1934 reads: "The Reich Film Producer [*Reichsfilmdramaturg*] has the following tasks: … [He is expected] to prevent in good time topics from being treated that run counter to the spirit of the age."[26]

Frank Leberecht, in his *Der Kampf um den Himalaya* (The Struggle for the Himalayas, 1937), celebrated the courage of the German Nanga Parbat expedition to conquer the unconquerable. As the forward song went: "Even if the goal is unreachable—youth will still conquer it." What the correspondent of the journal *Der deutsche Film* once wrote without a sense of irony applies to all those Alpine roped parties of German directors. He argued that it was less a matter of merely documenting dangerous climbing expeditions than of highlighting a "mental attitude" and "an idea to which the climbers were sworn" that flared up when they wrestled with the mountains. Thus, *Der Kampf um den Himalaya* was said by this journalist to have become "a general German symbol of the will to overcome all difficulties of life in order to reach the light."[27] Titles like *Der Aufstieg aus der Tiefe empor* (Ascent from the Depths, 1912) or *Uns zieht es zu höherem hinauf* (We Are Attracted Toward Something Higher, 1916) accordingly represent allegorical transfigurations of a lower ideology into the higher spheres of belief. These examples also demonstrate how the cultural film, walking a tightrope toward the documentary, became a Nazi organ, a party organ.

Technical Perfection with the Aim of Increasing Visibility

> *In this sense the moviegoer not only participates in what is being offered to him substantively, but also in the technical means by which things are being transmitted. This participation is justified.*
>
> Alfred Kerr[28]

Like abstract and expressionist art, imagination was banned in the Third Reich as something critical and dangerous. The Nazis perceived that they might lose control over content and over what constituted beauty if forms and the "natural" gestalt of things became open to interpretation. As early as 1918, Max Weber had denounced expressionism as an "intellectual narcotic."

How much more vigorously did the Nazi arbiters of art identify this sin against the prevailing spirit of the times with the destruction of order—in the eyes of any dictatorship, the most serious sacrilege. Consequently, it was wrong to "allow imagination to run wild! Imagination must be bound to the eternal laws of nature, and the utopian vision of such films must provide its own corrective. Senseless fantasies would result in a type of film that we saw so frequently in earlier days and in which *Unkultur* was given free rein."[29]

The cultural film, by contrast, took a Goethean view of life: "When you get it, it is interesting." The *Kulturfilm*'s striving for universality confronted it "with new tasks every day." These were "to transmit on film in comprehensible fashion what would otherwise not be accessible to the eyes of millions of its enthusiasts." The cultural film's camera "made us the partners of the most elusive beings on this planet; its time accelerator allowed us to experience the miracle of plant growth from the germinating seed to full blossom; its slow-motion technique made it possible to capture the flying bird in the air; with the help of x-rays it penetrated the secrets of life; and in the science lab we witnessed how nature and its laws were being outwitted."

Probably no less suited to underwrite the German *Kulturfilm*'s mission is another observation by Goethe in which he rejects a "separation of art and science." As Heinrich Koch and Heinrich Braune added: "The cultural film has discovered our homeland, and under the magic touch of the camera even monuments in marble come to life." This genre "is a much more important aspect of contemporary life than we surmise. As an educator of millions of people, it has profoundly changed our conceptions about the mysteries of life and given the *coup de grâce* to many superstitious prejudices."[30]

The optical and mechanical systems for improving visibility mentioned above (telephoto, time accelerator, slow-motion, microphotography, etc.) took an important step with the further development of the time lens which, from 1937, opened up new fields for scientific-technical cultural films. To optimize frequency and to facilitate extremely slow-motion pictures, prisms are put before the existing camera lens that permit a fracturing of incoming light. As a result, the object that is being viewed appears in an array of identical images. The staggered individual images are then sequentially exposed. Thus, by taking some 300 pictures per second it becomes possible to observe a falling raindrop; at 30,000 pictures per second we can study the tensions in a crystal at the moment of rupture. At 80,000 pictures per second we can trace the trajectory of a bullet. This was also the title of a film (*80.000 Bilder in einer Sekunde* [80,000 Pictures per Second]), produced by the AEG electrical engineering firm in 1938, that gave a good impression of such an event.

The educational film that provided exact data and scientific documentation satisfied a quest for learning in an age that developed a craving for compensatory counterimages to the uniform and ideologically anaesthetizing pictures that the Nazi regime presented. There is a world of difference between the idealistic definition of the cultural film as "an educator of millions of people" and the social function of the documentary as defined, for example, by Hans Richter who postulated the development of a "societally responsible film." Since the growing wealth of information constantly augments man's interest in recognizing the reality around him, the documentary opens up an opportunity to provide this latent cognitive interest with information that is true. Even if Susan

Sontag believes that "the purpose of art is not to help us with the finding of truth, be it a particular and historical truth or an eternal one,"[31] artistic ambition should nonetheless not obscure the substance and content of what is contained as immanent truth in those pictures or of what they demonstrate and of what can be objectively transmitted. Instead, the aesthetic element will have to confine itself to the role that becomes the overriding factor under the heading of transmission. The tension between art and real life, the confusion of appearance and reality that we frequently encounter in Nazi films, had been dissolved into social documents in the documentaries of early pioneers like Vertov, Flaherty, and Ivens which may be taken as yardsticks. Quite as Richter defined it, the documentary should "draw concrete life into the artistic sphere" so as to promote "the cognition of living relationships."[32]

What Richter understood to be the inclusion of "concrete life into the artistic sphere" the Nazis did not wish to see confused with attempts to individualize through aesthetic means. To them, "concrete life" was a useful life only if it was lived in the anonymous national community (*Volksgemeinschaft*). Film was to strengthen the conviction that had become increasingly virulent in Germany that only the individual who had joined the Nazi movement was capable of realizing himself—as a part of the whole. The documentary in particular was expected to make its persuasive contribution to this self-assessment gained through self-insight. The common denominator was the notion that the individual was nothing and the nation was everything. As Peter von Werder defined the "secret leitmotiv of films" in 1943: "Put in a nutshell, the self-image of the individual and the conception of the natural, cultural, and civilizational environment may be reduced, especially in the field of artistic expression, to one basic denominator. This is the image of man that predominates in a particular piece of art that represents at the same time the telos of a race, of a nation, of an ideological movement, or of a social stratum."[33] He believed, as he continued sibyllinically, that such a simplification is called for whenever "a range of individual traits is to be scanned over in order to recognize basic lines and to discuss matters of style."

Kulturfilm Weeks were organized in all major cities of the Reich with the aim of deploying this genre as a morale booster to counter a defeatist mentality that was being predicted in wartime. Cultural films were used prophylactically but also as part of a strategy of distraction. Two films gained general admiration in this respect, *Bunte Kriechwelt* and *Thüringen*. Both were produced in Agfa Color in 1940 and launched in September 1941 in Munich amid much publicity. The second "Reich Week for the German *Kulturfilm*" in November 1942 registered a mainly allergic reaction to the predominance of propaganda films, such as the trashy paratrooper epic *Sprung in den Feind* (Jump into Enemy Country, 1941) by Wilhelm Stöppler. The 1943 Film Week, held in the *Künstlerhaus* at Munich's Lenbach Square, had a better reception. With over one hundred films submitted, it became a sort of short film festival, featuring many *déjà vu* topics. Accordingly, Goebbels awarded prizes to rather unexciting movies like *Welt im Kleinsten* (Micro-World), *Netz aus Seide* (Silk Net), *Dämmerung über dem Teufelsmoor* (Dusk over Devil's Bog), *Kopernikus*, *Künstler bei der Arbeit* (Artist at Work), as well as the color animated films *Verwitterte Melodie* (Faded Melody) and *Armer Hansi* (Poor Jack). All these films were marked by the conspicuous absence of the swastika flag. Films loyal to the party line did not receive prizes this time, among them *Das deutsche Wort* (The German Word). Cultural films made at the very end of the Third Reich provided an even bigger escape into the idyllic: *Im Reich der Wichtelmänner* (In the Realm of the Dwarfs), *Kraniche ziehen gen Süden* (The Cranes Are Flying Southward), *Hochzeit im Korallenmeer* (Wedding in the Coral Sea), *Der letzte Einbaum* (The Last Dugout), *Romantisches Burgenland* (Romantic Burgenland), or *Im Tal der hundert Mühlen* (In the Vale of the Hundred Mills).

The replacement of Reich Film Superintendent Fritz Hippler by SS-Gruppenführer Hans Hinkel in the spring of 1944 no longer had a visible impact. It is, in any case, difficult to see how the cynic Hinkel, who had been responsible for the production of *Der ewige Jude* (The Eternal Jew), could have been outdone.

The Documentary

*What complicates the situation so much is that any simple "repro-
duction of reality" says less and less about that reality. A photo of the
Krupp Works or of AEG tells us virtually nothing about these companies. Actual reality has slipped into the functional. The reification
of human relations, as, for example, a factory, will no longer let these
relations go. There is hence a building job to be done for something
"artificial," for something that is "put up."*

Bertolt Brecht[34]

The Forerunners

The first sixty-foot German documentary was made at the end of
the last century by the German film pioneer Oskar Messter when,
on a sunny November afternoon in 1897, he put up his tripod in
front of Berlin's Brandenburg Gate. Messter had introduced the
Malteser Cross in Germany the year before and had thus facilitated
flicker-free screening. His number one film is described as follows
in the 115-page catalogue in which he announced some eighty-four
of his own films: "At the Brandenburg Gate in Berlin. The columns
of the Brandenburg Gate are visible in the background."[35]

Messter had recognized even before his foreign colleagues the
value of film as a biographical document. The "writing" of lively
history became possible only with the development of the documentary. What kind of visual images would we have today of
great statesmen and inventors without it? As early as 1897, Messter portrayed Emperor Wilhelm II in a "living photo" and later he
also did one of Bismarck in retirement. He was the first to use the
closeup and the time-accelerator dramaturgically. In 1902 the German princes had "their picture taken mutoscopically by order of
the All Highest [the Kaiser]." Only the town of Posen is revealed in
the simple report about the Imperial splendor when, "headed by
His Most Serene and Royal Highness Prince Albrecht of Prussia,"
people arrived on 5 July 1902 at Marienburg which had just been
restored. Ten years later, the Kaiser hovered at length in the aura
above the people on the occasion of the twenty-fifth anniversary of
his coming to the throne. Eight different production companies
were involved in the making of *Der deutsche Kaiser im Film* (The
German Emperor in Film, 1912), Max Reinhardt's Ambrosia-Film

among them.[36] The members of the royal house who can be seen strutting through the contemporary world almost as a matter of course give the appearance of exotic stopgaps for the real novelties that newsreels evidently could not get hold of.

From the early period of the silent film, Hans Cürlis has left us shorts of the portrait-painting Liebermann, of Slevogt, Corinth, and Zille, and it was only in 1957 that he put them together in his *Schaffende Hände* (Creating Hands). Probably the oldest portrait of an artist, a genuine *trouvaille*, is by Sascha Guitry: in 1919, just before Auguste Renoir's death, he documented a few moments of the almost paralyzed impressionist painter, representing the first known tentative forays of the camera toward the authentic subject.

Prior to World War I, the German Express Film Company began to market war newsreel material under the title *Der Tag im Film—Erste deutsche tägliche kinmatographische Berichterstattung* (The Day in Film—First Daily German Cinematographic Reporting). In 1913 its reporter shot footage at the front line in the Balkan War when, "in a hail of bullets," he succeeded in filming "an entire campaign including its culmination point as a real battle." Friedrich von Zglinicki reported in his book *Der Weg des Films* that the "Kaiser was given a private screening of "original footage of infantry bayonet attacks, cavalry patrols, firing guns, and Red Cross activities."[37]

Similarly the *Eiko-Woche* of 1913, which started even before Messter's venture, demonstrated with its first film what kind of elements a five-hundred-foot newsreel had to contain to be a popular success: "Balloon Rally; Accident Due to Gale-Force Winds; Jog in the Grunewald; the Brunswick Palace; The Empress Travels to Berlin; Homage Visit of an Air Squadron; The Romanian Crown Prince and Crown Princess in Berlin; The Modern Rotation Press at the Scherl Publishing House; Visit of the Württembergian Royal Couple; The German Crown Prince with Prince Carol of Romania." Half of the topics were concerned with royalty.

Before Messter once again employed his cameramen for documentaries and, in 1914, as war correspondents, he fully devoted himself to making feature films, discovering in the process many later "stars" such as Henny Porten (*Das Liebesglück einer Blinden* [The Love of a Blind Woman, 1910]), Lil Dagover, Adele Sandrock, and Emil Jannings (*Vendetta*, 1916). As Messter explains in his book *Mein Weg mit dem Film*, his excursion into feature films had very pragmatic reasons: the expensive newsreels had to be financed from the profits made with features—with the creation of fictive worlds that appealed to contemporary tastes.[38] In 1912 Egon Friedell, the cultural critic, characterized the cinema as giving aesthetic expression to the spirit of the age: "To begin with, it is brief, fast, and put in code words, and it does not linger. There is something curt, precise, military about it. This fits our age which is an age of extracts."[39]

Soon after the beginning of World War I, feature films with a heroic content, such as *Auf dem Felde der Ehre* (On the Field of Honor, 1914) or *Wie Max das Eiserne Kreuz erwarb* (How Max Gained the Iron Cross, 1914), acted as boosters of patriotism along with some footage of documentary material. In the 2,446 cinemas that existed in 1914 as the only place of diversion, the folks back home were to be told what they owed to the soldiers at the front. As Adolf Hitler later put it in his book *Mein Kampf*: "What the German people owe to the army can be summarized in one word: Everything!"[40]

In *Auf dem Felde der Ehre* a father disowns his son who was given a dishonorable discharge as an officer. The son is rehabilitated by his touchy father—an arrogant man with the frame of mind of a heel-clicking subordinate—only after he has become a volunteer and conquered a flag from the enemy. At the beginning of the war, Heinrich Mann called this species the "master race of subjects."

On 24 July 1914, *Eiko-Woche*, Messter's strongest competitor, advertised its pictures of the Sarajevo murders under the heading of "sensational program": "Archduke Francis Ferdinand's Last Reception in Sarajevo as well as the Funeral Arrangements from Sarajevo to the Family Mausoleum." Harbingers of World War I; murder as a marketing device. Language dropped to the level of propaganda. In his conversations with refugees, Brecht reminded us that in the German language wars merely "break out" like a pest. "This," he added, "is because no one has started those wars, and no one has been able to prevent them."

The newsreels of *Messter-Woche* then created the "Documents on the War" which from 1 October 1914 until the end of the war put on the screens back home "extracts" of heroic events from all parts of the front. At this point at the latest, the boundaries between documentaries and newsreels began to disappear.

Censorship certificate No. 36,732 of 3 October 1914 provides a good impression of the propagandistic force contained in the very first *Messter-Woche*. Its bullying words are given here in full in order to document the mind-set of heroic German chauvinism long before Hitler.

Subheadings:
1. The City of Domnau (East Prussia), a Document of Russian Destructive Rage.
2. Market-Place in Domnau: Mayor May, Who Has Escaped from a Russian Camp, Heads the Procession of Returnees.
3. The Grave of Sgt. Abelt in Domnau. Abelt Was the Last Heroically to Defend the Town and Died for the Honor of the Fatherland.
4. A Church Destroyed by the Russians in Allenburg (East Prussia).
5. The Town of Darkehmen (East Prussia) as Ravaged by the Russians.
6. Looking after the Wounded under the Protectorate of Princess August Wilhelm. The Princess Attends a Film Showing for Invalids at the Palace Theater near Berlin's Zoological Gardens.
7. The Berlin Choir League Organizes a Patriotic Concert at Berlin's Königsplatz.
8. "A Call Roars by Like a Thunder Clap."
9. The Brave Crew of the German "U 9" Submarine That Sank Three British Battle Cruisers in the Morning of 22 September 1914 Is Being Decorated with the Iron Cross.
10. Captain Lieutenant Otto Weddingen, the Commander of the Submarine.
11. "Dear Fatherland, You May Rest Assured."
Length: 500 feet.

The newsreels of the militarist Messter were nothing more than propaganda that took its cue from Prussianism. Thanks to his connections with the Imperial Court, the Supreme Army Command finally commissioned Messter to censor all pictures from the front. Apart from his own productions, these were primarily the films of four other companies and their eight cameramen who had permission to make films at the front, among them Carl Froehlich of later fame.[41] Messter's cameramen were also used by the General Staff in aerial reconnaissance to provide target photos. It was much more difficult to provide such photos from the trenches either because the equipment was too heavy or because soldiers and cameramen had to guard against being spotted by the enemy. Thus, cameraman Martin Kopp complained in the Berlin journal *Der Kinematograph* of 12 May 1915 how difficult it was "to film scenes from the trenches because the construction of the trenches did not provide a good view. It was even more difficult to film actual combat scenes since the cameraman naturally is not given any information about a planned attack."

Although the drama is often missing, World War I comes across in the newsreel on the whole as something horrific; however, it does not appear as the catastrophe that it was. To be sure, the soothing books by Werner Beumelburg (*Ypres*) and Paul Ettighofer (*Verdun*) were even less capable or willing to capture this aspect. On the contrary, they glorified the war as a cleansing storm of steel. As Friedell put it: "The imagination of the most sober and block-headed viewer is still a hundred times more gripping and mysterious than all the printed books in the world."[42]

In his memorandum on film as a means of political propaganda, written prior to the war, Messter drew attention to foreign competitors to induce the Imperial authorities to take countermeasures. As he wrote, the program of the French companies *Pathé-Journal, Gaumont actualité*, and *Eclair révue* contained "much that was beautiful and grandiose. But all of this had happened in France and England and not at all in Germany. They are showing exhibitions, parades, athletic contests, christenings of ships, maneuvers, fashion shows, etc., as well as beautiful landscapes; but all of them lie beyond the Rhine River. And if these good films contain something about Germany at all, it is bound to be something degrading. There is a system in all this. And these French newsreels are being supported by foreign governments."

Messter-Woche continued to exist under its old name after World War I until 1922, even after Messter's production company had been taken over by Ufa. Only thereafter was it renamed as *Deulig-Woche*. The first sound-film newsreel was issued by Ufa on 10 September 1930 as *Ufa-Tonwoche No. 1*. No less a person than Emil Jannings was the speaker. The first American sound-film newsreel, called *Movietone News*, dated back to 25 April 1928.

How effectively the documentary can subtly manipulate images of reality that are photographically authentic is demonstrated by the intensive use of this genre in Nazi propaganda. There is no better example to show how the dialectic use of authentic material during the editing process can deprive individual elements of reality of their "veracity" and turn them upside-down, when subjected to an ideological superstructure.

As we know from the early 1920s montage experiments by Pudovkin and Kuleshov, the authenticity of individual elements of reality can be voided by this technique, i.e., by means of simple cuts. The Nazis later perfected this basic pattern of manipulative tricks: they falsified facts by shifting the context in a speculative direction, by twisting causal connections through a change of chronology, by bending the visual truth with the help of corrections in the text, and used (heroicizing) music to add "what the images were lacking in power" (Goebbels).

Nazi propaganda was generally not at all interested in objective arguments. Joseph Goebbels, the Reich Minister for Popular Enlightenment and Propaganda, wanted to see production only of such documents that exclusively portrayed those aspects of reality that harmonized with Nazi ideas and goals. As Goebbels said before the Reich Culture Chamber in 1933, only "what serves National Socialism is good and must be supported."[43] In his view, propaganda was the "most honest proclamation of the best truth."

This view of truth reflects Darwin's basic premise pushed to its logical conclusion, i.e., that the evolution of life runs purposefully towards a better state of affairs. Since this evolution is based on what Darwin called "natural selection"—and this is nothing else than the competition of the animal races among each other—the "better" is equivalent to the "stronger" that has survived in the competitive struggle. Darwin did, in fact, develop the vision that at some future date "the civilized races of humanity" would everywhere replace the more "primitive" ones.[44]

It would be wrong to assume that those parts of humanity who consider themselves "civilized" will soon have exterminated those parts they regard as "wild;" at the same time, we are not too far from the destruction of the cultures of the so-called Third World. And yet this development does not confirm Darwin's ideas; rather it highlights the perversity of equating quality with power.

The Influence of Open Propaganda

> But the most brilliant propagandist technique will yield no success unless one fundamental principle is borne in mind constantly and with unflagging attention. It must confine itself to a few points and repeat them over and over. Here, as so often in this world, persistence is the first and most important requirement for success.
>
> Adolf Hitler[45]

The Nazi Party determined what was to be of interest to the German people. Being its most powerful political weapons, documentaries and newsreels were charged with preparing Nazi ideology as clearly as possible, which meant to say that it had to be comprehensible even to the most obtuse among the *Volksgenossen*. It was not Hitler's aim to convince the minority of intellectuals, who in fact were to be neglected. His primary target were the broad masses; he wanted to conquer the soul of the ordinary people. This is why all propaganda "had to be popular and its intellectual level had to be geared to the receptivity of the most limited minds among those whom it is designed to address.... The more it exclusively takes into account the feelings of the masses, the more penetrating will be its success.... The art of propaganda lies precisely in the fact that, in having the proper appreciation of the emotional world of the masses, it attracts the attention of these masses in a psychologically appropriate form and then finds its way into their hearts." As far as the documentary is concerned, it is therefore no longer the artist who leaves his imprint on the epoch, but the politicians—and in wartime, the military.

Hitler concluded from this that "all effective propaganda must be confined to a very few points to be turned into slogans until even the slowest person perceives the slogan as something desirable."

What then were those "very few points" of Nazi ideology to which all other items in the party program were to be subordinate? Andreas Hillgruber has identified a striving for world domination and a racist doctrine as the core of this ideology.[46] All other elements of Nazism have a merely functional value. Their primary role is to realize the two main objectives. A third core component is the Führer principle that overarches the two key objectives. It includes a notion of how the state functions in all its branches, institutions, and laws.

Eberhard Jäckel assesses the specific elements of Nazi ideology in a similar way: "The state and all its aspects including the Party and its program are only means to an end: an end, however—and this is absolutely crucial—which is very clearly defined, namely the realization of the twin goals of territorial policy and anti-Semitism.... Germany had to conquer new living space in the East, and it had to remove the Jews—and all the other aspects of public life had to serve as means to those two ends."[47]

The ideological hopes and expectations of the German people that were to be generated through indoctrination formed the psychic foundation that Hitler urgently required to implement his two main objectives. He needed it, firstly, in order to conduct his wars of conquest over a longer timespan without inducing paralysis in the wake of a rising defeatism among the population. Secondly, there was the "Jewish Question" to be resolved by means of the so-called "Final Solution." It was not the *Leitartikel*—a series in Goebbels's weekly *Das Reich*—that Hitler regarded as the primary instrument of indoctrination. In his view, the audiovisual media were a more powerful means to gain popular support for his aims. Accordingly, he used the full weight of the Propaganda Ministry above all for the production of newsreels and documentaries, with Goebbels personally setting the ideological parameters. At a time when the population still regularly went to the movies to find diversion, the newsreel and the short documentary, prominently placed in every showing, became the Party's most reliable mouthpiece and its most important and punctually delivered means of mass communication.

Nazi newsreels and documentaries exclude two areas as a matter of principle. To begin with, there is the private sphere: no extolling of an idyllic family life here; nor are deprivations treated. Instead of showing people in their daily lives or after work, Nazi propaganda shows the private existence of men and women only when they are cheering. However, the reverse side of this coin does not appear on the screen either. Anti-Jewish pogroms, book burnings, deportations, forced labor, and concentration camps are not shown. Nor do sterilization and euthanasia come up as themes. Atrocities and deadly facts are quietly passed over.

The early documentaries of Soviet propaganda show the hero of labor in his individual existence and portray him as the representative of a system that will bring happiness. The Nazi film, by contrast, reduces the individual to the status of a purely numerical element within the larger *Volksgemeinschaft*.

It is therefore logical that documentaries and newsreels represent all persons in uniform as embodiments of Nazism. It is part of the dramaturgy of Nazi propaganda, which is presented with an effective understanding of psychology, that even Hitler, in his apparent omnipresence, is not portrayed as an individual with his own development, but—as Kracauer put it—only "as the embodiment of enormous impersonal powers—or to be more precise, as their focal point. Many respectful closeups [of Hitler] notwithstanding, these films that are supposed to glorify him cannot adapt his physiognomy to actual human life."[48]

In contradistinction to the feature film with its actors conjuring up a fictive world, the newsreel camera captures real people living within a real world and depicts them as real phenomena. From all we know about audiences, the filmed world will be received as an authentic document. Nazi propaganda knew how to exploit for its purposes this widespread illusion concerning the facticity of what was being presented as documents. The contemporary viewer and *Volksgenosse* took at face value what in fact was merely presented as an extract of reality. The dramaturgy of lies to be found in the Nazi newsreel is based on this insight. As Kracauer explains:

> The effectiveness of Nazi propaganda results from the viewer's delusion that the evidence presented is genuine: everyone is inclined to believe that pictures taken on location are incapable of telling a lie. But of course they can. Let us assume that a documentary that has been billed as nonpartisan does not contain any purposefully staged scenes [and] simply confines itself, as it should, to reproducing reality ... and yet it may highlight certain aspects of a given situation at the expense of others and thus influence attitudes toward that situation. The shots that are being shown are bound to be a selection from a range of pictures.[49]

Never having seen the unedited truth and hence not missing it either, the moviegoer may accept the pictures as perfectly truthful even though they have been put into the wrong context or are based on material that has been tampered with; the manipulation of reality is perceived by the viewer as being authenticated by the documents. The truthfulness of the documents may show a bias only if the commentary is tendentious because the full truth in those pictures could either damage the reputation of the Party or undermine Hitler's image.

However, Nazi propaganda pursued as its main objective the suppression of all negative images and indoctrinated the masses with optimistic pictures that were presented as "genuine." It also aimed to impress Nazi ideology upon the people by this most powerful means, until everyone had become convinced that he or she was the proud witness to a globally historic moment. This was the mandate of documentaries and newsreels. What they offered in the way of information was determined exclusively by their propagandistic value. The appeal to have faith in the Führer and confidence in his ideas and ideals was to be served up until this propaganda had been totally internalized. As Hitler put it: "The German people must be educated to accept one absolute, stubborn, self-evident, and firm belief [that] in the end we shall all achieve what is necessary. But this can only succeed if we constantly appeal to the power of the nation, if we extol the positive values of a people and ignore as far as possible the so-called negative sides."[50] This is why it was especially necessary that published opinion "subscribes totally, blindly to the principle: the leadership is acting correctly."

As early as 1933, Hans Traub, an interpreter of Nazi propaganda films, had defined "active propaganda as the conscious application of tendentious means for political purposes," as the "implementation [*Zielwerdung*] of a mind-set." He then enumerated the main characteristics of "exemplary propaganda": "(1) The possible subjective appeal to the 'world of emotions'; (2) the restriction of content; (3) confrontationism [*Kampfansage*] from the start; (4) repetition in 'permanent and regular uniformity' (Adolf Hitler)."[51] As to the fields in which the educational film could act in an "enlightening and propagandistic way," Traub recommended portraying "life in the camps of the Labor Front, views of Reichswehr maneuvers and exercises, pictures from the daily routine and Sundays in the navy, work in individual occupations, a day in the life of the Reich Chancellor.... We [also] need educational films about World War [I] battles...."

In order to popularize the Führer principle as something natural, it was deemed necessary for the individual to be submerged in the nation—with the Nazi film providing the early example. Once a sufficient number of people had seen and internalized explicit propaganda movies, the *Volksgenosse* was to become *de facto* a part of the whole nation also—a small (anonymous) cog in Hitler's movement. The vulgarity of the national whole is depicted with gusto, and not merely in Riefenstahl's films, as a quantitative ornament through marching columns or through packed blocks of humans (*Menschenquader*) who listen to the Party's rhetoric. On the occasion that an individual is shown, it is in the shape of a "worker intimately bound to a machine" or of "a soldier wedded to his arms," as Ulrich Kurowski wrote. Gustave Le Bon added: "The moment they become part of a mass, the uneducated and the scholars are equally incapable of being observers." There were to be no differences between a member of the Academy and a water carrier.

When asked which art genre was up to the challenges of this epoch, Eisenstein replied:

> The medium of cinematography alone! An intellectual cinematography alone. A synthesis of emotional, documentary, and absolute film. Only the intellectual cinema will be capable of putting a stop to the "disuniting of language"—more particularly on the basis of

the dialectical language of film. Only an intellectual cinema of a kind that has never before existed and whose social function is open; a cinema of highest intellectuality and extreme sensuousness that seizes hold of the entire arsenal of optical, acoustic, and bio-motoric stimuli in order to influence the viewer.[52]

The Russian Montage as a Technical Model

The montage is just as essential an element of film as all others. After the campaign for the montage and the storm against it the time has come to approach the problems of montage de novo and without prejudice.

S. M. Eisenstein

Goebbels regarded Sergei Eisenstein's *Battleship Potemkin* (1925) as the prototype of a powerful propaganda film and wished to produce a Nazi film that would have a similar impact. He was convinced that "if some theater here in Berlin would screen a film that would genuinely reflect this age and be a real National Socialist 'Battleship,' it would be sold out for a long time."[53] Addressing Goebbels as "Herr Doktor," Eisenstein replied in the Soviet journal *Literaturnaya gazeta* of 22 March 1934 that truth and Nazism were incompatible: "Whoever stands for truth will find himself on a different path from that of National Socialism. Whoever is for truth, will be against you!"[54] And under the heading "No Thoughts Wasted for What Is Inexorable," Brecht wrote about *Battleship Potemkin*: "I have seen how even the exploiters next to me were seized by emotions of approval when they viewed the actions of the revolutionary sailors. In this way, even the scum participated in the irresistible seductiveness of the possible and the powerful joys of logic."[55]

However, Goebbels also took something usable from the montage theories of the Russians and drew opposite conclusions from their insights. According to Lenin, film is the most important of all the art forms; in Stalin's view it was therefore supposed to play an important role in the cultural revolution not only "as a means of comprehensive educational work and Communist propaganda," but also as "a means of educating the masses in the arts, [and] of offering them purposeful relaxation and diversion."[56]

As Mayakovski succinctly defined the function of Soviet film in 1922: "The cinema serves the proliferation of ideas." After 1933, this was also the maxim that Goebbels tried to realize. In the meantime, he had changed his mind with regard to boring "Socialist Realism" and hoped to popularize his Nazi ideas with the help of an aesthetic that Riefenstahl was in the process of developing. In both systems the camera is sent out on patrol to size up the existing order. Maxim Gorki, it is true, had first coined the term "Socialist Realism" in 1921 and charged it with the task of "consolidating for the present what has been achieved by the October Revolution and of illuminating accordingly the aims of the socialist future." However, it was only at the 1934 Moscow Writers' Congress that the term was turned into binding doctrine by Andrei Zhdanov who simultaneously condemned the aesthetics of formalism. According to Vsevolod Pudovkin, formalism was "a comprehensive term that includes everything that distracts the artist from the actual life of the people and its needs."[57]

The patriotic Ukrainian filmmaker Alexander Dovshenko, whose film *Earth* came out in 1930, made the shift toward partisanship in good time without sacrificing the lyric base and powerful sensuality of his films to Socialist Realism. His 1935 movie *Aerograd*, he reveled, was borne by the idea "that life is beautiful, that this part of our country is beautiful, and that foreign flags will never fly over here."[58]

However, the documentaries and newsreels that had so impressed Goebbels, like Vertov's *The Camera Eye* or *The Man with the Camera*, were products of the 1926–1929 period and thus originated in the period *prior* to a dogmatized Socialist Realism. During his tour of Europe in 1931, Vertov had shown these films to large audiences. At the same time, he revealed his insights into the construction of film like a *homo faber*: "I create thousands of people according to different schemes and plans. I am the camera eye. It is from one person that I take his hands—the strongest and most agile; I take the legs from another one—the prettiest and most well-proportioned. From a third person I take the head—the most beautiful and impressive." The same manifesto by Vertov also contains the quintessential *contradictio* to his montage of "superman": "The camera eye represents camera truth"—a statement that did no more than to articulate a fundamental truth about the nature of film. After all, the camera eye is the camera, and nothing else can be shown in film other than what the camera "sees." That the moviegoers take what is put before them as reality to a greater degree than in other media stems from the fact that they are forced to adopt the camera's view as the only one from which the world that is being depicted can be seen. However, with this, nothing has as yet been said about the use of formal means and possibilities that are inherent in film. After all, Vertov does not assert that the "camera eye" represents *the* truth; he only speaks about the *camera* truth. However, unlike "genuine" truth, the latter is absolute. Whereas in reality things and events may be viewed from different angles, film consists merely of the multitude of its pictures. And these have been taken by the camera and cannot be perceived from any other perspective.

Although his formalism was often extreme and included experimental visualization, Vertov pursued the aim of making political ideas transparent from their substance. For him, this also comprised the notion that the viewer must join in reflecting about the conditions under which political events are perceived. This is what he called the perception conditions of film. Eisenstein called these experiments "formal antics" and "senseless vagabonding with the camera." Even where Vertov aimed to win over illiterate viewers—the land laborer from Azerbeidjan, or the shepherd boy from the steppes—for socialist reforms, critics like Victor Shklovkij reproached him that the facticity of individual scenes had disappeared due to the predominance of scenes that were invented or staged. Thus, even the succinct metaphor which had gained Vertov and his audacious montages so much admiration has remained controversial: the young pioneers who hoist the red flag in a village camp are not thought to represent what Vertov calls "spontaneously" filmed life. Rather, such scenes are said to exhaust themselves in providing a calculated, purely aesthetic composition that aims at achieving a visual effect. As a result, the authenticity of the moment that he had had in mind is robbed of its impact. In an objective sense, this scene is nonetheless politically true in that it certainly happened in a very similar manner. Joris Ivens is similarly known for setting up scenes in his documentaries, as long as he thought it served the document. Accused of formalism, Vertov hardly received any commissions back home during the Stalin era, while his ideas remained virulent in Western Europe.

Among the Germans, it was above all Walter Ruttmann who was inspired by Vertov's syntax, according to which the filmmaker was urged to think in visual rather than literary or verbal categories. However, Ruttmann used montage techniques to develop formal progressions rather than ones concerned with content. The wealth of forms he deployed culminated in a brilliant fireworks whose dynamics, produced as they were through montage, drove the various parts and cadences into a chain reaction. It was this that gave *Berlin—Symphonie einer Großstadt* its artistic quality and turned it into a sensation. There is a parallel piece of 1930, entitled *Apropos de Nice*, which Jean Vigo montaged with Vertov's brother Boris (Kaufmann) and which ignored all sense of reality by relying on a self-propelling movement that is developed in masterly fashion. And yet the two films do not merely represent an explosive *l'art pour l'art*. By combining concrete images, they succeed in distilling and thus making transparent the phenomenon of the city as a space in which humans live closely and precariously together. Alberto Calvacanti's *Rien que les heures* (1926), which traces the course of a day in Paris in kaleidoscopic fashion, also falls into the series of city portraits cast in a poetic and reflective mood. Regarding much of this as artificial, René Clair called these films "visual exercises."

Ruttmann, whose work with Riefenstahl on *Triumph des Willens* ended prematurely, did offer the Third Reich his cooperation, but not his talent. His propaganda films *Metall des Himmels* (Metal of the Sky, 1934), *Altgermanische Bauernkultur* (Ancient Germanic Peasant Culture, 1939) or *Deutsche Panzer* (German Panzers, 1941) represented a tame, technically perfect afterglow of his earlier work; he escaped into formalism without even attempting to reach a critical level. Nor, in his very last wartime booster, did he succeed in cutting the "Gordian knot" that Ernst Jünger had tied in his 1925 book *Feuer und Blut* (Fire and Blood): "… we must transmit what is within us to machines; this requires distance and an ice-cold brain that transforms the convulsive flashes of the blood into rational and logical energies …" Finally, Ruttmann was not killed at the Eastern front in 1941 while shooting his film *Sieg im Osten* (Victory in the East); he died in a Berlin hospital in 1942.

Enter Leni Riefenstahl

> *Aestheticism that politicizes itself will always be radical, precisely because of bellezza. It is quite common to confuse radicalism with depth. Nothing is more incorrect. Radicalism is beautiful shallowness—a liberal cult of gestures that leads directly into choreography …*
>
> Thomas Mann[59]

Leni Riefenstahl was of a different caliber. By systematically excluding rational elements in the films she made for the Third Reich, she succeeded in finding the balance between propaganda and its aestheticism and in combining both in a perfect symbiosis. Indeed, without the help of a theoretical program and completely intuitively, she founded the fascist film aesthetic in her first movie, about the 1933 Nazi Party rally, entitled *Sieg des Glaubens* (Victory of Faith). She then so perfected it in her *Triumph des Willens* (Triumph of the Will) a year later that she set with this film binding standards that remained unsurpassed up to the end of the Third Reich.

Paul Rotha observed for the documentary in general what the Nazi film later pursued to excess: it had, he said, always been one of the grave weaknesses of the documentary that it excluded the individual.[60] Eisenstein also knew from experience that "the mass acts mechanically; it amounts to no more than a numerical factor." Henceforth, the community of faith, the mass became degraded to the position of a movable cadre pure and simple, that, as it moves along, is guided and directed artistically by Riefenstahl in accordance with the creative criteria that she has developed. With the help of *tableaux vivants* that have been pressed into firm blocks of humans and banner-carrying columns and which she utilizes aesthetically as geometric patterns, she creates emotional spaces that include the viewer in the cinema. For a director who is obsessed with rhythm, the formalized masses that have been molded into compact units of movement are supposed to symbolize the physiological marching in step that evolves, aesthetically transfigured, into the harmony between Führer and people. Riefenstahl's accelerated dynamic rhythm, which drives the images forward, does not give the viewers any caesuras that allow them to grasp new developments and situations; does not give them time for cogitation or room for catching their breath; in short, does not leave them any "half seconds" as formulated by cognitive psychology. Moviegoers are to be overwhelmed by the breathtaking events that Nazism generates around them; they are to be captured by its fast tempo.

It may sound paradoxical, but in the rapture of geometry Riefenstahl celebrates the contrast with abstract art. Thus, as Walter Benjamin had predicted, the aestheticism of politics triumphs in *Sieg des Glaubens* (1933) and *Triumph des Willens* (1934): aesthetics becomes a manual of downfall, becomes the imminent unleashing of a global conflagration. Riefenstahl always rejected the reproach that she had allowed herself to be abused as the handmaiden of ideology. She is right. After all, she was the standard-bearer of the

Führer in fascist film that, according to Susan Sontag "glorified sub-ordination, celebrated blind obedience, and heroicized death."[61]

In Riefenstahl Hitler had found a congenial choreographer of his "Movement." Just like herself, he, too, was the "director who aesthetically directed the masses as in a choir." Within the *Gesamt-kunstwerk*, within this "most grandiose Wagnerian opera of all times," the German *Volksgenossen* represented the "actors and the extras" at the same time.[62]

However, her films are not intended to celebrate themselves in the inimitable aesthetic structure. They do not represent *l'art pour l'art*, but have been turned into functional carriers of propaganda. They want to exert emotional influence and, with their visual and verbal messages, have taken sides in a great cause. Siegfried Kra-cauer is mistaken in this respect if he insists that such "patterns" represented nothing that was precise and hence reinforced "the impression of a vacuum." Even if it is true that the images are supposed to confuse the viewer "in order to subject him more eas-ily to certain suggestions," we must nonetheless contradict Kra-cauer's conclusion that "many images are in effect nothing but an empty break between two propagandistic insinuations."[63] Kra-cauer's absolutist notion of reality assesses film exclusively from this one-sided perspective that denies the aesthetic variety of film and accepts only what "gives the impression of reality which leads the viewer to believe to see events that happened in real life and that were photographed on location."[64]

Martin Loiperdinger has examined what he called Kracauer's "emphatic notion of reality" and demonstrated that the latter "val-idates it only for democratic realities."[65] Loiperdinger rightly sur-mises that Kracauer's theorems—starting with his assumption that fascist propaganda lacks an "informative character" to the idea of a "metamorphosis of reality"—are rooted in his desire to deny German fascism any political legitimacy by "declaring it a 'pseudo-reality' and as such obsolete."[66]

Hitler's Party rallies were not "pseudo-realities," but experi-ences of a bitter reality. They were not a "travesty." The legend that Kracauer has spread that Riefenstahl organized the 1934 Nurem-berg rally only to serve "as the backdrop for a film" that was then to assume "the character of an authentic document,"[67] is a fatuity that many historians of film have perpetuated. What Riefenstahl's art did was to encapsulate an extra-aesthetic reality with aesthetic means in such a way that the people who lived in this reality rec-ognized themselves in it—as parts of a crowd. Reality was thus not utilized aesthetically in order to pretend what it was. After all, Riefenstahl was herself piously fixated on this actually existing National Socialist reality.

Excursus: Reich Party Rallies and Their Transfiguration

In the actual act of deception, among all the preparations, the horror in the voice, expression, gestures, amid the striking scenery, the belief in themselves overcomes them. It is this that speaks so miraculously and convincingly to the onlookers.

Friedrich Nietzsche[68]

Why did Hitler attach so much importance to the films about the Nuremberg Party rallies? What did these rallies mean for the Nazi movement? They served a dual purpose: to maintain inner party discipline and to portray the movement to the outside world. The decisions of the leadership that were ratified by acclamation at these rallies were to be transmitted to the smallest local organizations by hundreds of thousands who had been there. The fighting spirit was to be charged up with ideological power and gain a fresh moral impetus—until the next mass rally came along.

Pierre Bourdieu has hinted that under Nazism such forces were at work even in the body language and the expressions of the masses that did not merely serve the movement: "All social orders systematically exploit the fact that the human body and language can serve as storehouses for ready-made ideas."[69]

This, he added, may be instrumentalized, explaining the care with which mass festivities are prepared and why the attempt is made to put order into ideas and to suggest emotions, such as laughter and sadness, through the regular patterns of human bodies. Varying an observation by Proust, he concluded that "arms and bodies are full of hidden imperatives."[70] Pudovkin was one of the first to define film as one of the means of making an impact upon "body and soul." He called film the best teacher, "because its lessons do not merely appeal to the mind, but to the entire body"—or to be more precise: the propaganda movie is the best instructor in this sense.

The first Party Day took place in 1920, at that point still organized by the precursor of the Brown Shirts, the National Socialist German Workers' Association. Subsequent rallies were held during the *Kampfzeit* years at Munich in 1923, at Weimar in 1926, and at Nuremberg in 1929. In 1926 Hitler was able to have both the general parade as well as the consecration of the flags in Weimar, a city full of symbols where the National Assembly had met in the National Theater in 1919. As Albrecht Tyrell put it, "the theater was dominated by the Party flag." With some three hundred of these flags on the stage behind him, Hitler repeatedly spoke of their symbolism, but in subtle nuances: "Red—the symbol of a social attitude; white—our nationalism of action, not of empty phrases; black—the spirit of labor, that will always remain opposed to the Jews and protective of the [German] race." The 1930 rally was canceled, and after the seizure of power all of them were held in Nuremberg, the last one in 1938.

In the Party's historiography, the chronology of the Party Days tends to start with the "great [1923] rally of infinite power and confidence" (Hitler) in Munich. This is when the basic pattern became established. Thus, the ritual of flag consecration, which was designed to mobilize members' emotions for a variety of messages, was inaugurated in 1923, though later modified. All members were supposed to give life and limb for the swastika flag and for all that it had come to symbolize. As the vow went: "I swear to you, our Führer Adolf Hitler, to stay with my flag until the last drop of blood."

The rallies did not represent a decision-making body for programmatic concerns. From the start Hitler had prevented their "parliamentarization." After all, his speeches were not be put in doubt by ballots, however farcical they would have been. The task was to instill the Hitler myth deeply into the hearts of the faithful. It was more important to organize a festive, indeed a sacral, atmosphere than to have discussions. As rituals that had been interspersed in the rally, the fireworks and the invocations surrounding the flag had a self-fulfilling magic and served as diversions. "Two lines of tradition from the font of nineteenth-century national festivities and the end of the Wilhelmine Empire came together" at Hitler's Party Days.[71] They included the popular traditions of public festivals, as they were held by bourgeois associations, singing clubs, rifle associations, athletic organizations, the Youth Movement, and working-class organizations.

Consecrations of the flag, memorial services, nighttime torchlight processions, delegates of the military, militias, standard-bearing march-pasts, as well as military music and songs from the Youth Movement were common elements of such events and were part of a festive ritual. The Nazi Party salvaged many of these old-fashioned traditions for its all too obvious purposes and updated them for ideological use. Thus, the *Niederländische Dankgebet* (Netherlandian Thanksgiving Prayer) was secularized with the aim of emotionalizing Hitler's Party Days. Even liturgical elements of Christianity were recast into Nazi symbols. Similarly, the wilted charm of the "blue flower" of Romanticism reappeared in a new guise at Hitler's campfires.

The public impact of Hitler's collective, immense spectacles was relatively small prior to the Nazi takeover. Even documentaries on the subject did not strike much of a chord. To begin with and owing to a lack of funds, they were technically imperfect and fell short on aesthetics. Until 1930, sound was missing. Cinemas were not interested, since the public refused to see party-political films as an aesthetic experience. Nor were there reputable directors who would have been prepared or able to give a movie about a mass rally a specific aesthetic flavor or dramatic structure. As Benjamin had argued, fascist propaganda was less about the politicization of art than about the aestheticization of politics. This is why it was left to Riefenstahl's genius to do the impossible and to popularize the negative aesthetic of the state by means of a positive film aesthetic. As a result of her suggestive aestheticism of fascism, she supported the "rape of the masses," whom fascism "forces to the ground in its Führer cult." Riefenstahl thus did violence to her filmic "equipment" which she put in the service of cult values.[72] She succeeded in transforming the rituals of the rally with its boring speeches and uniform parades into a hedonistic feast, into an easily sellable art product. Hitler found through Riefenstahl true aesthetic energy, and she was firmly resolved to realize, at the height of Hitler's own ambitions, her goal of constituting a fascist aesthetic. There was no room here for societal sublimations and social improvisation.

In her *Memoirs*, she—in a way that is very revealing of her identity—used "My" when talking to Hitler about the production of *Triumph des Willens* that he had been pushing for: "My Führer," she reports to have said, "I fear I cannot make this film.... The whole subject matter is strange to me; I cannot even keep the SA and the SS apart."[73] How could the "subject matter" be strange to her after she had produced *Sieg des Glaubens*, the one-hour movie about the 1933 Party rally a year earlier? She must have known the "subject matter" extremely well, as all the laudatory reviews in the press confirmed. In this first film she had also proven quite capable of sorting out those nine thousand standard-bearers from the

SA and SS. After all, she celebrated Röhm's SA and Himmler's SS in separate sequences. And with the help of a number of extravagant cuts, she highlighted the role of Hitler's bodyguard unit (*Leibstandarte*) which goose-stepped past the Führer with steel helmets and in black uniforms. It was precisely through the geometric shape of the marching columns and the blocks of flag-bearers that Riefenstahl was able to capture with breathtaking images the principle by which the obedience that was reflected in the goose-stepping columns became integrated into the larger whole. As Walter Hagemann put it: "The goose-step proved to be one of the most effective tools of mass suggestion; it forced thousands into following the same movements and rhythms."[74] With her two Party rally films, Riefenstahl reinvented the "Nuremberg funnel," first developed in the seventeenth century, with which even the dumbest were instilled with Hitler's ideas.

Riefenstahl's third major movie was to augment Hitler's prestige in the outside world, and the 1936 Olympic Games in Berlin provided a welcome opportunity. A year after the Nuremberg racial laws had been promulgated, the task was to improve Hitler's battered image. The film, *Olympia*, which was completed two years after the Games, consists of two parts, "Fest der Völker" ("Festival of the Nations") and "Fest der Schönheit" ("Festival of Beauty"). As in the two Party rally movies, Riefenstahl's *theoretical* notion of beauty remains undefined in this 225-minute work.

The Third Reich produced innumerable documentaries that cinemas were obliged to show in conjunction with the main feature film. They can be roughly classified as attempts to promote the following themes: the Führer myth; Germandom; custom; blood and soil; Thanksgiving; the German forest; national health; sports; art, culture, and "Strength Through Joy" (the Labor Front's recreational movement); Reich Party Days; successes of the Party; the various Nazi organizations; Hitler Youth; the Nazi Girls' Movement; premilitary training; rearmament; the German soldier in peace, maneuver, and war; a nation without space; world enemies; enemies of the people; anti-Semitism; hereditary diseases; euthanasia; belated victories over the Versailles system; Hitler's campaigns; cult of the Nazi dead.

As eager stooges of Nazism, next to Riefenstahl the following directors lent their corruptible talents to the production of documentaries: Hans Bertram (*Feuertaufe*—Fire Baptism, 1940); Eduard von Borsody (*Früh übt sich*—Early Start, 1936); Hans Cürlis (*Arbeitsdienst*—Labor Service, 1933; *Arno Breker*, 1944); Arnold

Fanck (*Josef Thorak*, 1943; *Atlantikwall*, 1944); Wolf Hart (*Rüstungsarbeiter*—Armaments Workers, 1943); Carl Junghans (*Jugend der Welt*—Youth of the World, 1936; *Jahre der Entscheidung*—Years of Decision, 1939); Svend Noldan (*Deutsche Arbeitsstätten*—German Workplaces, 1940; *Sieg im Westen*—Victory in the West, 1941); Curt Oertel (*Die steinernen Wunder von Naumburg*—The Naumburg Wonders in Stone, 1933; *Grabmal des unbekannten Soldaten*—Tomb of the Unknown Soldier, 1935); Hans Steinhoff (*Gestern und heute*—Yesterday and Today, 1938); Karl Ritter (*Im Kampf gegen den Weltfeind*—Fighting the World Enemy, 1939); Walter Ruttmann (*Altgermanische Bauernkultur*—Ancient German Peasant Culture, 1939; *Deutsche Panzer*—German Panzers, 1941); Alfred Weidemann (*Soldaten von morgen*—Soldiers of Tomorrow, 1941; *Hände hoch*—Hands Up, 1942); Eugen York (*Danzig*, 1939). Gustav Ucicky had to give his name to *Wort und Tat* (Word and Deed, 1938) without having been involved in the making of this film.

Piel Jutzi threw overboard the humanist aesthetic of the proletarian movie to act as cameraman in Jürgen von Alten's tired military film *Gewehr über* (Shoulder Arms, 1939). G. W. Pabst returned from his American exile to produce without pressure tendentious Nazi stuff like *Paracelsus* (1943). Karl Ritter, who had produced *Hitlerjunge Quex* (Hitler Youth Quex) in 1933, gained the reputation of being the most consistent among the compliant protagonists of the sophisticated documentary. Among his productions were such infamous and inflammatory movies as *Verräter* (Traitor, 1936) and *GPU* (on Stalin's secret police, 1942), as well as heroic pieces extolling war like *Unternehmen Michael* (Operation Michael, 1937); *Stukas* (Dive Bombers, 1941), and *Besatzung Dora* (The Dora Force, 1943).

In his feature film *Kampfgeschwader Lützow* (The Lützow Fighting Squadron, 1941), Hans Bertram continues from his 1940 documentary *Feuertaufe* (Baptism of Fire) and thus with his lofty cockpit heroes, one of whom succeeds in salvaging a precious bomber on the runway before—his face marked by death—he gives up his immortal soul. After all, "even a dying man demonstrates what spirit is alive and well in the Air Force." During the war the fascist film instrumentalized death. When Bertram produced his *Kampfgeschwader Lützow* in 1941, Reich Film Director Hippler held up the heroic deaths to be seen in German film as something to be imitated. He referred to Lessing's dictum that death expressed the "condition of calm and insensibility," in other words, a condition that was more comforting than particularly

disturbing. Hippler then defined death in his own words as a
state of weightlessness, if there really was a sense to it:

> Poetry and visual arts that can only depict the process of dying
> rather than the condition of death will put it into a larger philo-
> sophical context that will elevate it from the senseless and depress-
> ing sphere of nature into the world of values and ideals; this means
> that the process of dying itself becomes irrelevant at this point (that
> is merely a matter of medical record). What alone is essential is that
> it is embedded in the larger picture that precedes or follows it, from
> which it becomes necessary or in reference to which it bears fruit.[75]

The constant presence of death is also reflected in relentless
fade-ins of sacred elements like church bells, war memorials, pictures of martyrs, and specific Nazi symbols like photos of the
Führer. They represent the ubiquitous icons just as swastika flags
become the visual incense. The background music of spheric har-
monies or pseudo-religious choral songs provide for suitable ele-
vation. Carrying Hölderlin in his backpack, the poet pays homage
to the death-defying soldier, offering romantic verses during an
unromantic time.

The poet transforms the genuine fear of death into something
metaphysical. What Hitler needed for his German freedom struggle were films that educated people for war (*Kriegserziehungsfilme*).
They are designed to explain war as a means of developing the
highest manly virtues; for "war is the father of all things," as
Nicholas Kaufmann, Ufa's *Kulturfilm* expert put it in his article on
"Ufa's Cultural Film Production."[76] He added: "*Kriegserziehungs-
film* and *Kulturfilm* exist under the totality claim of the German
freedom struggle ... These films are faced with great tasks as we
try to explain, in simple words, the many measures that have been
taken for the protection of our national life and, above all, for the
exemplary and circumspect care of our armed forces. It is precisely themes of a state-political or party-political character that
have seized hold of the cultural film during recent years."[77] It is
not just spectacles like *Feuertaufe* or *Sieg im Westen* that offer typical examples of this kind of movie; there are also shorts like *Unter
der Kriegsflagge* (Under the War Flag, 1934), *Unsere Infantrie* (Our
Infantry, 1940), *Balkanfeldzug* (Balkan Campaign, 1941), *Die Funker
mit dem Edelweiss* (The Wireless Operators with the Edelweiss
Flower, 1942), *Junker der Waffen-SS* (The Lords of the Armed SS,
1943), *Front am Himmel* (Front Line in the Skies, 1944), *Endkampf
um Berlin* (Final Battle for Berlin, 1945).

No less important for any verdict on the Nazi regime are also, of course, all films that were refused production permission, even though the above-named directors would no doubt have made them in masterly fashion. However, just as there were no secession movements in Nazi art, it was equally impossible to produce movies against the regime. As Eisenstein put it in 1934 in his open letter to Goebbels, "this required courage and bravery." He continued: "The honey-sweet phrases in your speeches notwithstanding, you have put your arts and culture into the same iron chains in which you also hold the remaining thousands of incarcerated people in your hundreds of concentration camps."[78]

Leni Riefenstahl's Film Olympia

Politically, I did not know what was important. I only asked where the best material could be found, where intensifications might be possible. I concentrated on blending images and movements.

Leni Riefenstahl

Leni Riefenstahl's theoretical notion of beauty remained diffuse, whereas the ideal of beauty that she shows in her pictures can be deduced quite easily from her movies. However, we must differentiate between the median of what came to be portrayed as the ideal of the new man and man as the sum total of an idea that Riefenstahl set up in formations of columns and their preferably geometric movements. Riefenstahl's standards for her stagings of the beautiful and sublime take classicism as their original model, when symmetry, natural proportions, and harmony still constituted the canons of beauty. And what she selects from these models is then dressed up with elements of power and dynamic excitement to give the appearance of beauty. Her repertoire is the beauty of the masses, and these masses are not static but set in motion in ornamental fashion. Insofar as they wear brown shirts and carry swastika flags, she divests them of whatever may look threatening about them. She has even sensually captured the geometry of the anonymous marching columns and blocks of men and has rendered viewing them into an aesthetic experience.

As far as the beauty of nature is concerned, Riefenstahl takes her prejudgments from the platonic notion which postulated that the ideally beautiful be understood as the primordial image of everything that was beautiful in this world. If beauty was conceived by the Greeks as a complex being, as incarnation of the mythologically divine, Riefenstahl's camera forged from it her selection criteria for a kind of beauty that could be harmonized with the ideals of the Nazi movement.

The ancient Greek ideal of beauty, as reflected in the Venus de Milo or the Discus-Thrower of Myron, had been the foundation of the idealistic aesthetic since the Renaissance. Kant's definition of what was beautiful in the arts had had profound repercussions for German cultural consciousness. The beautiful was seen as the sensual manifestation of an idea.

Riefenstahl, with a sure instinct for what is effective in the arts, added a sizable dose of sympathy with nature in order to guarantee the emotionalization of the viewer. This viewer was thus to find it easier to identify with those ideas as they transported exemplars of beautiful, i.e., racially pure, men from the screen to the audience. In her movie *Olympia* Riefenstahl lets the camera revel in beauty. The lens is virtually glued to the beauty of athletic torsos and limbs with their muscle formations. She favors sequences that show an aesthetically beautiful movement, be it in long-jump, sprint, or discus-throwing. Even as it was tripping and falling over, the body was to display its beauty. To the natural elegance of a dart-like dive from the diving board her fanatical quest for beauty would add a subtle photographic point. The actual physical strain is suppressed when she shoots those sharply contoured portraits of extreme concentration in the starting hole, during target practice, or shot-putting and smoothes over the tense body lines. Indeed, many a champion on the field or the track becomes a plagiarism of nature, a simple copy of life before a camera that is concerned only with capturing radical beauty. By turning beauty into something absolute, she aestheticizes processes and thus robs them of their reality. The gospel of beauty that Riefenstahl reels off optically can award first prize to the perfectly shaped, steely body of the young man because the less attractive, old, and frail person is not permitted to compete in the stadium nor in the movie.

By excluding all phenomena that in her subjective perspective appear as ugly, and by thus also excluding the large majority of all men, she perpetrates a fraud on the image of reality. The lie is taken out of the set. The unwelcome reality remains *extra muros*; the green oval of the stadium is reserved for youth. Beauty exclusive. Those many millions outside Germany who saw this exalted picture with its optimistic emotions were treated to an idealized, sympathetic, and peaceful Germany with a relaxed and smiling

Führer—a true masterpiece of misrepresentation. This, after all, was the time of the Nuremberg racial laws; the first concentration camps at Dachau and Sachsenhausen had brutalized opponents of the regime since 1933; the preparation for war was started on the days after the opening of the Olympic Games in Berlin when Hitler decreed the dispatch of the Condor Legion to Spain to support Franco in his revolt against the Republic. In a secret memorandum, composed during the Games, Hitler ordered that for the next four years German industry was to be geared toward war and the armed forces to be prepared for an offensive in the East. By capturing the peaceful competition among the participant nations, Riefenstahl's *Olympia* movie thus stages a grandiose fraud: *Der Stürmer*, Streicher's anti-Semitic rag, had been taken off the newspaper stands during the Games and all signs demanding "Jews out" had been removed.

There remained one difficulty in which Riefenstahl had to outwit her opponent Goebbels. This was the delicate task of producing a rough approximation between the official ideal of beauty in Nazi art and her own optical products that frequently ran counter to the proclaimed Nordic image when she filmed athletes at the finishing line or on the winners' platform. At these points during the "Fest der Völker," as the first part of her movie was called, it was difficult to uphold Nazi racist views. Riefenstahl could not and did not want to omit the obvious fact that the nations of Africa, Asia, and other "non-Aryan" parts of the world had sent men and women to the Games who were, by the standards of classical antiquity, in an exemplary sense *beautiful* people. She therefore simply incorporated into her film whatever was usable in terms of her physical ideal. As far as propaganda was concerned, *Olympia* plainly was to be a "hymn to the power and beauty of man, a making visible of the healthy mind in a healthy body, illustrated by *exquisite* [!] youths from all over the world."[79]

Master Works by Outsiders to the Nazi Film Industry

Willy Zielke, the cameraman who shot the prologue to *Olympia*, remained an outsider as a director. Apart from the short film *Arbeitslos* (Unemployed, 1932) dealing with the fate of the jobless, he produced one other film that made him known only after the war. Fascinated by the machine, Zielke transformed his script for a commissioned exultation of the Reich railroad into a fortuitous synthesis of documentary and feature film whose segments are amalgamated by experimental transitions. The 45-minute movie appeared in 1935 under the title *Das Stahltier* (The Beast of Steel). Its theme is provided by an idealistic engineer who tells his colleagues during their coffee breaks amusing or dramatic episodes from the history of the railroads during the past one hundred years. Zielke translated these episodes into formally brilliant images, some of which remind the viewer of famous inventors, like James Watt, Francis Cugnot, or Stevenson. The film represents a dynamically edited celebration of the machine, which is used as a metaphor for the idea of progress and a glorification of technology. And yet the attempt to make its usefulness for the development of mankind visible remains underexposed, despite some partly expressionist fireworks. The dominance of formalistic elements was probably also one of the reasons why the movie was banned in the Third Reich.

Curt Oertel is the name of the other highly gifted outsider of the documentary who was not prepared to pander to Nazi aesthetics for the sake of achieving early fame. In 1932 his camera work had helped to make *Die steinernen Wunder von Naumburg* a success. This came after Oertel had given his visual talents as ingenious lighting director to Pabst for the latter's 1925 movie *Die freudlose Gasse* (The Joyless Street) and to *Geheimnis der Seele* (Secret of the Soul) a year later. Oertel quickly gained an international reputation. In 1940 Tobis and the Swiss Pandora launched a monumental coproduction under the title *Michelangelo*. In it, Oertel ingeniously united the life and work of the "Titan" (1475–1564) in a historical portrait, using the latter's sculptures (tombs of the Medici) and buildings (St. Peter's in Rome) as well as his paintings and drawings. Through a dramaturgy of light and shadows that gave life to figures, objects, and landscapes, he created a masterpiece that was received with reserve in the Third Reich because of its eccentric formal qualities. Accordingly, the press was directed to play this movie down. It was only in 1950 that the film achieved international acclaim under the title *The Titan: The Story of Michelangelo*, when Hollywood awarded it an Oscar.

Zielke's and Oertel's movies were diametrically opposed to the propaganda-soaked documentaries that were elevated to Nazi art not only with the help of Hitler's swastika flags, but also because they happily sported the flag in their titles, such as *Unter der schwarzen Sturmfahne* (Under the Black Storm Flag, 1935), *Unsere Fahne ist die Treue* (Loyalty Is Our Flag, 1935), *Unter der Fahne der Jugend* (Under the Flag of Youth, 1935), *Fäuste an dem Fahnenschaft*

(Fists around the Flag Pole, 1935), *Wir tragen die Fahne gen Süden* (We Are Carrying the Flag Southward, 1939).

The Compilation Film

The microcosm of the montage had to appear as a unified picture that falls apart under the inner pressure of its contradiction so as to reconstitute itself at a new level into a new unit that was qualitatively more advanced.

Sergei Eisenstein[80]

The compilation film, with its artificial structure and its violations of aesthetic rules, ignores traditional genre boundaries. The dramaturgy of this parasitic genre combines materials that have already been used in other movies that are then put into a thematic and stylistic context different from the original one. The disparate parts and heterogenous ingredients are removed from their original aesthetic context and reality to achieve a specific didactic purpose; they may even appear as diametrically opposed to their original context due to a montage that changes their entire orientation. They represent particles in a reconstructed film reality that appear to be realistic; they develop their impact only in their complementary role or in a correspondingly aesthetic combination.

The reality content of these films was changed simply by eliminating the original context. The old "truths" percolated through the sieve of the new ideology. The blending of many rudimentary realities produced a new, quite different filmic reality, and, as far as the Nazis were concerned, this new reality was geared, above all, to its ideological impact. The eclectic layout of the compilation movie is not only structured by its thematic presuppositions, but in particular also by the genres that have been chosen. As Svend Noldan's two-part *Der Weltkrieg* (The World War, 1927/28) and the anonymously produced *Deutschland—mein Deutschland* (Germany—My Germany, 1932/33) demonstrate, these may consist of combinations of silent feature films, silent newsreels (taken from the Reich Military Archives and to some extent also from Hugo von Kaweczynski), animated film elements, as well as sequences, reflecting the appropriate contemporary climate, that were especially shot for the occasion. Compilation films are strung together synoptically, but rarely with the aim of staking out an aesthetic claim or of creating a tangibly modified new form. In his retrospective on World War I, Noldan invented the general staff map, which was enhanced by technical tricks, and used it to provide moving visual images of the war's logistics. His new techniques made it possible for four years of war to become visually more graspable.

Such arch-reactionary compilation films as Johannes Häußler's *Der eiserne Hindenburg in Krieg und Frieden* (The Iron Hindenburg in War and Peace, 1929) and *Blutendes Deutschland* (Bleeding Germany, 1933) provide examples of how unable the directors were to master the wealth of material (by mostly unknown cameramen), not to mention their inability to put some structure into them. Without the critical historical eye, a chain of visual events turned into a purely material conglomerate. Made from an inflexible, right-wing, patriotic perspective, these films pay sentimental tribute to the relics of the past. The emperor's long beard, so to speak, protrudes from everywhere. The iconographic past assumed an almost liturgical role.

Häußler's *Blutendes Deutschland* was the most frequently screened film of its day in this genre. Historic truth is blatantly falsified so as to enable the Nazis to see themselves as the sole heirs of Prussia's heroic virtues. History has become a semantic space; the Nazis appear as alert jugglers with words and pictures under whose fingers history is given a new shape at the cutting table. In three parts, Häußler's cheap product conjures up what he calls Germany's national uprising: (1) "Aus grosser Zeit" (Of Great Times), which runs from the birth of the German Empire, starting at Versailles in 1871, up to the "Storms of Steel of the World War"; (2) "Der Verrat an Deutschland" (The Betrayal of Germany), presenting the November Revolution, the Spartacist Uprising, the Versailles "Treaty of Shame," and the execution of Albert Leo Schlageter ("with original photos") by the French during the Ruhr Occupation in 1923; (3) "Deutschland erwacht" (Germany Awakens), starting the "fateful turn" of 30 January 1933 when Hitler was appointed Reich Chancellor.

These three headings constitute the technical pattern and the basic bias of the propagandistic compilation film during the years to come. The montage script and its technical realization at the cutting table put together various visual set-scenes, facts, half-truths, lies, false ascriptions, false or exaggerated emphases; in other words they do everything that Eisenstein defined as the model case of a "montage of attractions." An insidious compilation film of this type, which constructs an actually desired reality and presents images that have been torn from their original context, removes from this material all that does not serve the one and only truth. Its fake authenticity, generated from genuine materials, for example, from enemy newsreels, rests on the fact that it has been usurped by an ideology that is not concerned about truth. Changes in chronology and details that are either reported or omitted, and hence augment or reduce weight and meaning, also stem from this dubious approach.

Of course, the strictly ideological use of preexisting material that was typical of fascist compilation films does not apply to the genre more generally. Nevertheless, it is striking how rarely directors have succeeded in making such films aesthetically satisfying. As Ulrich Kurowski put it, this is because "the film material cannot be completely refashioned."[81] Thus, it may be possible only in exceptional circumstances to compile a movie about Nazism that is critical and analytical and relies primarily on Nazi material with its own peculiar aesthetic. Michail Romm's *Daily Fascism* (1965) may be such an exception. It is barely feasible to counter the power of the pictures with the acoustics of the commentary. History—seemingly supported by the visual documents—remains overwhelming. As a rule, the word tended to overlay the pictures in Nazi compilation movies and thus to dominate the overall thrust. Vague commentaries are employed to spread historical falsehoods in a quite literal sense. The conglomerate that consists of heterogenous memory fragments, contradictory visual material, and anachronistic chronologies is held together by a unifying idea or ideology, by the brackets of the director's dramaturgy, and by a text that insinuates symbiosis. This hodge-podge that aims to reconquer the past may be made up of silent film and sound film, of 35 mm, 16 mm and super-8 film, of 16 and 24 pictures per second, photos, facsimiles, newspaper cuttings and posters, black-and-white as well as color film, animation and moving maps, aggregate data, interviews, and newly shot sequences. All these elements and, as Alexander Kluge called them, "self-contained grammalogues," that at best represent miniatures borrowed from divergent styles and currents, are strung together to be handled as gratuitous pictorial proofs. It is only in the rarest of cases that they form a mosaic that is also superior from a film-aesthetical point of view and has a synergetic impact.

While making his film *Strike* in 1924, Eisenstein was one of the first to articulate how important the context is into which individual shots and whole sequences are being put: "The essence of a film

must not be sought in individual sequences, but in their interactions
… the expressive impact of a film is the result of combinations."[82]

From Esther Shub to Jean-Luc Godard

> *Production advances all the time with fresh confidence and in the*
> *clear consciousness that the traditional Ufa standards have to be, and*
> *will be, upheld and that, with an unquestioned sense of duty, cultural*
> *films will come out of the Babelsberg studios in sufficient numbers*
> *and established quality: scientific films and technical ones, entertain-*
> *ing and historically important ones, political as well as unpolitical*
> *movies, films in black-and-white and in color. They are all designed to*
> *discover life in its manifold variations, to discover nature and its mys-*
> *terious laws that never cease to stimulate man to investigate them*
> *anew and further; they are also designed to entertain and elate people*
> *and to expand their knowledge for the benefit of the German people*
> *and the world.*
>
> Nicholas Kaufmann[83]

The model of the aesthetically structured compilation film was
created between 1925 and 1928 by the Russian director Esther
Ilyinichna Shub with her trilogy *The Fall of the Romanov Dynasty*,
The Great Road, and *The Russia of Nicholas II and Leo Tolstoy*. In three
years of work, Shub, who was Eisenstein's montage assistant for
his *Strike*, put together a filmic triptych from old newsreels dating
back as far as 1896 and from the private collections of the Tsarist
family. Meandering through its chronology and adhering strictly
to a partisan point of view, she traces the development of Russia
from the Tsarist period down to the tenth anniversary of the Bolshevik revolution. The approach is decidedly selective and gener-
alizes partial aspects and small points of information. Thus, Shub
contrasts sequences about impoverished peasants with images of
wealthy people who are (apparently) amused by the former's misery. At this point, she does not come through exactly as an advo-
cate of truth. She uses the "Kuleshov Effect" as a stylistic means.
She described her work on this project in these words: "When
doing the montage, I tried to avoid classifying the material
according to its inner value; rather I evaluated it with its documentary importance in mind. All details had to be subordinated to
this principle."[84]

In 1923 Lew Kuleshov, who saw film as a synesthetic art, had made an experiment to demonstrate the manipulative power of the montage. With the help of a simple cut, he confronts the stoic face of the actor Ivan Moshuchin alternately with the picture of a soup bowl, a corpse, and a nude beauty. The viewer believes that he sees in the actor's face consecutively the expression of hunger, fear, and lust.[85]

Similarly to Kuleshov, Vsevolod Ilaryonovich Pudovkin, in the early 1920s, gave impressive proof to how easily the reality of a particular angle can be changed when juxtaposed with others. He chose three angles, with two showing the same woman, first smiling and then in shock. The third picture is a closeup of an unsecured revolver. By choosing the sequence, woman in shock—revolver—smiling woman, he gives the impression of a courageous woman who is in control of the situation. Meanwhile, the reverse sequence would have suggested panic.[86]

Pudovkin wanted to demonstrate how easy it is to reverse meaning by changing the content sequence. Both experiments typify the simple means by which the public can be duped and demonstrate how effortlessly the manipulators can instrumentalize the montage for demagogic purposes.

Dziga Vertov had designed the basic dialectical pattern of this genre some six years prior to Esther Shub. Under the title *History of the Civil War* (1921/22), he made a film that was less concerned with presenting an objectivized array of facts than with using these facts for agitation. Probably without knowing it, Vertov took Nietzsche's dictum literally, according to which there are no facts but only interpretations of them. It was a famous formula that John Grierson later expanded in his *Creative Interpretation of Facts*. Vertov in his *History* interpreted the Bolshevik party line by reference to selected and one-sidedly presented sequences in which the official party doctrine was nostalgically laid out in no less than thirteen acts.

With this movie Vertov anticipated the program of the later *Kinoki* who proposed to compile their works "from facts." They used intermediate texts to avoid giving the impression that they were *not* meant to agitate, with the counterrevolution, of course, as their target. The introductory sentence of the *Kinoki* manifesto may serve as an example of the thrust of their work: "The power of the workers and peasants had to conduct a long, drawn-out struggle against their class enemies within the country after they had freed the nation, which was bleeding to death, from the clutches of the imperialist war."

Vertov experimented constructively with a formula that Soviet movies later deployed very methodically, i.e., that putting two images next to each other generates the suggestion in the mind and consciousness of the viewer that there exists a connection between them. Once the viewer becomes conscious of this connection, "construction sets in and its laws begin to have their effect," to quote Victor Shklovsky.

How clearly Communist functionaries had recognized very early that they could use for propaganda purposes historical material that reproduced facts that had been declared to be such, is confirmed by a reference in the first German compilation film, which had been commissioned by the KPD. Under the title *Weltwende* (The Beginning of a New World), Carl Junghans compiled a one-hour movie from newsreel material for the benefit of the Communist Party in 1918. This movie copied the principles of the Russian model, though without coming anywhere close to Vertov's advisory that the camera must register "the world more variedly from the most divergent angles and more perfectly than the human eye." Instead of enlightening the viewer about Marxism, Junghans rather turned it into a puzzle.

To this day, we do not have any generally accepted syntactic rules for the compilation film. Its authenticity is created less by the persons and historical events it portrays than by the context into which the film puts its extracts, making them truthful by means of a lie (*sie wahr lügt*). It was not only the Nazis (though they above all) but other countries as well that put the compilation film into the service of political agitation. They, too, turned the cutting table into an experimental ground for (subjective) history. Thus, we were rarely given a true picture of reality during World War I, which Paul Virilio called the "first mediatized war." What we mostly received instead was an image that propaganda said was "truthful." In other words, films were made that "confused the last with the first" (F. Nietzsche). After all, pictures and texts do not make an aesthetic parallelogram; nor do form and content lead to a symbiosis.

Toward the end of World War I, the Americans spread worldwide their propaganda versions of the war's origins and consequences in films like George Crul's *America's Answer to the Hun* (1917). During the same year, the Allied powers produced *Under Four Flags,* and in 1919 the British followed suit with *The World's*

Greatest Story. All these movies satisfied the respective "syndrome of expectations." Given that the compilation of the selected parts into a merely chronological or formal sequence without any dialectical tension amounts to pure tinsel, the monosyllabism that is generated becomes the sister of boredom and fails to induce reflection.

Jay Leyda has reported that Joris Ivens and his friends frequently borrowed copies of newsreels from cinemas. They then edited them "during the night in order to highlight their class character and to screen them before a working-class public." At the end of the weekend, the copies were then revamped into their original state before they were sent back "with a few friendly words on Monday." It was due to this influence that Henri Storck was able to conceive the idea for his first short compilation film, *Histoire du Soldat Inconnu* (History of the Unknown Soldier), made in 1932, with a 1959 sound version.

The growing signs of preparations for war in 1932 are taken by Storck, Belgium's pacifist pioneer of the documentary, as an occasion to write a satire about the Kellogg-Briand Pact. Signed by more than 120 countries, this agreement aimed to outlaw wars of aggression. Storck drew his material for this satire from the 1928 newsreels that celebrated the Pact. He believed these films to be suitable to serve the unreconstructed militaristic attitudes and the rearmament fever that was spreading throughout Europe in the early 1930s.

One of the smaller and macabre episodes contained in this movie is the exhuming of an "unknown soldier" whose skull had clearly been pierced by a bullet. This is followed toward the end by a pompous ceremony at the Tomb of the Unknown Soldier in front of the "Flame of Memory" flanked by two lions in stone seemingly ready to pounce. The film concludes with shots of Brussel's "Männeken Pis," which do not seem out of place in this context. It is meant as a metaphor for what a soldier's life has really been worth to governments. The contexts into which Storck puts representatives of the bourgeoisie, the churches, the army, capitalism, as well as "the silent majority" hint at his latent Marxist sympathies; but French critics later accused him more of anarchist and surrealist proclivities.[87]

Temporal distance from events portrayed by the material makes it easier to manipulate them. This is because the material can no longer be scrutinized by the accurate memory of the viewers. At any rate, at the moment of projection onto the screen, it is difficult to assess the truth content of the image of history offered in a documentary.

A typical example might be the American compilation film that Frank Capra made in 1943, entitled *Why We Fight*. The first two-thirds of this movie deal exclusively with the period prior to the outbreak of World War II to justify its title. The sequence showing infantry supposedly parading at the 1937 Nuremberg Party rally is based on archival material that must date from the beginning of the war two years later, since the soldiers wear war decorations like the "Iron Cross, Second Class." However, this fraudulent detail that is basically insignificant should not lead us to conclude that the entire film is designed to deceive. And yet, the knowing viewer is left with serious doubts as to the credibility of the whole enterprise.

With Luis Buñuel as the dominant influence, *Madrid '36*, an anti-fascist movie, was compiled that same year from newsreel material and photos from the Republican side in the Spanish Civil War. With Beethoven's symphonies as its music, it certainly succeeded in making an emotional impact.

Nicole Védrès's *Paris 1900*, made in 1947/48 with Alain Resnais as her assistant, must be considered one of the most influential movies since the genre developed in the direction of a more analytical structure. She does not simply pile the available pictures on top of each other. Instead, and in her own words, she "wants to penetrate the cover of the pictures that have been selected and to capture, without particular emphasis, that special expression that is always hidden under the surface of the images. [Thus] this bearded gentleman, a politician, struts about with a smile and an air of *joie de vivre*, and yet we sense his mendacious malice. He does not show it; his photo does."[88] This is the sophisticated context of self-revelation in which Nicole Védrès presents, without any commentary, contemporaries like Monet, Renoir, Bernhardt, Carpentier, and many others. The pointed music by Guy Bernhardt makes anything else superfluous.

Often the privileged persons that are portrayed are used to leave the viewer with the bitter feeling of exclusion from their world. This is true not only of *Paris 1900* (though it is particularly marked here), but also of many other movies that were cobbled together from newsreel material. The film then compensates for this "loss" by giving viewers the impression that, as spectators, they have become witnesses to moments of historic encounters, at least after the event. As Hans Magnus Enzensberger concluded from similar situations, being no more than an onlooker reinforces "the viewer in his belief that paradise begins beyond the barriers. The viewer does not see through the macabre irony of this parasitic flashlight business, i.e., that those on display have themselves been cheated, that the celebrity is his own extra, and that the empress is her own model. It never occurs to him to doubt the dignity of the empress who poses before the camera, and so it is he who is putting clothes on the model that doubles for her."[89] In *Paris 1900* people of different class backgrounds act like divergent factors within a societal parallelogram of forces.

Major directors of the *nouvelle vague*, such as Frédéric Rossif (*Mourir à Madrid*, 1962) and Jean-Luc Godard (*Les Carabiniers*, 1963), are similarly not interested in the great men of the age but in the consequences they left behind. Both of them have made montage into the montage movie; both invoke what Habermas would later call the "subversive power of reflection." Moreover, both of them use the same material with the aid of which they hoped to gain access to the Spanish Civil War from the perspective of the victims. Such films indirectly contradict the view that the eye is the ultimate authority. Rather, it is the viewers' intellect. Godard believes that the corpse that is shown in his *Les Carabiniers* triggers a sense of unease, whereas the same dead person enthused the viewers of *Mourir à Madrid*. What causes the unease is that the corpse "remains what it is: insignificant, i.e., it gains no importance, whereas it is given an importance in *Mourir à Madrid* that probably did correspond to its life...."[90] Godard rightly calls this a fraud, "even if it has been perpetrated with clean hands." And, so we are tempted to add, perpetrated with emotional power and visual beauty.

Bashing the United States and the Soviet Union

> ... for contrary to earlier times, in this war we Germans have learned one virtue that will make us invincible: the confidence in our own power.
>
> Joseph Goebbels[91]

So far we have surveyed the genesis of the compilation movie on the basis of a number of typical examples from the history of film in order to demonstrate that this extremely ambivalent genre was not an invention made in Dr. Goebbels's diabolical laboratory, even if the Nazis appear to have invented it. What must be stressed, however, is that the cinematographic falsifiers of history and the atrocity propagandists of the Hitler regime studied the relevant techniques of manipulation and mechanisms of popular seduction in detail. They appropriated whatever was useful for their negative designs and perfected it psychologically.

The compilation films that were produced against Hitler's "world enemies" after the beginning of the war provide especially telling examples of the kind of demagogic deception that the Propaganda Ministry engaged in with its uninhibited use of the "art" of montage. These films were shown not just in the Reich, but also in the occupied territories. They were designed to justify why Hitler was allegedly forced to wage a holy war against the "beasts," plutocrats, and Jews that were represented.

Thus, the 1942 movie *Amerika sieht sich selbst* (America Looks at Itself) lays out a depressing picture of the country with unreferenced excerpts from American feature films of the late 1930s and early 1940s. Juvenile crime is rampant and indirectly contrasted with visually tangible Nazi ideology under which young German criminals do not have a chance. The revamping of evidence relating to the physiognomy of American society culled from American thrillers to provide material for Goebbels's propaganda, blended with original German commentaries, provide the elements that have been craftily constructed from a dramaturgical point of view. It is this texture that made this film so effective when it came out in 1942. Slum scenes, evidently portraying New York's East Side, have been taken out of their original context in the gangster movie *Dead End* (1937) and compiled as authentic documents to fake American reality. These and other fictional images of the United States achieved a higher degree of reality than the best *German* propaganda material could ever have copied, since director William Wyler had originally presented this milieu with artistic license in a way that was aesthetically convincing. Consequently, the German compilation, its formal brilliance notwithstanding, turned into a casuistic example and a propagandistic fraud. The scenes from the American feature film that the German makers had interconnected displayed a marked tendency to turn the function of self-criticism in *Dead End* into its opposite.

In 1943, then, when Goebbels proclaimed "total war," the caricature of Roosevelt which is cobbled together from the President's different public appearances for the movie *Herr Roosevelt plaudert* (Mr. Roosevelt Chats) is used at the same time to personify the Jewish "world enemy" whom it is necessary to extinguish; for

"Roosevelt, the warmonger, has developed an appetite for [gobbling up] the whole world." Again, and without indicating the source, the film included a scene from John Ford's *The Grapes of Wrath* (1940), which effectively rang true because the drastically shown capitalist methods of exploiting the farming population appear, in the deceptive context of newsreel material, as a reliable report of facts.

Together with the Jews, Bolshevism had been declared "world enemy No. 1." Hence, during the Nazi-Soviet Pact, Hitler alone was in a position to declare a thaw that lasted from the fall of 1939 to June 1941. The SS-journal *Das schwarze Korps* (The Black Corps) explained the renewed reversal in 1941 to its readers as follows: "Only Adolf Hitler was able to lead the German people to this change of fronts, and it was only upon the German people that the Führer could impose at that moment the expectation of an unconditional willingness to follow him. Even if there was never a question of an ideological reconciliation or even rapprochement between National Socialism and Bolshevism, superficial observers could nonetheless easily gain this impression."[92] Not surprisingly, anti-Soviet propaganda pieces had long been lying in Goebbels's drawer, to be taken out punctually when Hitler tore up the Nazi-Soviet Pact. Subsequently, the Russians are portrayed as a devilish and inferior race in films that are even more perfidious than the ones against "plutocrats" and Wall Street. Movies like *Das Sowjet-Paradies* (The Soviet Paradise, 1942) or *Im Wald von Katyn* (In Katyn Forest, 1943) not only excoriate the Communist system, but the nations of the Soviet Union as a whole.

The former film begins with an aggressive commentary that sets the tone for the rest of the movie: "Where once stood prospering villages, the gray misery of the collective farm predominates today. This is where the Soviet peasant lives as a slave." And: "Some eighty people must vegetate in fifteen rooms." The editors evidently had fun composing a potpourri of misery from the sinister documentary material. The horror images certainly demonstrated what the commentary had promised, i.e., "the disastrous results of twenty years of a bloody regime run by a Jewish-Bolshevik terror clique." The misery was coded with the help of attributes like "caked in filth" (*"dreckstarrend"*), "unkempt," "enslaved," "liquidated," etc. In conjunction with the film *Soviet Paradise*, Goebbels organized an exhibition with the same title in which a monster that was made up of Jews and Bolsheviks was declared "world enemy No. 1" and then sent around the Reich.

Helmut Krausnick has documented in his book *Hitlers Einsatz-gruppen* the catastrophic consequences that the equating of Jews and Bolsheviks had, especially for the former. It appeared in the literature and film published by Goebbels's Propaganda Ministry and Alfred Rosenberg's Ministry for the Occupied Eastern Terri-tories in aggressive slogans such as "Jewish-Bolshevik terror clique."[93] Anti-Jewish pogroms began immediately after the inva-sion of the Soviet Union, following on the heels of the racist liqui-dation programs that the Nazis had initiated in Poland in 1939. Jews were murdered in the thousands in bright daylight and before everyone's eyes. This refutes the contention that it was only the dreaded "Gestapo on wheels" who were responsible for the mass murders of Jews. Rather, it was Wehrmacht generals who either covered or even ordered the deadly excesses against Jewish civilians, since "a crusade had to be conducted against Bolshevism and hence also against the Jews who were more or less equated with Bolshevism."[94] The actions of Gauleiter Erich Koch alone, in his role as Reich Commissar for the occupied Ukraine, reached the proportions of genocide when he ordered hundreds of thousands of Jews from Bialystok and the Ukraine to be liquidated by bestial means while implementing his "Germanization" policy in his realm. According to Alexander and Margarete Mitscherlich, the vanquished loses his quality as a human being in the eyes of the victor. He may be persecuted without inhibition after everything that is evil and dangerous has been projected onto him: "The defeated becomes the prey of boundless bloodthirstiness."[95]

The two-part movie *Im Wald von Katyn*, which is subtitled "documentary film," turns us into witnesses of superficially buried history. It exhumes in a very literal way the crimes of Katyn Forest where in April 1943 German soldiers came across the mass graves of 4,143 Polish officers. They had been murdered there in 1939 during the occupation by the Red Army which had marched into the eastern half of Poland as part of the deal with Hitler under the Nazi-Soviet Pact. The litany of pictures of corpses, exhumed by Polish prisoners, is accompanied by interviews with Poles who "stand shattered in front of the blood of their former comrades." These kinds of testimonies are designed to "objectivize" the hate-filled German commentary. The second part shows mass graves of Ukrainians as "witnesses to Soviet bloodthirstiness." A Greek-Orthodox bishop sprinkles holy water across the sea of corpses. In the words of the commentator, Bolshevism appears here as "a Jew-ish organization for the extermination of the intelligentsia and the culture of Europe and the world." The Soviets are not simply portrayed as enemies, but as a bestial brood. This film with its horrifying photos was supposed to act as a diversion from the mountains of corpses in Hitler's concentration camps. In the debate that the Berlin historian Ernst Nolte unleashed in the 1980s concerning the origins of the "Final Solution of the Jewish Question," we have been hearing unacceptable arguments that challenge the uniqueness of the Holocaust when by quantifying Hitler's and Stalin's victims for "objective historical writing," the deaths of sixteen or more million Ukrainians and kulaks who perished are alleged to weigh, statistically speaking, more heavily than the six million Jews who died in Nazi gas chambers.

The Eternal Jew *(1940)*

He calls death more sweetly.
Death is master in Germany.
He shouts that we should play our violins more darkly,
Then you will ascend into the air as smoke,
Then you will have a grave in the clouds,
Where it is not cramped.

Paul Célan[96]

SS-*Hauptsturmführer* Dr. Franz Hippler was the most eager and unscrupulous among Goebbels's film experts who knew how to arrange the most disparate clips and most antagonistic arguments into a triumph of dialectical destructiveness. It was he who put together the morally most perfidious, intellectually most underhanded, and ideologically most perverse mishmash that has ever been produced. This was *Der ewige Jude* (The Eternal Jew), made in 1940. Only human scum could bring out such a diabolical work. Together with *Jud Süß* (1940) and *Die Rothschilds* (1940), as well as the book by Hans Dieboro with the same title, *Der ewige Jude* raised the pogrom mood against the Jews to boiling point. These films and a number of other books were calculated to justify in advance the mass murder of the European Jews.[97] The film was premiered in Berlin on 28 November 1940. Deportations to the camps in the East followed without delay. When the film was first shown in the "Casino Cinema" in Lodz at the beginning of January 1941, some two hundred thousand Jews who had been crammed into the local ghetto were liquidated shortly thereafter. Under the impression of the Polish premiere, the Berlin journal *Film-Kurier* wrote of Lodz as "a place which, so to speak, symbolizes this film; for it was here that a large part of this movie was made."[98]

There then followed this aggressive text: "The camera wandered [through this ghetto] before the ordering hand of the German administration intervened to clean out this Augean stable in order to obtain a true, undiluted picture of this cesspit from which world Jewry was steadily supplied." This is where the camera discovered those "types of Jewry" and those "depraved faces" that are shown in the film. Once "they moved as peddlers and parasites through this city." And finally: "The movie left a very strong impression."

Succinctly and approvingly, *Deutsche Allgemeine Zeitung* of 29 November 1940 gave a description of the emotional streams of hatred that the film unleashed: "The viewer breathes a sigh of relief when the film reaches its end. He returns to light from the darkest swamps."[99]

The *Illustrierte Film-Kurier*, another synchronized journal, played the same propaganda tune: "In shining contrast [to the "rats"] the film, following these terrible scenes, ends with pictures of German people and German orderliness. They fill the viewer with deepest gratitude that he belongs to this nation whose Führer is in the process of developing a fundamental solution to the Jewish problem."[100] In January 1942 the Lodz Casino Cinema showed Gustav Ucicky's hate-filled concoction *Heimkehr* (Homecoming, 1941). In it, the return of the Germans from Volhynia is said to be indebted to a dive bomber attack: "Against the background of a world-historical decision, the fate of the ethnic-German men and women from the late summer of 1939 who are depicted in this great and moving film leads to the cause of the fateful struggle that has been imposed on us." These were the words of the *Völkischer Beobachter* on 24 October 1941. Meanwhile, the demagogic texts in the Polish language were to have a psychologically humiliating effect.

The tremendous impact of both these films is due to several factors that provide an apparent authenticity, systematically concocted in the laboratory of destruction. *Der ewige Jude* combines individual parts of the argument in a demagogic commentary and a montage that is artfully welded together by synthetic forces; it does so in such a fashion that the individual segments mutually magnify their pitilessness. The shots taken for Hippler's work in the ghetto "at the source of all evil" exclusively show faces that were designed to confirm the prejudices about the "subhumans" that Julius Streicher had spread in his anti-Semitic rag *Der Stürmer*. The dilapidated and filthy milieu for which the Nazis, having crammed twelve people into one room, were themselves exclusively responsible is presented in "genuine" pictures as an "Augean stable" that was typical of the Jewish "race" and that the Jews had merely brought upon themselves. Among this "evidence" were also excerpts from Joseph Green's *The Purim Player* (1937) and *Yidl Mit Fidl* (Jew with a Fiddle, 1936). In a perfect fade-over, several Jews "metamorphose" from men in orthodox dress to people in West European tailor-made suits without beards and sideburns. This is supposed to demonstrate the Jewish art of perfect deception. In order, nevertheless, to be able to identify *the* Jew, he had to wear as the mark of Cain the Star of David, first introduced in Poland on 23 November 1939 and in the Reich on 19 September 1941.

All these scenes of denial are escalated in this film into a guide for action by a commentary whose cynicism can hardly be surpassed. The result was many spontaneous outrages against Jews, not to mention all the ones that had been officially organized. Through insertions, various partial truths are further truncated and lies are refashioned into truths. In short, as Theodor Adorno put it, "everything that isn't, is nonetheless promised by the fact that it appears." The theme of extermination is buttressed by "arguments" that look convincing in their primitivism. For example, an analogy is made between a bunch of disgusting rats and Jews massively swamping the civilized world and in turn conjuring up dangers of pest epidemics and festering sores. Just as in the case of other contrapuntal montages, the indoctrinating commentary is important here: "Where rats appear, they spread disease and carry destruction into the land. They are wily, cowardly, and cruel and appear mostly in large numbers—just like the Jews among the humans."

The scenes of ritual slaughter of sheep and other animals in this film may look cruel to Christian souls, even if the commentary is disregarded. But the impact is worsened in its polemical anti-Semitic effect because faces of Jewish butchers who go after their profession with apparent voluptuousness have been faded in. Nor does the film's montage technique shrink from defaming famous Jewish artists. Thus, scenes from Fedor Ozep's *Der Mörder Dimitri Karamasoff* and Fritz Lang's *M* (both made in 1931) are brought in to personally identify Fritz Kortner and Peter Lorre with the psychopathic roles they played in these movies as seducer and as murderer. Within this hate-filled context, emotions are fanned by an irrational chauvinism in order to turn the Jews into scapegoats on patriotic grounds as well. In these ways the producers tried to justify what Foucault has called the "stigmatization of the victims and the demonstration of the punishing authority."[101]

Nazi racism, as depicted in film, reached its terrifying climax in *Der ewige Jude*. It is no coincidence that the machinery of genocide was set in motion at the same time that this "documentary" justification of mass murder was released. The power of the words and the wizardry of the pictures provided the ammunition for a large-caliber anti-Semitic weapon. As Albert Memmi put it, "Racism is no doubt one of the cogs in this diabolical engine."[102] He continued: "Man is the only being that systematically despises, humiliates, and exterminates members of its own species physically and existentially for the purpose of self-justification. In large part this occurs through language, and this linguistic aspect of racism is certainly not just perverse. Man is endowed with language, i.e., he draws, communicates, stresses, and erases his experiences in images and words."

In Memmi's view, racism at the level of symbols is a continuous laboratory in which the destruction of the victims is being prepared. Films like *Der ewige Jude* were supposed to justify at a symbolic level Hitler's racist fanaticism worldwide. Cinematographic instruments that worked so insidiously and manipulated the consciousness of the masses as effectively as possible secured a consenting silence on a massive scale. Racist anti-Semitism may arise through "the generalized and absolutized valuation of actual or fictive differences to the advantage of the accuser and the detriment of the victim with which privileges or aggressions are to be justified."[103] In this anti-Semitic world, Hitler was the "cement" of his Nazi movement.

Fritz Hippler's *Feldzug in Polen* (The Polish Campaign, 1940), Hans Bertram's *Feuertaufe* (Baptism of Fire, 1940), and *Sieg im Westen* (Victory in the West, 1941) by Svend Noldan and Fritz Brunel pursued identical objectives. What differentiates them from most other compilation films that have been mentioned here is that all events take place on the "field of honor." This means that they rely almost exclusively on German war newsreel material, which in turn was made up of many individual contributions from a variety of cameramen. The thinking and feeling of these men were pervaded as strongly by the spirit of Nazism as their films. Their authenticity is reinforced by the attempt to use captured newsreel in order to produce a friend-foe dialectic. This is done with perfidious perfection in *Sieg im Westen* by omitting the context in which the latter originated. In this way and for the purpose of proving the point, "foreign matter" from the opposing side is incorporated into the narrative.

German War Film Compilations, 1939–1945

From the long-term perspective, war propaganda that exclusively serves truth is the best.

Joseph Goebbels[104]

In a strict sense, every single newsreel represents a compilation film. However, the photo material is more homogeneous than in other montages insofar as all of them are permeated by the same heroic spirit and are wedded to the same cause, i.e., to win victory for Hitler. These films exude an enthusiastic mood that is enhanced by marching songs. To this extent, all of these films with their adoration of the Führer belong to the same category of equally crude propaganda pieces. Paul Virilio's assessment of *Feuertaufe* in the armed forces journal *Signal* applies *praeter propter* also to the other war films: "[These are] pictures without immediate dramatic tension whose judicious editing, which combines events occurring more or less far apart, and whose commentary are designed to expose the viewer to the vibrating rhythm of the grand historical event."[105]

The same ends as in *Feldzug in Polen* also justified the means of *Feuertaufe*, according to the subtitle of Hans Bertram's "film about the deployment of the German air force in Poland." Bertram released his documentary a few months after Hippler's movie. Bertram was severely wounded on location and lost one eye. Above all, like most other cameramen attached to the air force, he became intoxicated with flying. These men were trained to wield both the camera and the machine gun and were able to switch positions if required. As Major Carl Cranz, the commander of the first Air Force Propaganda Company reported, thanks to this training "our war reporters are full-fledged soldiers."[106] This company had gained its first relevant experiences only a few months earlier during maneuvers in West Prussia and Pomerania and during the occupation of Sudetenland. Perhaps without realizing it, these men implemented in the baptism of fire high above the

Vistula and Warthe rivers the idea of the "armed camera-eye," albeit in a totally different way from what Vertov had envisioned.

Virilio no longer saw the war of the twentieth century as a war of weapons, but as a war of perception. In his view, battles are only secondarily decided on the battlefields; the actual conflict takes place as a map maneuver in the command centers. The effectiveness of such scenarios is dependent on the exact location of the enemy positions—it is a perception that determines victory and defeat, life and death.

And indeed, combinations of guns and cameras, e.g., cameras mounted on top of machine guns, were quite widespread in World War II. Whoever operated the gun would automatically also trigger the camera. As Virilio wrote, "For the soldier the function of the eye merges with that of the weapon."[107] He added that war has shown to the camera-artist that "military technology in action [is] the highest privilege of art." Soon the air war appeared to many airmen as the French writer Antoine de Saint-Exupéry had described it in his *Flight to Arras*—as no more than "an experiment in a laboratory."[108] Saint-Exupéry, who had tried to elevate the machine as a symbol of the spirit, failed to return from a sortie in July 1944. The poetry-writing hero thus ennobled his work through his death.

Bertram presents his report on the eighteen-day blitzkrieg against a Polish army that was greatly inferior and totally unprepared primarily from a bird's eye perspective and elevated also in ideological terms. The sequences in the film's preamble identify Britain as the main warmonger that instigated the Poles to unleash pogroms against ethnic Germans: "The West European plutocracy—Free Masons and Jews—have sworn an oath of truce to combat National Socialism."[109] The film then provides the response: "Like a sword in the sky, our air force is ready for take-off."

We also know Hitler's reply: "From now on we shall retaliate bomb for bomb." The inferno had thus been prepared. Göring's two air fleets systematically destroyed Polish airports, railroad tracks, roads, ports, military installations, and towns, allegedly "in order to prevent the concentration, supply, and retreat of the enemy." As the speed of bombers increased, not only the aerial views changed all the time, but also the angle at which films were shot. As a result, the walls of ruins assume the ghostly shape of isometric projections. When the film presents the horrifying pictures of devastated Polish cities as a pleasurable panorama, the commentary adds sneeringly that whoever "sees the true measure of the impact of air warfare will also recognize the extent of the guilt that Britain has to shoulder."[110]

Wilhelm Stoeppler's lines, composed in 1939, are recited:

> We flew to the Vistula and Warthe rivers,
> We flew toward Polish land
> We hit the enemy army hard
> With lightnings and bombs and fire!

Göring's boastful delusions of revenge are supposed to provide the crowning commentary for the movie: "The promises the German Air Force has made in Poland will be fulfilled in Britain and France.... We shall prove to Mr. Chamberlain that islands no longer exist. The hearts of all airmen beat faster when they are cleared for take-off: We are flying against *Engelland*." And with relentless optimism, the bomber pilots sing themselves into the apotheosis at the end of the film, in Stoeppler's words and with music by Norbert Schultze:

> We confront the British lion
> for the last decisive attack.
> We sit in judgment. A global empire is breaking up.
> That was our proudest day!
>
> Comrade! Comrade! The girls will have to wait.
> Comrade! Comrade! The order has come through. We're off!
> Comrade! Comrade! You know the password:
> Close up to the enemy! Close up to the enemy!
> Bombs for *Engelland*!
> Do you hear the engines sing: close up to the enemy!
> Does it resound in your ears: close up to the enemy!
> Bombs! Bombs! Bombs dropped on *Engelland*!

Sitting in front of the screen, the spectators are sucked into the fighting and the assurance that the enemy's potential has been destroyed; they are included as a sympathizing mass that, through its sons, brothers, and fathers, has been made part of the victory. The stirring marching band music similarly swept people away and absorbed them emotionally. Many joined in the singing of the "Bombs for *Engelland*" song or at least quietly hummed it. This powerful emotional push toward victory and this popularity among the masses were aspects of propaganda that became decisive in Nazi filmmaking.

Jerzy Bossak and Vaclav Kazmierczák have included in their 1961 montage, titled *September 1939*, the whining engines of dive bombers from *Feuertaufe*. They have also used the choir's happily sung lines: "For we are flying against *Polenland* ... with lightnings and bombs and fire"—which had been prognostically changed to "against *Engelland*" only toward the end of the movie. The two Polish filmmakers then replay the cutting voice of the original commentator who orders death and destruction for Poland. As Bossak explained: "This passage enables us to say a great deal about the spirit of fascism."[111] From the limited material that was available to them, he and Kazmierczák compiled a 60-minute retrospective that offered more a passionate historicization than a sober argument about the Polish campaign. Consequently, they have used prewar newsreels and Göring's glorifying air force movies rather inorganically. What they have produced is a mechanical sequencing whose anti-fascist message is carried alone by the commentary, without reaching a new qualitative level. As the two directors added: "The editing makes it impossible for us to feel and think with them. If a particular scene is unusually drawn out, this is not in order to produce tension and cogitation, but only because the montage in question just happened to be that long." This approach is responsible for the film's inorganic structure that leaves the viewer no room to make associations.

Eduard von Borsody's *Wunschkonzert* (Request Concert, 1940) was the first German feature film to fade in original documentary clips as part of the action. These authentic sequences from Riefenstahl's *Olympia* as well as war newsreels have been so perfectly blended with the main narrative that the fictive persons become credible. There is, for example, the Olympic Stadium in Berlin where Inge (Ilse Werner) and the dapper lieutenant Herbert Koch (Carl Raddatz) discover their love. "Germany is coming," Inge says enthusiastically as the German Olympic team, dressed in white, turns into the homestretch. The editing suggests that the Führer is watching the same scene as Inge and Herbert. Just as the Olympic bell is faded over, pictures of the Olympic fire lead into the film's second part. We find ourselves in the war which ends with another symbol-laden technique: a fade-out with swastika flags *in cumulo* that promise victory.

In the second part, Herbert, the air force officer who has meanwhile received the Spanish Cross and now acts against the backdrop of original war newsreel, looks as if he has just returned from a sortie in the heated air battle with the enemy. The request program of "Greater German Radio" contributed to this illusion of authenticity. Using contemporary show-biz darlings, the *Wunschkonzert* is broadcast as if the movie were "by chance" witness to this Sunday afternoon ritual of the nation. It was a ritual that was to keep soldiers as well as the "home front" in good spirits, with the help of light music and obligatory morale boosters like the operetta star Marika Röck and the schmaltz baritone Wilhelm Strienz.

This movie certainly is an example of the attempt to blend the simultaneity of the nonsimultaneous, as well as play and reality, front and home front into an optical unit by deploying bits of newsreel as alternating visual stimuli. Thanks to the blurring effect of a heavy dose of sentimentality, the viewer generally did not notice how the nonidentical had been made totally identical. Adorno has called this realism resulting from a loss of reality. Attendance figures prove how much films were loved at this time that were categorized as "popular" and "valuable" from a "state-political" and "artistic" point of view: up to the end of the war *Wunschkonzert* had been seen by 26.5 million people.

By relying upon recognition effect, the stereotypical final ceremony of the request program provided a million-fold opportunity to identify emotionally with the sentiment that the popular showmaster Heinz Gödecke had prepared:

> The Wehrmacht request concert is now coming to an end,
> The home front stretches out to the front its hand,
> The front stretches out its hands to the home front.
> We say: Good night, *auf Wiederhören,*
> Until we return next time—
> The Fatherland says *auf Wiedersehen!*

Allied War Film Compilations, 1940–1945

> *We live in an obsessed world ... It would not come as a surprise to anyone if the madness would some day suddenly turn into a rage into which this poor European humanity would lapse, stunned and insane; while the engines are still purring and the flags rustling, the spirit has disappeared.*
>
> Johan Huizinga[112]

Michail Romm's impressive symbiosis of aesthetic quality and enlightenment in the sixteen sections of his *Obyknovennij fasizm*

(Daily Fascism, 1965) has been unsurpassed in its impact to this day. Indeed, it signifies a crossroads on the well-trodden path of compilations about fascism. Romm is himself convinced that his work is a criticism of movies about fascism in which the bitter reality of Nazism has been transformed into an artistic reality, since the critical perspective became imprisoned by stereotypical images and powerful concepts. At the same time his film is a "critique of movies about many other historical themes." He adds:

> We have movies about the "Great Patriotic War," the history of the Revolution, about a variety of countries.... They are all the same. I am convinced that as a consequence of the principles that underlie them they are all profoundly untrue. And none of them is a success with the viewers. They are successful only with those who commissioned them. Thus, the latter will already be happy if all has been enumerated and reported. Meanwhile, the viewer is terribly bored: "Everything is included and nothing else!" ... We watched one documentarist movie about fascism, the war, and the Soviet Union after the other; we then switched off the sound, and our attention was drawn to the unintelligent and uniform language of the pictures. It was not the primitiveness of the montage; [on the contrary,] this was all neatly and expertly done; it was the uneducated language of art [that struck us]. It was no longer what is called "colds cuts" over here....[113]

Romm does not simply show images of atrocities taken from German and Soviet newsreels in order to emotionalize the audience through shock treatment. The original material from those Nazi films is not suited for his ambitious enterprise to develop a typology of a terror regime. In Romm's view, those films are in any case "incredibly monotonous.... Among six million feet of film we did not see a single picture of ordinary man."[114] And yet it is this ordinary man, the follower, on whom his interest is focused.

Why did this man join in and why did he remain an obedient link in the chain of the mass movement to the bitter end? All material Romm draws upon is designed to unmask the propaganda methods, including the aesthetic transformation of ideological content into a motivating force, which the Nazis marshaled in order to use the German people for their sinister purposes. Romm is not interested in the tabulation of history. He wants to grasp the socio-typical moment behind the pictures, to get hold of the phenomenon of fascism in its totality. He hopes to make visible the motives of blind obedience. This is why he tears the veil from the artificial aura surrounding the adventurer Hitler. He uncovers the mechanisms of Nazi ideology through picture and commentary, in which he combines "the language of the angry journalist with the pungency of the satirist, the stylistic sensitivity of the artist with the wisdom of the humanist."[115]

Romm chose a method that is both intellectual and emotive to investigate the truth about the Hitler period and to make it accessible: "If we all cooperate to describe the historical events not just superficially and with didactic commentaries, but try to stop and think when dealing with every individual phenomenon, we shall sooner or later come close to the truth."[116] However, this goal can be achieved only if the limits of the genre are broadened beyond the confines of the massive material that is available. In 1965 Roman Karmen turned the Soviet movie *Velikaya Ochesvenaya Voina* (The Great Patriotic War) into precisely such a mammoth enterprise that he, as the organizer of the whole compilation, evidently lost his thread. This film about a period of great tragedy for the Soviet people strings together all sorts of episodes to produce an arbitrary conglomerate of impressions that are all similar. This is achieved with the help of Nazi newsreels and Soviet documentaries that Karmen himself was involved in. Thus, he was the cameraman for Leonid Varlamov and Ilya Kopalin's *Victory Against the German Armies before Moscow* (1942) and during the same year directed, with Yefin Uchitel, the documentary about *The Struggle for Leningrad*. This latter film was shown under the title *Moscow Strikes Back* in the United States and was awarded an Oscar in 1942 for best documentary. Still, in Karmen's case and even with a film that runs for 130 minutes, it should have been possible to avoid contrived transitions and repetitions in such large numbers, if only he had developed a professional pictorial grammar.

Karmen was always directly on the front line, facing the enemy. He reached Berlin with the first Soviets tanks. Thus, he used scenes from his *The Struggle for Leningrad* (1942) and *Stalingrad* (1943) both for his *Great Patriotic War* and for *Sud Naradov* (Judgment of the Nations, 1947), a movie about the Nuremberg Trials of the major war criminals. And "jointly with the judges and the Allied nations we documentarists rendered the verdict: death by hanging."[117] However, it is only after Stalin's death that Karmen also explicitly takes the view that "barbaric fascism" rather than the Germans was the enemy of the Soviet Union. In his *Great Patriotic War* Stalin had already been dethroned.

Ten days after the Japanese attack on Pearl Harbor on 7 December 1941, Roosevelt issued a Presidential Letter on 18 December in which he appointed a "Coordinator for Government Film," though without executive powers. This is the background to an initiative by the U.S. War Department authorizing Col. Frank Capra to begin a propaganda film offensive. The idea was to counter the weapons produced in Dr. Goebbels's cinematographic munitions factories. A film series seemed most suitable, not only to justify the United States's entry into the war, but also to depict it "as the inevitable reaction to serious crimes." Under the title *Why We Fight,* a seven-part series was to be made that would be based on firsthand evidence and factual accounts because they, above all, were deemed to have persuasive power.[118] In the first instance, this implied reliance on newsreels from around the world. Capra's films were shown to GIs before they were sent to Europe, but also in cinemas back in the United States and the British Commonwealth. Churchill personally introduced the Commonwealth version. The movies were designed to give a conclusive answer to the question of "Why we fight" by contrasting, in a psychologically adept manner, the "Free World" with the "Slave World" of the Axis Powers. The seven installments of, on average, sixty minutes were to safeguard not only chronology and systematic interpretation, but also continued popularity.

The series broadly followed Roosevelt's somewhat vague proclamation in his State of the Union Address of January 1942. In it, the President identified as central points of the war and *raison d'être* of the American entry: "the American way of life," and, secondly, the "character of the enemy—his ideology, his motives, his methods." Furthermore, he mentioned the United Nations and their Allied armed forces and the need to secure, from "the production front" supplies for the ultimate victory. Finally, there were the responsibilities of the civilian services at the home front and "our troops, our Allies and sympathizers."[119]

"Prelude to War," which appeared in 1942 as the first title in the *Why We Fight* series, covers the years of Hitler's rise up to 1938. The next part, "The Nazi Strike," reports with biting irony the Wehrmacht's march into Austria and Czechoslovakia as well as the invasion of Poland. "Divide and Conquer" (1943) documents Hitler's war in Western Europe. The evacuation of the British Expeditionary Force from Dunkirk after the fall of France in June 1940 and the air raids on London and Coventry are at the center of "The Battle of Britain" (1943). "The Battle of Russia" (1944) shows the Soviets as brothers in arms and spreads sympathy for the suffering population under the motto: "Generals may win battles, but people win wars." The 1944 installment, "The Battle for China," was removed from circulation because relations between the Communists and Chiang Kai-shek were precarious. "The Battle of Russia" was withdrawn during the McCarthy years of anti-Communist hysteria in the United States.

Among the seven *Why We Fight* movies, Anatole Litvak's "War Comes to America" (1945) is probably the most impressive. Although opinion polls with "common people," official statements, and historical facts are neatly interpreted in conjunction with newsreel materials and dialogues, the constant fade-ins of interviewees and the statistical evaluation of their answers by Gallup do become somewhat unnerving. By including newsreels and even clips from *Triumph des Willens*, Litvak succeeds in portraying a cross section of contemporary American history. These images are confronted with Hitler's wars of conquest and Japan's raid on Pearl Harbor, resulting in the American declaration of war. Sentimental texts about the American countryside in deep peace and its lyrical transfiguration take the German *Kulturfilm* as their model. But then the trivial tone is replaced by warlike language: "We shall fight to the last man." The movie also contains interesting sequences about fascist movements outside Hitler's sphere of influence, among them Nazi rallies and large numbers of swastika flags in New York's Madison Square Garden. No doubt the answers to the overriding question of "Why we fight" have been carefully documented here; and yet it is not a "dramatic, exciting … and extremely convincing film," just a very patriotic one. A statement by George C. Marshall, as chairman of the Joint Chiefs of Staff, concludes the movie: "Victory of the democracies can only be complete with the *utter defeat* of the war machines of Germany and Japan." The film then shows the Stars and Stripes with a fade-over of American children who, with hand on heart, sing the national anthem.

In "Prelude to War," the first part of the series, children in Nazi Germany, Italy, and Japan are shown from the opposite angle—how they are put under the state's tutelage at an early age. There is a German blackboard with the words in Gothic script: "We are living for Hitler, and we'll also joyfully die for him. With the Führer unto death, for he is our God." A Japanese cemetery is headlined: "To die for the Emperor means eternal life." However, Americans also do not shrink from a willingness to face death: "Give me Liberty or give me Death." Through judicious editing, Frank Capra put together a dynamic propaganda film for which he recklessly exploited Riefenstahl's movies, German newsreels, and American anti-Nazi films. "Prelude to War" comes across as a well-rounded whole, supported by John Huston's commentary and Dimitri Tiomkin's music, that is skillfully deployed from the viewpoint of dramaturgy. Clearly, this is one of the best-made propaganda films of World War II.

The same crew also made "The Nazi Strike" a success. Bismarck is introduced as Hitler's precursor with the words: "We shall dominate the world." This is then echoed in the song "Today Germany Belongs to Us, and Tomorrow It's the Entire World." Scenes from Party rallies are designed to demonstrate the threat posed by a tightly organized dictatorship and to reveal the psychology behind Hitler's military mass parades, which tries to "demoralize his enemies" with these techniques. Using Nazi newsreels and Riefenstahl's films to buttress the basic argument, the film summarizes all major events in Nazi Germany that until 1942 caused the rest of the world to hold its breath. A critical commentary is added to Hitler's negotiations with Chamberlain and Daladier in 1938 that led to the Munich Agreement. Next we see Polish cavalry advancing against German tanks—probably using film from Polish maneuvers. Capra calls the Nazi-Soviet Pact of August 1939 "the kiss of death for the Poles." Churchill's statesmanlike speech is juxtaposed with footage showing the faces of desperate people next to their dead. The film ends with the V(ictory) sign.

The Battle of San Pietro is a much more shattering movie than words could express, showing pictures of the front line in the devastated mountains of Cagliari province in Italy. It is no exaggeration to say that this movie is a *document humaine* that, because of its sincerity and grim authenticity, reveals all heroicizing Nazi propaganda as absurd. John Huston depicts the horrors of war from the perspective of the victims. Their boundless suffering is reflected in the faces of innocent women and the angst-filled eyes of children that provide a physiognomical commentary from the ruins of the village of San Pietro, the site of fierce fighting. The extent of the destruction and the number of victims appear in starkest contrast to the strategic significance of this battle. Huston does not shrink from exposing the viewer to closeups of dying soldiers and the most extreme moment of their life, i.e., their violent death. Huston thus breaks the great taboo of the documentary, i.e., to show the dying. The camera underwrites their death certificates. The scene assumes a very human dimension because all this is done without zealous pathos. During a brief pause in the fighting, the dead are put into body bags before they are buried far from their homeland. Highly decorated with the Legion of Merit medal, Huston can claim to have cast doubt on the meaning of war in an American propaganda film.

According to Richard Griffiths, top Pentagon officials then edited the material so that a badly truncated version was ultimately released to the public—pompously advertised as "the big picture" and dedicated "to the American soldiers who fought and died in San Pietro." Not a single shot of the dead and dying in the original was to be seen in this version. Equipped with a new leader, the film capitalizes on its Hollywood maker: sitting under the Mexican sun with a stetson, Huston is interviewed during the shooting of his Western *The Unforgiven* (1960). In other words, fifteen years after the end of the war he contextualizes the documents of the battle of San Pietro. He remembers this period as "a time when life had almost ceased to exist there." He continues laconically: "Most of the soldiers that you will see on the screen are dead, have died in battle. All men who served their colors and humanity." In Huston's memory, they are all heroes who advanced until death or their injuries stopped them. Huston then lifts his stetson and *The Battle of San Pietro* begins.

Although the movie has been severely cut, it nevertheless represents an authentic report of the fighting around the villages of Lungo and San Pietro during the fall of 1943. With Huston's introductory statements in mind, the viewer will note more attentively the closeups of GIs whose faces are marked by death than would have been the case without this macabre preknowledge. The rotation of the camera (held by Jules Buck, among others) resulted in frequently blurred pictures, explained in the text with the words that the soil "never stopped trembling." For a while, the camera closely follows those shock troops whose fate Huston comments on with the sober words: "Not a single member ... ever came back alive." During a fire break, the survivors nail the identification tags of their fallen comrades to a wooden cross: "The lives lost were precious lives to their country, to their loved ones, and to themselves."

The leader of the second documentary that the Pentagon commissioned Huston to make reads like a medical bulletin.[120] As an invisible witness, the camera yields shattering images of six soldiers who had suffered nervous breakdowns with symptoms including loss of speech, loss of memory, partial paralysis, an end-less flow of tears. In this case, this indiscretion as a legitimate filmic means of uncovering truth had a deep ethical impact. Because it unsparingly undertook psychiatric interviews with American invalids of differing IQs who had suffered shell shock at various sections of the front, it was only in 1948 that the film was released under registration No. PMF 5019, to be screened before audiences of clinical experts.

As early as 1933, Eugen Hadamovsky, a *Stabsleiter* in Goebbels's Reich Propaganda Office and director of the *Deutschlandsender*, had defined "sobriety (*Sachlichkeit*) as a danger for weak charac-ters." Later he viewed the care of injured Americans from the atrocity perspective of his office when he denied that the Allies offered their veterans humanitarian support:

> Whereas Soviet invalids simply go to the dogs and invalids in the Western democracies live a miserable life as beggars depending on the charity of the plutocrats, National Socialist Germany, under the leadership of outstanding physicians and psychologists, tries not to condemn to an unsatisfying life as pensioners even those who by general standards are severely wounded, but to give them the opportunity to reintegrate themselves into professional life.[121]

In 1941 Canada started its *World in Action* series, with John Grierson taking charge of production. Among the legions of Allied propaganda films, the series, despite the enormous amounts of material used, excels as a work that combines irony with intelli-gence. Director Stuart Legg avoids all crude attempts to shape viewers' opinions. By providing associative connections between the different parts, he gives the impression of objectivity, thereby augmenting the propaganda value of the series. And yet it is diffi-cult to overlook that this intelligent series, too, is commissioned and primarily operates to a certain matrix.

From 1940 onward France was partially occupied, and the cine-matographic infrastructure, where it had not been smashed by the Germans, was strictly controlled by them. As a result, few impor-tant films, for example, by the Résistance against the Vichy regime and the German occupiers, were made. From his London exile, Charles de Gaulle had made the *Croix de Lorraine* the official flag of his *La France Libre* organization in the spring of 1942. However, de Gaulle proved to be an awkward ally for the British, and the French themselves failed to follow him with the exception of the French colonies in Central Africa and the Pacific. The British, therefore, hesitated to recognize the self-appointed leader of the "true France." It was only at the Casablanca summit of Roosevelt, Churchill, and de Gaulle in January 1943 that *La France Libre* received the Allies' blessing after they had agreed to work for the unconditional surrender of the Axis powers. In May 1943, then, de Gaulle was finally nominated spokesman of *La France Libre* by the groups that had formed the National Résistance Council. Still, the image of a heroic resistance army successfully fighting the fascists was more a reflection of "wishful thinking than of historical reality."[122]

To launch a French film propaganda campaign, de Gaulle lacked resources comparable to those that Roosevelt and Churchill had at their disposal. Consequently, the only two important movies about the French Résistance were produced by Hollywood. In 1942 *Réunion in France* was made under the artistic supervision of Metro-Goldwyn-Mayer (MGM), followed in 1943 by *The Cross of Lorraine*. Based on Hans Habe's 1941 novel *A Thousand Shall Fall*, the latter is a feature film by Tay Garnett, which was partly shot in France. The leader shows the rustling flag of de Gaulle's *La Libre France* with the Lorraine Cross. There are two narrative threads running through this film. The first reflects the divergent moral responses and physical conditions of French prisoners in German labor camps; the second depicts French soldiers who had escaped to France among Résistance fighters near the village of Cadignon as they join General Cartier's army.

Réunion in France by Jules Dassin offers an ambivalent critique of the causes behind France's precipitous capitulation in 1940 and identifies what Andrzej Szczypiorsky called the "moral dilemmas" of the *Grande Nation*. On the one hand, Dassin advances the hypothesis that the generals and industrialists had betrayed France to the Nazis since they were collaborating with them; on the other hand, he praises the activism of the Résistance movement exclusively from a rightist perspective.

Etienne Lallier's French-made documentary *Réseau X* (1944) portrays the "Secret Service" trying to rescue Allied pilots who had been shot down. *Camera sous la Botte* (Camera under the Jackboot, 1944) relates kaleidoscopically the liberation of Paris. Even if these films had possessed a different technical and aesthetic quality, there was no chance to show them to larger French audiences.

However, there are at least two documentaries dating from this period that continue to be historically significant. In 1943 Luis Daquin, Jean Grémillon, Jacques Becker, Pierre Renoir (Jean's brother), and others had founded the *Comité de Libération du Cinéma Française* which included a team of technicians. Operating under a constant threat to their lives, this latter group took pictures of the Paris uprising from its first beginnings on 19 August 1944. The documentary that emerged from this was shown immediately following the withdrawal of the German troops from the occupied territories under the title *La Libération de Paris*.

One of the few prominent directors of France was Jean-Paul Le Chanois who had made a name for himself before the war through his work with the Prévert brothers and with Jean Renoir, and who actively participated in the resistance movement. Operating in the midst of the fighters of Vercors Massif in the French Alps, the center of the French Résistance between 1942 and 1944, he filmed the covert and open guerrilla activities of the *Maquisards* against the German occupation. However, this important document could only be shown in 1946, after the war, under the title *Au Coeur de l'Orage* (In the Eye of the Storm, 1945).

The Genre Is Upvalued by Well-known Names

The person who is being filmed is no more than the raw material for the filmic phenomenon that is put together later on through montage. The individual angle is no more than a single word. "Montage sentences," the individual scenes and episodes and, finally, step-by-step the completed work, the film itself, emerge only from the artistic shaping of this raw material. However, this "step-by-step" should not merely be described; the director must use it as an effective instrument.

Vsevolod I. Pudovkin[123]

Many big names can be found among the authors of compilation films, as well as writers who did not think it beneath them to produce from other material "essayistic" movies, as Hans Richter called the genre in 1940 before the new term came into use. Richter recommended this type of movie to illustrate "intellectual conceptions" and to make visible what "is basically invisible." Here, he argued, it was possible to draw upon an immeasurably larger reservoir of expressive opportunities than was available to the pure documentary. The director was not bound to a reproduction of external phenomena or to a particular chronological sequence. On the contrary, the illustrative material could be drawn from anywhere in order to be left moving freely in time and space.[124]

The following names may suffice as examples of feature film directors who, by making compilation films, moved into foreign terrain: Edwin S. Porter (*The Life of an American Fireman*, 1910), Carl Junghans (*Weltwende*, 1928), Walter Ruttmann (*Die Melodie der Welt*—The Melody of the World, 1929), Luis Buñuel (*Madrid '36*, 1937), Frank Capra and Anatole Litvak (*Why We Fight* series, 1943ff.), John Huston (*The Battle of San Pietro*, 1944), Alexander Dovshenko (*Victory on the Right Bank of the Dnieper*, 1945), Luchino Visconti (*Days of Glory*, 1945), Carol Reed (*The True Glory*, 1945), Sergei Yutkevich (*Liberated France*, 1945), Joris Ivens (*Song of the Streams*, 1954), Alain Resnais (*Night and Fog*, 1955), Erwin Leiser (*Mein Kampf*, 1960), Chris Marker (*Description d'un combat*—Description of a Battle, 1960), Jacques Prévert (*Paris la belle*, 1960), Sayajit Ray (*Rabindranat Tagore*, 1961), Alexander Kluge/Peter Schamoni (*Brutalität in Stein*—Brutality in Stone, 1961), Jerzy Hofman (*Fatherland and Death*, 1961), Frédéric Rossif (*Le Temps du Ghetto*—Ghetto Times, 1961), Paul Rotha (*Das Leben Adolf Hitlers*—The Life of Adolf Hitler, 1961), Jean-Luc Godard (*Les Carabiniers*, 1963), Jerzy Bossak (*Requiem for 500,000*, 1963), Jean Aurel (*La Bataille de France*—The Battle for France, 1964), Lionel Rogosin (*Good Times, Wonderful Times*, 1965), Michail Romm (*Daily Fascism*, 1965), Marcel Ophüls (*The Memory of Justice*, 1975). Well-known photographers and intellectuals like Henri Cartier-Bresson (*Le Retour*, 1946) or Joachim C. Fest (*Hitler—eine Karriere*, 1977) have also tried their hand at this genre.

The Newsreel

The newsreel shall no longer be a more-or-less interesting and randomly compiled hodge-podge of pictures from all over the world; rather it is to be shaped into an artistic whole that is self-contained. Its optic effect shall be cultural and propagandistic education and construction, without the viewer realizing it.... We intend to use, by means of a newsreel that is artistically rounded, the possibility of spreading state-political, ideological propaganda and popular education.

Hans Weidemann, Vice President of the
Reich Film Chamber, July 1935

German Newsreels before World War II

"The meaning of propaganda is the excitement of ecstasy!" Thus spoke Adolf Hitler as quoted in Hans Traub's 1933 booklet *Film als politisches Machtmittel* (Film as a Means of Political Power). And like his models Hitler and Goebbels, Traub warns against the dangerous blending of propaganda, entertainment, and art. Again he quotes Hitler as his master, this time in a conversation in Berlin with the actress Tony van Eyck: "True, on the one hand I want to use film fully as a means of propaganda, but only in such a way that all viewers know: 'Today I'll be seeing a political film.' Just like in the *Sportpalast* where he does not have sports mixed with politics either. I find it revolting if politics is made under the guise of art. It's either art or politics." The purpose behind this restraint is also made very clear: "We have to realize that a basic function of the cinema, i.e., of entertainment, begins to swerve in its foundations, if we deploy in the daily program the open, active propaganda feature film that can make its full impact only when it is shown before closed audiences or in special public screenings. The challenge will be to concentrate on the overall production of films and their successes in individual cinemas if, by judiciously mixing political and general feature films, we want to keep the public enjoying the movies ('*kinofreudig*') and willing to go there ('*kinowillig*')."

As early as 1931 we find in a memorandum issued by the Party's Reich Film Office that one should not lose sight of the production of "covert NS films" as "a very considerable propaganda factor." It was Georg Stark who was responsible for drawing up, in May 1931, principles of Nazi film propaganda that appeared in

Chapter B (Internal Propaganda), with the above quotation to be found under the heading "Covert Films" on page 12.[125]

"Kinofreudig" and *"kinowillig"*—these were the magic words. Hitler, Goebbels, and their aides were very serious about supplying the cinemas with as much "unburdened" entertainment as possible. The feature film that pursued clear propagandistic aims was to remain the exception. The most powerful weapon was the production of a good mood and its constant proliferation.

There can be no question that strict limits were set to the freedom of cultural expression. A doctoral thesis, completed in 1938, formulated this with striking frankness and without the author realizing the cynicism of his words: "It is not in the interests of National Socialist cultural policy to act patronizingly toward cultural and artistic creativity. The state merely [!] demands of every cultural producer, just as of every German, that the National Socialist *Weltanschauung* be the lodestar of all his work."[126]

Kinofreudig and *kinowillig* was what the Germans were expected to be; then they would also be able to enjoy exemplary propaganda. As Traub put it: "The first law of all propaganda reads that people must be kept receptive and capable of enthusiasm." *Kinofreudigkeit* was thus the precondition for Nazi propaganda's favorite tool—the newsreel—and conversely this genre stimulated the cinematic interests of the masses.

To be sure, the rulers of the Third Reich never tired of giving public assurances that the newsreel must not be misused as a means of propaganda; for it was wrong "always to beat the drums.... The public will slowly get used to the sound and then fail to hear it."[127] However, if we analyze the care that was taken with the newsreel in subsequent years, it is easy to recognize that it constituted the Nazis' most important propagandistic means of convincing people.

The aspects of the Nazi newsreel that are to be discussed here, with reference to a few typical examples, demonstrate how easily reality can be falsified with the help of sequences that are, as such, authentic. However, as is well-known, this statement does not just apply to Nazi newsreels. Thus a study, commissioned by UNESCO, about newsreels from all over the world came to the conclusion that the viewer "has to concentrate so much on the fast sequence of pictures that any response that goes beyond simple reception is forced into the subconscious. Even if the viewer is critically disposed, he has no opportunity to check or compare the information that is offered to him."

This is precisely what Goebbels and his accomplices in the Propaganda Ministry knew so well, Dr. Fritz Hippler being one of them. He wrote in 1942: "In comparison with the other arts, film, from a mass psychological and propagandistic viewpoint, has a particularly deep and lasting impact because of its property to affect the visual and emotional, i.e., the nonintellectual."[128]

The following brief summary is designed to show that National Socialism remained a "propaganda movement" even after the seizure of power in 1933. When Goebbels took over the newly founded Ministry for Popular Enlightenment and Propaganda on 13 March 1933, he assumed supervisory powers not only over the press, radio, and theater, but also over film. The Ministry's film department was characterized by some remarkable continuities. Thus, Dr. Seeger, who had been a lawyer with Bufa in World War I until 1917 before serving as director of the Film Censorship Office, was appointed as its director. After World War I, Seeger had acted as director of the *Film-Oberpüfstelle* in the Reich Ministry of the Interior which also had censorship tasks. Goebbels similarly used experienced people in the newly established division for "Film Technology and Film Reporting." It was led by Eberhard Fangauf who had joined the Party in 1931. During World War I, he had been a war correspondent and later had been involved with the production of documentaries at Ufa. Some 92 percent of the personnel in Goebbels's Ministry were longtime party members. As he once remarked: "For me, a National Socialist is only that person who has come to us *before* 30 January [1933]. There are over 300 members in my Ministry whose membership numbers [in the NSDAP] are below 100,000."[129]

Fangauf had well understood the signs of the new times. He quickly built up an efficient and fast coverage of events so that in film and photos tribute could be paid to the new masters and the pompous ways in which they presented themselves. These "film reporters," who were given green armbands, IDs, and all sorts of special passes, received support from many offices. Thus, the chief newsreel cameramen participated in the dress rehearsals for mammoth rallies and other events. Their working conditions were ideal. The wishes of the cameramen were taken into account as far as possible so that the "intellectual content" of Nazi speeches and the parades that advertised the movement so effectively could be turned into impressive pictures.

As early as 10 February 1933 Goebbels had exclaimed enthusiastically when he gave a radio report on Hitler's first appearance as Reich Chancellor: "At the foot of the podium stands an army of photographers, an army of film technicians. The entire speech is to be put on sound film to be used propagandistically during the next few weeks."

As soon became clear, the *Gleichschaltung* (totalitarian integration) of film occurred with terrifying speed and thoroughness. *Licht-Bild-Bühne* had this to say about the work of the newsreel men on 1 May 1933, the day that the Nazis had meanwhile converted from the traditional Labor Day to a "Day of National Labor": "The newsreel coworkers have the great task to put the celebrations of this day on sound film and to preserve them for later periods and subsequent generations [as well as] to make them visible in the five thousand movie theaters of Germany for all those who were unable to participate."

And week after week, propaganda was disseminated with newsreel in these five thousand theaters. As Hippler, since 1939 the director of the film department in the Goebbels Ministry, admitted after the war, this was not a matter of "objective reporting, of balanced neutrality, but ... of [providing] optimistic propaganda that spread confidence in victory and was designed to strengthen the spiritual fighting potential of the German people. Commentator and language, texts and music had to conform to this objective."[130]

Before 1945 Nazi propagandists like Hippler expounded very different claims. Thus, Hans-Joachim Giese, author of the book *Die Film-Wochenschau im Dienste der Politik*, published in 1940, turned the matter on its head when he asserted that the hostile Entente powers had developed their newsreels into "an extremely effective instrument" of propaganda, whereas "the German newsreels were to convince through truthful pictures."[131] Giese went on: "Very many things can accidentally give a tendentious coloring to pictures on the long path that film has to traverse from the moment the camera begins to shoot to the screening in the movie theater. Newsreel will therefore never be a mirror of an event that conforms to reality to the last detail." Giese then inadvertently lapsed into a self-accusatory mode: "This is why newsreel can be called a 'document' only in a conditional sense."

Indeed, already in the infancy of the newsreel, events that the camera had failed to capture were later staged for the benefit of the moviegoer. A telling example of this is provided by the genial Georges Méliès when in 1902 he produced a credible studio version in Montreuil of the coronation of king Edward VII. With the help of ships' models in his bathtub, Edward H. Amet restaged the destruction of the Spanish fleet by the Americans in 1898.[132] A few years later, Pathé similarly remade the battle between the Russian and the Japanese fleet outside Port Arthur on 10 August 1904 by setting it up with models on a small pond.[133]

The thematic structure of the Nazi newsreel corresponded to its gung-ho tendency. Let us take a production phase that can be surveyed relatively easily. During the period from 1 June 1935 to 31 May 1936, Ufa newsreels showed on average per reel some 180 feet of parades, 180 feet of speakers, 100 feet of armed forces, 90 feet of fighting in the Italo-Ethiopian War, 90 feet of other political events. Hardly a single precious foot of film was squandered with unpolitical topics.[134]

As late as two years prior to Hitler's seizure of power, Siegfried Kracauer bemoaned the opposite trend in Weimar newsreels. Newsreel, he said, avoided political and social implications and instead wasted its time with natural catastrophies, acrobatics, pictures of happy children and zoo animals:

> By retreating, time and again, to the portrayal of untamed nature, their viewers gain the impression that social events are as inexorable as some flood calamity. He who has natural catastrophies constantly served up to him, will inevitably transpose its causalities to human affairs and will willy-nilly confuse the crisis of the capitalist system with an earthquake.[135]

Nazi newsreel is even better at distracting the viewer from reality by mythologizing the Nazi *Volksgemeinschaft* as a social ideal and by producing indistinction instead of insight when it shows the regimented masses with their flags. Instead of picturing man in his individuality, Goebbels's newsreel presents him as the formulaic part of a larger composition. His life becomes a phantomlike presence in the milling crowd.

For comparison purposes, the statistics of *Deulig-Ton-Woche* may be of interest here that cover the period from 30 January to 11 March 1933, i.e., the weeks before the establishment of Goebbels's Propaganda Ministry—relevant information from around the world: 41.8 percent; sport: 17.6 percent; customs and fashion: 13.2 percent; military affairs: 13.2 percent; economic questions: 4.4 percent; entertainment: 2.2 percent; and a meager 8.8 percent for reporting of current political events. In this connection, Hugenberg used his company mainly to highlight the "National Revolution of 30 January" which he portrayed as a fruit particularly of the policies of his party, the DNVP, and of policies marked by a Prussian spirit, while playing down the Nazi share.[136]

Having lost his cabinet post in June 1933, Hugenberg's dismissal by Hitler was probably accelerated by the fact that Hugenberg's Deulig Newsreel No. 76 of 14 June 1933 highlighted excerpts from a speech by Vice-Chancellor Franz von Papen, Hitler's cabinet rival, and incurred the wrath of Hitler and Goebbels. Here are the words that Deulig reported from Papen's speech at Naumburg on Saale on the occasion of the leadership meeting of the Langemarck League, the student wing of the *Stahlhelm* veterans association:

> The word about the revolution of our time is on everyone's lips. A nation, that experiences itself anew; that becomes newly conscious of its past, its values, its power and its hopes. We would fail to do justice to the heritage of Langemarck [one of the mythical battle sites of World War I—Transl.] if we were only to uphold the tradition of this patriotism. Of course, the object of this love, this Germany, is dear and sacred to us. But the moral greatness that we encounter in this commemoration of the Langemarck sacrifice should be just as sacred to us.

It was with such words that the German Nationalists around Hugenberg tried to transfigure the misguided idealism of the Langemarck League.

Hugenberg's *Deulig-Ton-Woche* thus strictly avoided showing a single clip of Hitler between the middle of May and the middle of July 1933 when the Reich Film Chamber disenfranchised it. Nor were any of the Führer's words reproduced. Instead, the newsreel showed Hugenberg or Hugenberg together with Papen, who had been Reich chancellor for six months in June 1932.[137]

In 1934, then, Goebbels issued an executive order via the Reich Film Chamber that all cameramen working in the Reich had to be a member of this institution if they wanted to receive a labor permit. This brought the cameramen into line.

The rest of this section will analyze five *Deulig-Ton-Wochen* and compare them with later Nazi newsreels in order to throw light on the first months after 30 January 1933 when the German electorate had the choice between two reactionary ideologies. Deulig, incidentally, was the first newsreel company that moved from silent to sound film in January 1932, one year prior to the Nazi seizure of power. It was a system that was one of the best in the world at the time.

Deulig-Ton-Woche No. 57 (passed by censor on 1 February 1933):
This newsreel covering the period from the end of January to the
beginning of February is not yet dominated by Nazi propaganda.
In contrast to later reports that were *gleichgeschaltet,* there is a cos-
mopolitan variety of themes whose information value is, as was
usual, small: a ship is being demolished in a dock—islands along
the North Sea coast are being supplied with the help of a Ju-52 airplane—a Japanese rent-a-crowd bids farewell to soldiers going off
to the Manchurian front—horse races in the second-largest city of
India, Calcutta, before local high society—skiers doing *salti mortali*
in the Bavarian resort of Garmisch—international riding competition in Berlin with dresses from the time of Frederick the Great
and review to the tune of the Hohenfriedberger March.

The transition to a scene that was to assume great historical significance is then surprisingly casual: "The Reich President
appoints the [Hitler] Cabinet of National Concentration." The corresponding pictures are as innocuous as these words: Relaxed and
dressed in civilian clothes Messrs. Hitler, Hugenberg, Göring,
Frick, Papen, Krosigk et al. pose, like the presidium of a private
club, for a group photo, with a newspaper headline fade-in
announcing the "new Hitler-Papen-Hugenberg Cabinet." The
occasion apparently silenced the commentator. Nor was Hitler
given an opportunity to say something, like Papen had done in
Deulig-Ton-Woche No. 23 of 9 June 1932 when he had been nominated Reich Chancellor. The film treats as self-evident that Hugenberg and Papen hold leading positions in the Hitler government.
Nor does the newsreel make much of the thousands of Storm
Troopers and SS men who formed an endless torch parade
through Berlin when Hitler's seizure of power became known.
This historic torch parade that was used in many later documentaries is accompanied by a "balanced" commentary that is
unlikely to have pleased Goebbels: "After the news became
known, members of the *Stahlhelm* [veterans association] as well as
SA and SS formations gathered for an enormous torch parade that
lasted for hours." Prussian marching music and the national
anthem, but no Nazi songs, accompany the demonstrators on this
winter evening. Peter Bucher has noted that the inscription "*Der
Stahhelm*" on one of the flags that had been filmed in more favor-
able daylight was probably edited into the newsreel after the
event.[138] The answer to the question of what Goebbels's propagandists might have done with this event may be found in Riefenstahl's *Sieg des Glaubens* (Victory of Faith, 1933). In this model of a

Hitler cult film, she developed a new pictorial language that was aesthetically daring.

Deulig-Ton-Woche No. 63 (passed by censor on 15 March 1933): This newsreel begins with a report on Franklin D. Roosevelt and his assumption of office on 4 March 1933. With Deulig at this point still firmly in Hugenberg's hands, this issue is then devoted to the imposing rallies of nationalist associations and organizations of Hugenberg's DNVP in Berlin and Munich that met to cultivate the past in cult-like fashion. As late as six weeks after Hitler's assumption of power, this newsreel continues to give much space to heroic reminiscences in connection with right-wing rallies on Memorial Day in Berlin and with celebrations of the Fallen Soldier (*Heldengedenkfeier*) on Wartburg Castle at which the DNVP's leadership intones a hymn to the flag: "Ascend to the top of Germany's Wartburg Castle, you noble colors of the Bismarckian Empire, you glowing flag in Black-White-Red, sacred to every German heart through the millions of heroic sacrifices that have been made in your name! And you ascend, too, banner that has been chosen as its flag of conquest by a powerful nationalist movement that is determined to fight! Be [our] witness before the entire world that the German nation has awakened and that it is setting out, loyally following the call of its dead, to fight for life, freedom, and honor!"

Deulig-Ton-Woche No. 62 (passed by censor on 8 March 1933): This newsreel similarly moves in the wake of the German Nationalists and gives more sympathetic coverage to the mass parades of the *Stahlhelm* than to those of the Nazis: "In the days prior to the [Reichstag] elections, SA and SS formations held numerous propaganda marches. On the afternoon of election Sunday [5 March], 26,000 Stahlhelmers marched through the Brandenburg Gate, surrounded by popular jubilation." Looking at these columns, Heinrich Mann, the leftist author and brother of Thomas, demanded: "The time has come for real human beings to become visible behind and beside all these parades. The actual labor, the real deprivation, attitudes toward life, and the direction of popular moods that prevail in reality—all this ought to be expressed in pictures. It is not just in newsreels that this is called for...."[139] However, the newsreels did not take heed of the truth.

Meanwhile, *Emelka-Tonwoche No. 14* of 14 April 1933 devoted seven and a half minutes to the "Day of Potsdam" when Hindenburg and Hitler appeared with many other right-wing dignitaries for a memorial service in the town just outside Berlin which symbolized the old monarchical Germany. But most of this newsreel is devoted to entertainment, the more so since the producers could not resist including, in two places, the usual nonsense reserved for April Fools Day. And yet authenticity is not taken literally. There is a sentimental scene showing deer in the park of Nymphenburg Palace being fed in deep snow. In the meantime, it had been thawing for a month, and the pictures had thus been deprived of their asserted topicality.[140]

The Potsdam report remains silent about an important "omission" in the story, not only by its one-sided selection of pictures, but also by its failure to comment on important facts. Thus, it neglects to mention that Hitler had originally refused to attend the service. Nor is reference made to the absence of the Social Democratic Reichstag deputies, who—in the words of one SPD deputy—did not wish to be the physicians at the bedside of hospitalized capitalism. If we count the number of pictures of Hindenburg in comparison with Hitler, we may also gauge how little this newsreel had been poisoned by Goebbels's propaganda and exuded a conservative spirit instead: Hindenburg appears twenty times as against Hitler's ten. Moreover, Hitler is shown in various marginal situations. The legendary shot of the symbolic handshake between Hindenburg and Hitler was celebrated in papers and broadcasts at the time as sealing the alliance between the old Prussiandom and the young Nazi Movement.

Deulig-Ton-Woche No. 66 (passed by censor on 5 April 1933): Though Deulig was still privately owned at this point, this newsreel had clearly begun to take sides after the Ministry for Popular Enlightenment and Propaganda was established on 11 March 1933, and chicaneries were to be expected. There is a brief review of Pope Pius XI at the opening of the "Holy Year" of 1933, next to reports on an earthquake in far-away Japan and on the boat race between Oxford and Cambridge. The newsreel homes in rather casually on the new rulers of Germany: "Daughters of the Spreewald region [near Berlin] pay their respects to the Führer," the text announces. The boycott of Jewish shops is highlighted from a Nazi perspective. Posters scream the slogan "Germans defend yourselves! Do not buy from Jews!" and the commentator adds: "Despite the boycott, law and order in Berlin." The fade-over shows orthodox Jews in the United States to suggest the "progress" that the Nazis have introduced in this respect in Germany.

A longer sequence is devoted to the DNVP. Together with other national associations and delegations of the right-wing National Union of Student Governments, its members are seen standing at the foot of the Bismarck Monument in the Müggel Mountains near Berlin, demanding "Back to Bismarck." In his speech at this joint patriotic celebration, Goebbels extols the rally as a "miraculous sign of national revival."

Hugenberg's *Ton-Woche* is likely to have irritated its sympathizers for the first time when it reproduced the blaring sounds of the Nazi song *"Die Straße frei den braunen Bataillonen"* (Clear the Streets for the Brown Battalions). From the mid-1930s, stylistic elements taken from the American newsmagazine *The March of Time* temporarily exerted an influence on German newsreel production.

Deulig-Ton-Woche No. 279 (passed by censor on 4 May 1937): The Führer is introduced to fifty of the "best youth workers of Germany." Trivia are offered between this introductory sequence and further adorations of the Nazi leadership: a pedigree dog show in Munich; record pole vaulting in Los Angeles; a steeplechase in Wimbledon.

Referring to the 1936 Four-Year Plan, the commentator proudly reports that such a plan had first been presented "shortly after the seizure of power." Goebbels had his speech marking the occasion enriched with closeups to provide visual support for what is being proclaimed as "a show of German efficiency." Robert Ley's "Strength through Joy" organization is presented during the 1 May festivities. Cheerful spectators are shown in an overcrowded stadium. Reich Youth Leader Baldur von Schirach reports to his Führer the opening of "the largest youth rally in the world." Emil Jannings receives an award from Goebbels for his title role in the film *Der Herrscher* (The Ruler). Friedrich Bethge is given a book prize.

When Hitler, in addressing the German youth, discovers *"joi de vivre* in their faces," the camera provides reinforcement by showing blue-eyed faces. His charisma is supported by visual effects. Hitler's enlarged figure is skillfully faded over smiling youngsters. Apart from a nebulous irrationalism and references to the "resurrection of the German people" the Führer's speech does not offer anything special. Nevertheless, his words are synchronized with the response of the masses, whose broad consent stems more from grandiose emotions than from intellectual insight. The ponderous concluding metaphor is provided by the May Tree, a birch that is taken from a tilted angle.

Meanwhile, Ufa's *Wochenschau* was calling the tune. Being the instrument of the Party and the mouthpiece of partisanship, it showed reality only with the intention of interpreting the facts and of proclaiming Nazi ideology. Objective meaning was wrapped in propagandistic commentary. Thus, Hans-Joachim Giese demanded that the newsreel be given a strictly partisan role as a carrier of ideology:

> During the years of struggle [prior to 1933] the NSDAP was able to use film only in a limited way. Now after the seizure of power, however, it consciously moved to put it in the service of one single great idea, the idea of the people's state, and to imprint upon it the characteristics of its *Weltanschauung*. In clear recognition of its suitability as a means of political leadership, it was above all the newsreel that was now geared to its actual journalistic task. The noncommittal pictorial news of the previous years was replaced by film reporting that was guided, in the first place, by state-political, cultural-political and popular-pedagogical considerations. This approach provides valuable educational reconstruction work without the individual viewer becoming conscious of it. Following the spiritual renovation of film, the German newsreel has to some extent already succeeded in exemplary fashion to communicate and deepen the insight among all strata and circles of the population within and outside the borders of the Reich just how vital and concerned with the preservation of the state (*staatserhaltend*) are the measures that the leadership has taken, and just how many fruits they can bear for the present and the future.[141]

In order to give events as much authenticity as possible, the newsreel confined itself to a strictly realistic reproduction. However incredible it may sound, the Nazi newsreel, its role as the primary media instrument notwithstanding, hardly ever staged an event; instead virtually all pictures were taken from reality.

It was only during the second stage that reality came to be manipulated. Thus, all elements of reality that were detrimental to the needs of the hour were deleted without further ado. The rest that was useful to the line of argument was given a suggestive commentary. It provided the intended propagandistic effect in order "to empower and to educate a nation to promote its vital claims," as Goebbels put it.

The remilitarization of the Rhineland by German troops on 27 March 1936 offers an example of how propaganda could be presented very effectively and in general staff fashion. This event was turned into a perfect show. According to eyewitness reports, journalists and photographers were asked to come to the Propaganda Ministry on the previous day. There they were kept waiting for hours until they were taken by bus to the airport and flown to

Cologne—all without a word of explanation. The cameramen who were also taken to Cologne with their equipment had a similar experience. It was only in Cologne that they were told that German troops were on the march. This method was extremely successful: the event could be fully captured on film and then transformed into an impressive journalistic feat.

The same year saw the establishment of a "War Correspondent and Propaganda Unit." The decision unleashed a bitter feud between Wehrmacht and Propaganda Ministry over who was in charge and who would assume supreme command over the system of war reporting in times of war.

Goebbels won an ephemeral victory on this point. When at maneuver time "total chaos" broke loose among the civilian reporters, the Wehrmacht had sufficiently strong arguments on its side to take charge of "war reporting." On 3 May 1938, the Reich War Ministry in its "Guidelines for the Cooperation between the Armed Forces and the Reich Ministry for Popular Enlightenment and Propaganda in Respect of War Propaganda" firmly insisted that a military way of reporting be instituted through propaganda companies.

Even before this date, newsreel reporters were mandated to wear uniforms. Apparently, the black shirts of the Italian reporters during Mussolini's visit in 1937 had left a deep impression. Long before Hitler, Mussolini had called propaganda "the best weapon in the struggle for interests." However, the Propaganda Ministry failed to convince the Wehrmacht that German war reporters wear brown shirts or even SA uniforms. It was finally agreed to introduce a "pike-blue" uniform—so to speak, a "neutral" color. It was this uniform that is said to have made a big impression on the Italian population when Hitler visited Rome in the spring of 1938.

Ufa-Tonwoche No. 355 of 23 June 1937 is a telling example of how clumsily Goebbels's newsreels tried to produce in the mind of "the viewer connections between ideas by the montage of topics." Johannes Eckardt, writing enthusiastically in 1938 in *Der deutsche Film*, had this to say:

> If the newsreel puts images of the German Labor Service right next to gripping scenes from the Spanish Civil War, then almost every viewer will connect in his mind the two picture complexes, which as such have nothing to do with one another. However, in this way the reproduction becomes a symbol. It grows beyond its technical preconditions and completion and comes to be shaped in the realm of ideas—a realm in which we can actually speak of artistic creation.[142]

In October 1938 another milestone in the triumphant rise of the Nazi newsreel had been reached: Goebbels issued a decree mandating movie theaters to show his newsreels. He also stopped older newsreels from being available at a reduced price. This meant that all cinemas now screened the most up-to-date news.

In August/September 1938 a first training course was held to educate officers about the tasks of propaganda in case of war. Promotion of the willingness to serve (*Wehrfreudigkeit*), preservation of the will to fight (*Wehrwilligkeit*), raising the preparedness to make sacrifices (*Opferbereitschaft*), preservation of law and order among the indigenous population, and military camouflage—these were just some of the objectives that one hoped to achieve with the help of war reporting.

Increasingly, Germany's preparations for war were reflected in the creation of an effective contingent of war reporters. Numerous propaganda companies were built up in the summer and fall of 1938. In the winter of 1938/39 General Wilhelm Keitel, the chief of the Armed Forces High Command (OKW), and Joseph Goebbels signed an "Agreement Concerning the Execution of Propaganda in Wartime." The first sentence of this document pinpointed the importance that propaganda was given within the overall conception of Nazi warfare: "In its essential points the propaganda war will be recognized as a means of warfare that has equal status next to the military war." Up to the summer of 1939, the navy and air force also had propaganda companies attached to them. Both the War Ministry and the Propaganda Ministry were prepared for the coming conflict.

Ultimately, Goebbels agreed to a compromise by which all questions that "jointly concern politics and the conduct of war and that might have an influence on strategy (*Gestaltung der Kriegsführung*)" would be resolved in cooperation with the OKW.

Ufa-Tonwoche No. 439/1939 (passed by censor on 1 February 1939): The introductory sequence celebrates Franco's occupation of Barcelona. "Women and old men are the victims of the Bolshevik reign of terror" and are said to be "fleeing toward France." As an eyewitness reported during a symposium at Bar Ilan University in Israel in 1986, these victims were, in effect, fleeing the fascists. Pictures of air raid exercises in Paris are supposed to legitimate blackout exercises in Germany—seven months before the outbreak of war. There follow police athletics in the Berlin *Sportpalast* with a paramilitary program: Himmler admires daring *saltoes* across police horses, etc. Finally, the cameraman who is assigned to the

Olympic ski jump in Garmisch-Partenkirchen evidently recognizes only winners from Germany or the Scandinavian countries.

Some 60 percent of newsreel No. 439/1939 is devoted to the sixth anniversary of Hitler's seizure of power. Many swastika flags decorate the Reichstag building for the occasion. Hitler's infamous speech against the Jews serves as a signal for a broader anti-Semitic campaign: "If international finance Jewry succeeds ... this will be the end of Jewry" as a whole. Compliantly, Göring, in his capacity as Reichstag President, reinforces Hitler's apocalyptic words. From the midst of an endless torch parade, the swastika at the center of a large flag is faded in until it fills the whole frame. This euphoric scene is designed to be experienced in the cinema as if the viewer had been present at the meeting. The noise level from the crowds that cheer Hitler and Göring reaches hurricane force. What this newsreel has in common with so many other Nazi *Wochenschauen* is above all the logic of disjointedness. The synthesis of its parts is purely technical. The weakness of its dramaturgical scaffolding is papered over by the predominance of the commentary.

Hitler's Fiftieth Birthday in Berlin

> *The essence of propaganda consists in the concept of winning men over to an idea, an idea that is so gripping and so vivid that in the end they fall prey to it and find it impossible to emancipate themselves from it.*

> Joseph Goebbels

Ufa-Tonwoche No. 451/1939 (passed by censor on 25 April 1939): The above quotation from Goebbels seems to have been the guiding principle for the producers of this particular newsreel, with its emotional dramaturgy celebrating Hitler's fiftieth birthday around the world. Conceptually, the film has three main constituencies in mind: the Party faithful to gain self-assurance; the still wavering German population so that it would fall prey to the "great idea;" and finally foreign governments that were to be impressed by the display of military power. Whatever Hitler's and Goebbels's speeches and whatever the words of these political frauds that exuded barbarism were unable to transmit was provided by this film. It was a concentrate of the new mentality whose prejudicial power was carried into the population more impressively than by all other media taken together. This was supposed to be the "rise of the people's will" through the selective portrayal of a jubilant population. Newsreel No. 451 is a masterful directory for this kind of propaganda.

With two hundred copies distributed on 25 April 1939, No. 451 was shown at 40 percent of all German cinemas up to the middle of June. This means that some forty million people became participants in Hitler's cinematographic birthday party, i.e., more than half of the German population of seventy million. That the rather linear dramaturgy did not miss a single important phase in the festivities was due to the rare fact that the script had been meticulously prepared and had been synchronized, with great logistical precision, with the tightly organized birthday schedule. The camera crews used up about seven miles of film of which a mere 1,500 feet were ultimately deemed suitable for inclusion in the final version.[143] Since it had become more and more difficult to deploy Hitler as the magnet of popular sympathies, the newsreel did not contain a single closeup of him. Only photogenic material was selected for mass propaganda purposes. In order not to undermine the image of a genius and hypnotic figure that had been so painstakingly built up over the years, Hitler was shown without imperious gesturing and uncontrolled facial expressions. Indeed, on his great day he did not utter a single word in front of the camera.

The prelude to the pompous show starts on the eve of Hitler's birthday. To the sounds of festive music by Wagner, Berlin's *Siegessäule* (Victory Column) is captured on film. There then follows a long glance at the avenue that runs from west to east through the Zoological Garden, which comes to form the central axis of the newsreel. This provides a foretaste of the great parade that has been planned as a major historic event. For a few seconds, the tyranny behind the façade shows its true face. Portentously, the camera shows the turning of the calendar page from 19 to 20 April 1939.

The bright sun celebrates Hitler's birthday; it is "Führer weather." The band of *Leibstandarte Adolf Hitler*, his bodyguard contingent, has the honor of opening the event. Next to various Nazi bigwigs, only Josef Tiso and Emil Hácha, respectively the Slovak puppet minister president and puppet president of the Reich Protectorate of Bohemia and Moravia conquered by Hitler during March, can be seen among the prominent foreign guests. Goebbels's children, all dressed in angel white, remain near Hitler reflecting decorative innocence so that some of their affection may fall on the Führer. The convoy of Mercedes cars begins to move through the enthusiastic crowds of the Reich capital. The words and sounds of the newsreel remain restrained. The commentary leaves it to the music to provide the sense of elation. The parade begins after Hitler has assumed the appropriate position under the canopy on the platform. The "largest parade of the Third Reich" takes four and a half hours. There are many aerial photos of the parade grounds and of the iconographic expressions of military power that look like toys from above. All services goose-step past Hitler. Hitler's physical stamina is shown as he salutes the troops with his arm either stretched out or half raised. Foreign military attachés and the diplomatic corps witness this demonstration of power, "astonished" or dumbfounded. Hitler had given his Foreign Minister Joachim von Ribbentrop the following mandate: "I ask you to invite a number of foreign guests to my fiftieth birthday, among them as many cowardly civilians and democrats as possible before whom I shall parade the most modern of all armed forces [in the world]."[144]

Time and again faces are shown from among the crowd that look as if they have abandoned themselves to this historic moment, a technique clearly designed to purvey affective enthusiasm. The camera's angle of vision is not that of the participants; it is the perspective from above. The static pictures are edited to give the impression of dynamic movement. Repetitions hardly make the montage more tolerable. The finale culminates in the inevitable ritual when the flags are lowered as the national anthem is intoned: "*Deutschland, Deutschland über alles in der Welt* ..." At this point content is dictating form.

The newsreel contains the following texts: "Preparations for the Führer's fiftieth birthday/Thanks and congratulations of the entire nation belong to the creator of the Greater German Reich/Presents are being delivered to the Reich chancellery all the time from all regions of the Reich and from all strata of the population/Guests arrive in Berlin from all over the world/On the eve of the birthday, Albert Speer, the Inspector General for the Reconstruction of the Reich Capital, opens the East-West Avenue with the Führer/The remodeled Victory Column sends a welcome from the middle of the *grosser Stern* rotary/On the morning of the birthday, the serenade by the *Leibstandarte* opens the *défilé* of the well-wishers/The Slovak minister president Dr. Josef Tiso, the president of the Reich Protectorate Bohemia and Moravia, Emil Hâcha, and Reich Protector Freiherr von Neurath (Neurath gets into the black limousine *before* foreign guest Hâcha)/Troops assemble for the march-past/The largest military parade of the

Third Reich begins/For four and a half hours formations from all the services march past their supreme commander/Paratroopers/A motorized infantry division/A tank contingent on trailers/"*Fahnenbataillon—Halt!*" There is no expectation that the moviegoers make their own differentiating, intellectual contribution to the consumption of this film.

Since the cameras are omnipresent, commentary becomes dispensable. Words would unnecessarily exert pressure on the efficiency of the optical language. It is only by aesthetic means that the event is raised to a festive level; the commentary has been reduced to providing sparse information. The quality of the Nazi idea is not to be expressed through verbal messages, but through its carriers—as a filmic message. The newsreel about Hitler's birthday, therefore, represents a demonstration of how film came to be instrumentalized by Nazi propaganda to create a reality of its own in the public consciousness.

Under the heading "*Parade als Paradestück*" ("Model Parade"), G. Santé published an instructive report on how the twelve cameramen who had been sent out to document the events of 20 April 1939 went about their work. Apart from describing the planning of the program in general staff fashion and its capture on film, his piece also offers a reliable impression of the mood, cast in the language of the period. Take, for example, how cameraman No. 2 followed his instructions:

> Move along the troop lineup. Capturing of the entire imposing parade lineup. These shots were among the best. The cameraman searched for and found new angles not by focusing his camera directly on the Führer, but by constantly leaving rows of soldiers between himself and the Führer's car. He thus obtained a complete panorama that looked both purposeful and sensible. We may therefore begin to mention at this point what, as the objective, pervaded the entire creation of the newsreel: [it was to be] a picture that in equal measure satisfied and gripped eyes and emotions.

The shooting of the parade alone used up some thirty thousand feet of film, and the cameramen left nothing untried that "could contribute to the augmentation of the impact": "The event contained a sufficient dynamism within itself; and still the attempt was made to reinforce it by using different focal distances. The cameras moved from the panorama to the closeup. From normal distance to reflect natural size they zoomed in on a contingent of soldiers and sometimes literally almost moved into their midst."[145]

Gerd Albrecht has quantified the various elements of the news-reel and has calculated that 64 percent of the newsreel's running time is devoted to depicting the program's military aspects. The treatment of the official ceremonies and activities that involve the crowds make up 36 percent. Some 81 percent of the film's total angles deal with military sequences; meanwhile, some 75 percent of the nonmilitary sequences represent closeups and blowups. What is of interest in an analysis of Nazi propaganda films in general is to see how far they were made up of symbols that were intended to impress.

In the first part, some thirty-five to fifty angles convey the symbols of this celebration. Among these are some twenty-eight angles of the Third Reich (flags, standards, swastikas, and Führer photos) and some seven angles with historic symbols (Brandenburg Gate, Victory Column) that cannot be deciphered by the fleeting glimpse of the moviegoers. They absorb everything as creations for the higher glory of the Führer. In the second part, we encounter the armed forces relatively seldom, four times altogether. By contrast, the SS is presented in twenty-eight angles and is clearly meant to reflect power. The population appears twenty-three times, in half of the cases as an unspecified crowd. What is striking in this part is that Hitler's car is shown in connection with the Wehrmacht on nineteen occasions, but only nine times in the context of the spectators. With reference to the fourth part, Albrecht reminds us that although cameras had been put up at all important points so that it was unnecessary to use a telephoto lens, such a lens is nevertheless deployed whenever the mass of parading soldiers was to be "compressed" in order thus to weld them into "a barely dissoluble unit." Albrecht counted no more than seven angles in the epilogue that return to the same places as in the second part. Here we should note the quick shifts in perspective that are achieved by the tilt of the camera.

Apart from Hitler, it is the flag that figures as a myth in this newsreel. When Hitler assumes his seat, the Führer standard is solemnly hoisted. A specially constituted flag battalion keeps swinging its enormous number of flags in waves all across the avenue, until it finally lowers the consecrated cloths respectfully and to the tune of the national anthem before the Führer. In a final and striking sequence, the flag ritual disappears behind a fade-over showing boys and girls of the youth organizations who look up to something without the object of their pious gaze being immediately evident. Only the next angle shows that it is none other than Adolf Hitler. He stands high above them on a balcony. It was with this metaphor that the film symbolizes the byzantine power relations that obtained in the Third Reich.

Newsreel No. 451 aims to be a hymn to Hitler's greatness, but it was also supposed to be an oratorio, created on the occasion of his fiftieth birthday, to the idea and reality of the Greater German Reich and to the unity of the new nation. The end product faithfully illustrates the advice that Ludwig Heyde gave in his booklet *Film im Dienste der Führung* (Film in the Service of the Leadership), published in Dresden in 1943: "The newsreel in particular is the proper place of propaganda work in order to elucidate the world of the Führer for all *Volksgenossen* and to make tangible his essence as the embodiment of the all-German existence"—as a fermenting mix of emotions.

The German Newsreel During World War II

Whether or not 10,000 Russian women collapse from exhaustion while building an anti-tank ditch is of interest to me only in the sense that the ditch will be completed for Germany.... If someone comes along and says: "I cannot build the ditch with children or those women; that's inhuman for it will kill them"—my reply is: "You are a murderer of your own kith and kin; for if the anti-tank ditch is not built, German soldiers are going to die and they are sons of German mothers. That's our blood."

From a speech by Heinrich Himmler at
an SS-Gruppenführer meeting
in Posen on 4 October 1943

The "great era" of the German newsreel started with the beginning of the war. Up to the outbreak of war there had still been four different companies: *Ufa-Tonwoche, Deulig-Ton-Woche, Tobis,* and 20th Century Fox. This soon changed. For a few months, a coordinated newsreel was shown with different credits; but from 21 November 1940 *Deutsche Wochenschau* became the only one that was being produced. Now it paid off that the public had been kept *kinofreudig*, as Goebbels had hoped when he administered film propaganda merely in cautious doses.

The Nazi propaganda machine operated as planned from the first day of the war. The techniques that had been tested during the march into the Rhineland in 1936 were now perfected as war enthusiasm became almost boundless. The German troops that invaded Poland on 1 September 1939 were accompanied by half a dozen propaganda companies. They gave the public a gripping image of the "lightning victories" on the Polish battlefields that were "true to reality."

When on 1 February 1939 Hippler was made director of the "German Newsreel Center within the Ministry for Popular Enlightenment and Propaganda," he also seized hold of *Deutsche Wochenschau* as a propaganda instrument. This Center was in charge of "the political and overall dramaturgical shape of the newsreels" and, in conjunction with the newsreel directors, decided on individual commissions.[146]

Hans-Joachim Giese, the Nazi analyst of the German newsreel in his book *Die Film-Wochenschau im Dienste der Politik*, formulated in timely fashion for the beginning of the war the axiom that "the newsreel was particularly suited for the political-spiritual direction and influencing of the public," even if Nazi propaganda had been tacitly guided by this axiom ever since 1933. Goebbels similarly had made a demand from the start that he imposed only later, on 15 February 1941, during the third war year: "Film has to fulfill a state-political function today. It is a means of educating the people. This means must be in the hands of the political leadership, and it is irrelevant whether this is done openly or covertly."

The Nazi newsreel gave an impression of facticity that was unaccountable. It mesmerized viewers and led them to believe that the film was taken directly at the front line and under life-threatening conditions. Accordingly, Kurt Hubert, the director of Tobis, confirmed in the fall of 1940 that the cameramen were soldiers who fully lived up to their soldierly duties. They operated from the most advanced positions, which, he added, "explains the realism that we show in our films." Heinrich Roellenbleg, the wartime director of *Deutsche Wochenschau*, characterized Propaganda Company (PK) reports as a weapon. It was said to be a means of "modern government that existed right next to the formations of the Wehrmacht in order to make its contribution to the final outcome" of the war.[147] Members of the PK were not only trained in the use of weapons, but in emergencies could also be deployed at the front. Thus, a PK reporter in the air force might occasionally have to operate a bomber's rear machine gun; others fought in the thicket of the battle. Up to October 1943, more than a thousand of these men had fallen, were reported missing, or had been mutilated.

Nazi literature on the subject likes to sing the praises of the courageous correspondents who were prepared to face death. It was in this way that their pictures and reports were imbued with the notion that being present and facing mortal danger had something heroic about it:

> Stemming from the traditional *Aktualitätenschau*, the newsreel has evolved into a unique document of the age. Only its [Nazi] bias endowed its tightly edited sequences with an idea, an objective, and a style of its own. It reached its high point in the German war newsreels. The extreme exertions of the men in our Film Propaganda Companies frequently created unique documents of manly courage in which the boundary between life and death was being transgressed.[148]

To highlight the heroism of the PK reporters, the credits marked with a cross the names of those who had been killed in action. In his *Das eherne Herz* Goebbels, writing in 1943, attributed the success of the newsreel exclusively to the PK men, adding explicitly that many of them gave their life in service to the German nation: "Here the modern way of conducting a war finds its highest manifestation with which the amateurish propaganda of the enemy powers cannot even begin to compete."[149] Goebbels was wrong. The first cameraman who was killed in action was a Frenchman. J. A. Dupré fell in 1916 near Verdun during a German artillery barrage. Four German cameramen met their death when filming on the Somme. The number of Soviet newsreel reporters killed on the German front was particularly high during World War II. Maria Slavinskaya commemorated their work in her documentary *Frontovoi Kinooperator* (Cameraman at the Front, 1946) with material by Vladimir Sushinskij, who was killed near Breslau toward the end of the war. As the Russian director Esther Shub noted, "the cameraman is the film's main hero."[150]

The determination of the Nazi leadership and the combat effectiveness of the Wehrmacht that the German newsreels suggested or demonstrated continued to leave the impression of army advances even at a time when it had long begun to beat the retreat. The statistics show how far the newsreel, even before its centralization within the Goebbels Ministry, was able to strike a responsive chord among the public simply by virtue of the suggestive power of its pictures from the Polish campaign. According to Giese, newsreel reporting pushed up cinema attendance by 90 percent in June 1940 as compared to June 1939.

Production figures confirm this picture of increased popularity. Before the war some 500 copies were made of each newsreel film. In 1943, if Hippler is to be believed, it was 2,400. Whereas no more than about 3,000 feet of film were taken per week before the war, after 1939 the figure rose to 150,000 feet per week. Again according to Hippler, a total of 40 million feet of film was used for the prewar production of newsreels; at the height of the war the figure was around 300 million. With the amount of material exploding and quantity becoming more important than quality, the average prewar length of 10 minutes was extended to 20 to 30 minutes during the war. During the period when it was still in a position to celebrate victories, the propagandistic quality of the German war newsreel was obviously higher than that of the Allies' offerings. Thus, the *Manchester Guardian* wrote the following flattering words: "We saw two German war films next to which even the best British newsreels that have been shown until now looked like immature schoolboy pieces. British newsreels compare with German ones like lukewarm water to a stiff whisky."[151]

Accordingly, the number of copies rose from 800 to 2,000 for domestic distribution, while the number distributed abroad increased from 30 to 1,000, dubbed in 15 different languages. A newspaper article, published in June 1941, had this to say about the subject: "The foreign edition of the newsreel is sent to all countries around the globe, including North and South America, and is flown there from Lisbon. We exchange newsreels with Russia. It is particularly widely seen in Japan. In Europe, the German war newsreel has editorial offices in Vienna, Paris, Madrid, Brussels, The Hague, Copenhagen, Oslo, Warsaw, Pressburg, and Zürich." Rudolf Oertel summarized the situation as follows:

> During the Polish campaign and during our victories in the West, millions of people stood in line outside movie theaters not because of the feature films, but because of the newsreels [they wanted to see]. This demonstrates how enormously important film has become as a report on contemporary events.[152]

The German newsreels that were circulated abroad had an exclusively propagandistic mission: the visual and verbal arguments that had been turned into a National Socialist iconography were designed to generate sympathy among neutral governments. Hitler wanted to secure this sympathy in order to buttress his plans psychologically and to be able to pursue his conquests without critical reactions from abroad.

As to the territories that the Wehrmacht and Armed SS had occupied, newsreels were supposed to contribute to paralyzing resistance efforts. They tried to promote German confidence in the final victory of Nazism and to stifle partisan activities as well as organized underground work. What Hitler said with regard to Germany in 1937 applied even more so to occupied Europe: "I have no use for opposition. That is why I have built concentration camps. I could have done all this through the courts; but for me this takes too long."

As early as the summer of 1939, the German population had been prepared through newsreel reports that a violent solution to the conflict with Poland was imminent. Thus, *Ufa-Tonwoche No. 468* (passed by censor on 23 August 1939) offered a tendentious "retrospective on Poland and Danzig since World War I" and wished Foreign Minister Ribbentrop farewell on his trip to Moscow. *Ufa-Tonwoche No. 469* (passed by censor on 30 August 1939), the last peacetime newsreel, informs the Germans about the signing by Ribbentrop of the Nazi-Soviet Pact that sealed Poland's fate. Reports about "the deprivations of Germans who had fled Poland" are given a prominent place, accompanied by a commentary that indirectly anticipated the invasion of Poland: "A glance at these refugees shows what terrible things they have experienced and what they had to go through before they chose the final way out ... the escape across the border." The refugees who are being heroicized in these pictures are then shown the newsreel that is dedicated to them in their camp. *Film-Kurier* carried a report on what happened next:

> Warmest sympathies are being extended to our German brothers and sisters. Almost all women pulled out their handkerchiefs; no one was ashamed of their tears. The men sit upright, their faces have hardened and show determination. Ten minutes of newsreel—an experience that will never go away.[153]

Ufa-Tonwoche No. 470/37 (passed by censor on 7 September 1939): The first wartime newsreel was released a mere six days after the beginning of the German attack on Poland. Many combat scenes and the hate-filled leader were later incorporated into *Feldzug in Polen* (Campaign in Poland, 1940). The 18-minute *Ufa-Tonwoche No. 470* is divided into seventeen segments. With the exception of clips from Hitler's speech before the Reichstag on 1 September, it uses almost exclusively material taken during the "lightning campaign" or from conquered Polish "enemy pictures."

Presented in segments 1 and 7, they are designed to create a prototypical Pole represented as a collective homunculus. The film speaks of a "Polish murder gang" that had killed such loyal ethnic Germans as the Storm Trooper Josef Wessel, who was shot in the back. Segments 9, 10, and 12 suggest to the German moviegoer that Britain, in fact, is the main enemy, the next threat to the nation that must be countered in time with anti-air raid preparations, blackout exercises, and munitions production. Hitler Youths are seen sandbagging the Pergamon Freeze in Berlin to protect it against bombs. The newsreel illustrates the tactical interaction between armaments and enemy actions.

Ufa-Tonwoche No. 472/39 (passed by censor on 20 September 1939): When this newsreel was given its first screening, Hitler and Stalin had agreed on the demarcation line between Germany and the Soviet Union which carved up Poland. Remnants of the Polish army are seen "crawling from their hideouts" near Gdingen. As the commentator says sneeringly, after such "scenes of chaos … security and order returned with the German soldiers." Confidence radiates from another sentence, according to which "all forces in the homeland rally to fight the defensive struggle." This is followed by idyllic sequences with blond maidens gathering in hay and women working for the Red Cross, underlined by lyrical tunes: "Women replace their husbands and contribute energetically." This is the new moral imperative. Neat female gymnasts of the "Strength Through Joy" organization do a display in front of men wounded in the Polish campaign. Everything is going perfectly in Hitler's war: supply trains carry munitions to the eastern front; the field bakery is busy baking bread. A French fighter pilot who has been shot down is buried "in chivalric fashion" and with full military honors: whoever fights honorably, unlike the Poles, will also be buried honorably in foreign soil. A captured British officer "volunteers" that he is being well treated, has good accommodation, and is fed well: he has "no complaints." Meanwhile, Polish prisoners of war are given an unsympathetic portrayal and are thrown together as negative prototypes of "inferior" Slavs. After having been put behind barbed wire, "the expelled ethnic Germans are able to return to their villages." Nor is the home front spared some horrifying pictures: "This man had his eyes gouged; this woman had her face mutilated; this man had his right hand pierced"—of course by Polish "subhumans." Jews with shovels are shown in the Warsaw ghetto: "For the first time in their life they are forced to work." This scene was later edited into Hippler's *Der ewige Jude.*

Hitler flies over the front in a Ju-52 airplane. Back on earth, he is seen affably eating some soup served from a field kitchen: "The Führer stays with his soldiers." Göring and Walther von Brauchitsch, the Army Commander in Chief, report to him at headquarters on the military situation. Next, Hitler inspects the town of Lodz "shortly after its conquest." This is how the folks back home like to see the Führer: "*Hitler and his soldiers—a community bonded together in life and death.*"

Finally, on 19 July 1940 Hitler said with reference to Poland:

> ... One of the creations of the Versailles *diktat* that was very remote from reality; politically and militarily an inflated bugaboo; behaves offensively toward a state for months and threatens to knock it out, to make mincemeat of the German armies, to move the frontier to the Oder or Elbe rivers and so on.... Germany patiently watches this behavior for months, although it would have required no more than a single movement of the arm to beat up this bubble filled with stupidity and arrogance.

Feldzug in Polen *(1940) and* Feuertaufe *(1940)*

The 40-minute report titled *Feldzug in Polen* (Campaign in Poland) that was compiled from several newsreels is a good example of trends in propaganda at this time. Through the demagogic use of words and pictures, Hippler tries to justify the invasion of Poland. The very much expanded newsreel movie begins with the obligatory omissions when it talks about the "*urdeutsch* character of the city of Danzig" that the "Polish robber state" had gobbled up. "With an ice-cold mind" the Polish government had pushed for war in order to "eternalize the injustice of Versailles." And: "It was Poland's task permanently to threaten Germany from the East. It is the proclaimed objective of Britain to uphold this threat."

A single burning hut was sufficient proof for Hippler that "the Poles are burning and devastating farmsteads of ethnic Germans." Looking from a very different perspective at the trigger that the Nazis had set up to justify their invasion of Poland, Günther Anders wrote after the war: "Following the ignominious farce at the Gleiwitz" radio station in Silesia where German *agents provocateurs* had been put in Polish uniforms to fake a Polish attack, Hitler "assaulted the East, razed villages and towns to the ground and murdered millions upon millions of people." The newsreel commentary, by contrast, reads as follows: "After Poland had taken up arms against German vital rights in a threatening manner, German troops marched across the German-Polish border on 1 September 1939."

Since the film was unable to provide realistic pictures to demonstrate the alleged threat—except for the burning hut that has been mentioned—Hippler relied on the persuasive power of a faded-in map. On it, Polish expansionist designs toward Germany's eastern provinces can be seen in the shape of giant tentacles. In this way, Hippler enables the viewer to witness the work of the general staff and its ingenuity. Having been incited to become accomplices to these policies, the population, it is hoped, will give support to its leaders. As to the border lines that appear on the map, the commentator offers a retrospective justification for Germany's alleged need to conduct a preventive war against Poland: "Excessive annexationist aims are proclaimed [by the Poles]." The latter "have visions of the Polish frontier running along the Oder river or even along the Elbe."

The panzer units that overrun Poland with the speed of a "lightning war" are shown without commentary. Only euphoric music by Herbert Windt accompanies the rolling commandos for about ten minutes. Unencumbered by distracting words, the viewer was supposed to be able to visualize the precision with which the general staff did its work at all stages. In this way, the German attack on Poland came to be extolled as a historic moment. The moviegoer on the home front was to be its witness.

Overjoyed by the swift victory that even Hitler had not thought possible, the regime compiled two full-length documentaries from newsreel material. Both tried to outdo each other in their overestimation of the German armed forces and of the air force in particular. After *Feldzug im Polen* by the party hack Hippler, there followed *Feuertaufe* by the professional Hans Bertram. Many film histories, even those by Kracauer and Courtarde/Cadars, erroneously list both movies as one and the same.

Feuertaufe (1939/40) shows the Führer getting out of his Mercedes car in the small hours of 1 September 1939 to make a thunderous speech to the nation broadcast over millions of *Volksempfänger*, the cheap radio sets that the Nazis had been marketing after 1933. His infamous words signaled the catastrophic consequences that followed: "For the first time Poland has sent regular fighting troops into our territory during the night; we've been shooting back since 5:45 a.m.! And from now on we'll retaliate bomb for bomb!"

Shouts of joy flare up. When we reach the prologue of
Bertram's *Feuertaufe*, action follows without delay. Standing along
the runway under the machine guns of their dive bombers, pilots
tighten their helmets. The camera revels taking in the neat technical gadgets that spell death: machine guns, control stick, wheel
hubs, emblems, etc. The engines are started. The aestheticism of
war takes its disastrous course. Like swarms of locusts, one
squadron after the other climbs into the steel-blue sky, accompanied by the noisy war chant "We are flying eastward!" written by
Wilhelm Stoeppler, with music by Norbert Schultze:

> ... the password is known ...
> Close up with the enemy!
> Close up with the enemy!
> Bombs for *Polenland*!
> We flew to the rivers Vistula and Warthe
> We flew over Polish land
> We hit it hard,
> The enemy army
> With lightnings and bombs and fire.

It was not just the conduct of this lightning war and the verbal
hurrah patriotism that Schultze's shrill music is supposed to under-
line. The roaring soldiers' songs also generate an affective tension
that binds the emotional response to the verbal message. Thus, the
trivial pathos of "Close up with the enemy!" will have its impact
on the viewers in the theaters many thousands of miles from the
front. To quote Frank Mahraun, they will receive the film as the
"heroic song of a service arm." Or as *Völkischer Beobachter* put it:
"Millions will catch fire from the glow of *Feuertaufe*." Bertram also
reports his "most unforgettable experience." This was his flight
along the Bzura river, "where the encircled Polish troops tried desperately and vainly to break out and the air force rained down
their bombs over a space of thirty square kilometers.... No one
escaped alive through this fiery curtain that our pilots put up along
the river banks. Wherever our air force attacks, its hits are fatal."[154]
Thus, the battle of annihilation near Kutno marked not only the
strategic but also the dramaturgical climax of the campaign.

By making direct camera contact with the enemy, the war
newsreel had developed its own martial standards; being part of
the offensive, it had itself gone on to attack. It "abandoned the
noncommittal attitude of the leisurely observer and moved into
firing range; and one senses that the camera that captures this or

that combat scene is guided by the same hand that will grab a gun in another moment."[155]

Films like *Feuertaufe*, *Feldzug in Polen* and *Sieg im Westen* wage the battles for a second time, this time to win them also with aesthetic means. By compressing the battle, picking some scenes and deleting others, constructing rudimentary contexts that never existed in reality in this density, these movies discard all that is undesirable from a propagandistic point of view. They show "images of horrific beauty" instead of brutal horror pictures. The opulent display of pictures is made to overlay the true misery of war and the legions of Germany's own fallen heroes, and in the viewer's mind the campaign is turned into thrilling legend. Frank Mahraun, writing in *Der deutsche Film*, No. 11, 1940, went on to describe its theme: "a single dark pyramid of smoke hovering above the burning city and even higher up the overarching dome of cumulus clouds glistening in the sun topped by squadrons of our fighter planes unloading their lethal loads into the clouds and smoke"—until Warsaw surrendered. The moviegoer back home is drawn in emotionally; he is himself a participant in the war without being exposed to imminent danger. By tampering with the reality of the actual war, the event is divested of its tangibility (*entdinglicht*). Thus, to many war became part of their experience in an aesthetically transfigured form.

The movie was compiled from some fifty thousand feet of documentary material and, in terms of its structure and approach, which adopted the high ground of the victor, did not differ much from the many PK reports that were to emerge from Hitler's "lightning war." They all confirmed from beginning to end what Goebbels had proudly announced to the world on 19 January 1940: "We have planned and thoroughly organized this war to the last detail." This was also true of Bertram's film, which turns the compilation of history into a masterpiece of film montage and, indeed, served as a model for this genre. As Goebbels wrote in *Der deutsche Film*: "World history was written here with the help of the camera."[156]

In a "Wehrmacht Order of the Day" Hitler expressed his thanks and appreciation to the soldiers of the Polish campaign for a fight that "tells of the best of German soldierdom." Nor did he forget to thank those who had fallen—just as two million men who died in World War I had given their lives so that Germany might live. "We stand together more closely than ever before and tighten our helmets under the flags that fly everywhere in Germany with proud joy."[157] Seven PK reporters who participated in the making of Bertram's *Feuertaufe* were among the fallen.

Deutsche Wochenschau No. 513/28 (passed by censor on 3 July 1940): This newsreel celebrates the Führer in a retrospective on the campaign against France. Hitler's appearance obviates the need for a general staff map. Thus, we see him "touring the Vosges Mountains," "in the midst of his soldiers who drown him in their cheers;" he is seen in Strasbourg and "on the battlefields of the Maginot Line.... The Führer's train rolls through the jubilant countryside; he encounters signs of love, devotion, and gratitude." Celebratory images and texts certify that Hitler's charisma is infallible. Having gotten back to his Reich capital, the "victorious leader is received by his people against the background of the festive ringing of bells"[158] that celebrate his strokes of genius. Many of these clips from France will reappear in *Sieg im Westen* a year later to provide another boost to collective morale.

Sieg im Westen *(1941)*

> *Think of the Führer by day and by night and no bullet, no bayonet will ever reach you.*

OKW leaflet

> *Victorious we want to beat France*
> *And die as a brave hero.*

Soldiers' song from *Musketier seins lust'ge Brüder*
(The Musketeers Are Funny Guys)

> *War moves across the fields*
> *Up and down the streets.*
> *Many a soldier's grave*
> *Lies in the dim woods.*

Song from *Sieg im Westen*

The campaign against France was likewise turned into a full-length documentary compiled from newsreel. The film sang the high praises of the Führer and his genius. The journal *Der deutsche Film* called *Sieg im Westen* the greatest of all German newsreels. Moreover, "by reproducing the most direct pictures that, in defiance of death, had been wrung from reality at the very front line, the breathtaking continuous illustration [of the fighting] has also yielded something of the spirit of the troops about which the war correspondents have been reporting in the press and on the radio."

With the help of maps, the "course of Germany's fate" (thus the accompanying brochure) was to be made visible for all "with utmost brevity" against the background of Hitler's strategic vision. In this way, confidence in the infallibility of the Führer and his ingenuity was to be strengthened that would also guide future actions.

Sieg im Westen is an epos that Svend Noldan and Fritz Brunel forged from newsreel through a cleverly organized structure. Having served as a prototype for many others, it is a movie in which the Wehrmacht figures as a "community of fate" that has been welded together by the belief in the "final victory." Close to one million feet of film were used to extract an ideal-typical portrait of the warrior—the image of the "German hero." This heroic character is confirmed by a closeup of a soldier's face that Kracauer describes as "soft," yet which "unintentionally betrays a close link between blood and soul, between sentimentality and sadism."

Because Hitler's heroes had to be portrayed as invulnerable, all documents were deleted that reported human and material losses. Clearly, the ideology of invincibility would have been nullified by scenes of cripples and corpses, which would also have put a damper on the delirious enthusiasm. However, corpses that are shown buried in the film look like bodies that are not part of the national community (*volksfremde Körper*). The optimistic portrayal of the war culminates in Hitler as the personification of all Wehrmacht successes and those of its generals. With the exception of the last two editions, Nazi newsreels turned Hitler into "superman."

In contradistinction to *Feldzug in Polen*, the heroism of the German soldiers in this film is mirrored in the courage of their opponents. The "hereditary enemy" France is not denigrated; the commentator explicitly concedes that the *"Poilu"* fought bravely. The Teutonic victory was not due to the weakness of the French, but alone to superior military leadership.

To the very end *Sieg im Westen* remains nationalist to the core, but it is not a typically National Socialist strip of the kind regularly produced by *Deutsche Wochenschau*. Even the oft-cited episode in which the camera lingers over captured Senegalese soldiers performing "negro dances" is presented without commentary. The moviegoer is left to draw his own conclusions. *Deutsche Wochenschau No. 513* of 3 July 1940, by contrast, added biting comments about the black barbarians who had been selected by the French to defend European civilization.

Der deutsche Film speculated that it was possible to see "naiveté" (*Ahnungslosigkeit*) in the faces of French POWs and compared their "playful private attitude" and their "aimlessness" with the diametrically different German mentality and its virtues. Thus emerged "the clear and noble image of the optimistic German soldier who remains upright even in the toughest battle and is used to being victorious." It was an image that was "also wonderfully highlighted by closeups."[159]

According to the accompanying brochure, the film's most noble task was "to make apparent the values for which we are fighting today." *Sieg im Westen* was commissioned by the Army High Command (OKH) and was designed to conjure up the power of the all-powerful. This glorification is divided into three chapters: the introduction, titled *"Der Entscheidung entgegen"* ("Toward the Decision"), the main part, called *"Der Feldzug"* ("The Campaign"), followed by the finale.

The introduction takes as its guideline the formula of the professional Nazi film ideologue Hans-Joachim Giese. In 1949 Giese published his book *Die Film-Wochenschau im Dienste der Politik* (Newsreel in the Service of Politics) in which he wrote: "This journalistic means of leadership, in fulfilling the basic axiom of all propaganda, does not represent the objective truth *per se*. But, using decent means, it does represent that side of truth that it is necessary to proliferate in the interests of the German people." Of course, the "necessary" version of "the encirclement policy of the enemy powers up to the [First] World War and the Versailles *diktat*" was, in Giese's view, part of this picture that he continued to spread even after 1945.[160]

The following sentences are taken from the leaflet advertising the movie:

> In Adolf Hitler, the German people gained a leader toward new unity and freedom. The injustices of Versailles are removed step by step; universal service is reintroduced; the lost German territories are liberated; Czechoslovakia is put out of action as an air base of the Western powers. Despite the Führer's repeated peace initiatives, war breaks out with Britain and France. Poland is destroyed within eighteen days. The Westwall [German fortifications in the West] is reinforced. In the North, Germany secures Europe from Narvik to Copenhagen.

The introduction starts off with the oath to the flag and shows the devout faces of those who have just taken the oath. The ceremony is given a festive exultation with rousing music. The suggestive impact of this prelude was supposed to induce young viewers to soon join those who were presented to them as models on the screen: "I swear that I will be prepared, as a brave soldier, to risk my life for this oath at any time!" This is followed by postcard-style clips of beautiful German landscapes that are presented as symbols of all that is sublime, for which Germany goes to war. Scenes from the idyllic homeland are continuously faded in. In their interaction with photos from the front, they are supposed to give the impression of a nation that is united in its struggle. There is also the statue of Saint Uta in the eleventh-century Naumburg Cathedral that is used as a symbol of the Germanic female. It serves as an object of identification just as the Horseback Rider of Bamberg was deployed in other documentaries. Both figures were designed to embody the myth of the Nordic ideal. As Alfred Rosenberg, the Party's chief ideologist put it: "The hero is always beautiful, but this means [he is] of a certain racial type."[161]

It is above all in the idealized sculptures of Klimsch, Breker, and Thorak that the fascist aesthetic of physical perfection celebrates its greatest triumphs. Their figures look like healthy nudes in homeopathic journals. To quote Traub's statement of 1933: "It is the first commandment of all propaganda to keep men receptive and capable of enthusiasm."[162]

Like Adolf Hitler, the Führer and Reich Chancellor, Bismarck, the "Iron Chancellor," is said to have fulfilled a historic mission, i.e., to weld the Reich together. In order to tie Hitler's greatness to Bismarck, the latter's "ingenious leadership" is pronounced as the heritage to be honored. Hitler's wars of conquest are legitimized as a task that is rooted in Bismarck's policy of expansion. With original clips from World War I, we move to the assertion that inflation and unemployment were a consequence of the "Versailles *diktat.*" As the commentator explains the ideological background, "it was in this period of decay that Hitler founded the NSDAP."

With the slogan "The Führer takes back what belongs to Germany," the optically opulent introduction was supposed to cover up the problems of legitimating the horrors that follow: the occupation of the Saar; the annexation of the Memel district; the Sudetenland; the occupation of the Czech territories, now cynically called the "Protectorate" of Bohemia and Moravia; the invasion of Austria; and finally the assault on Poland.

The "authentic" pictures fail to prove the film's contention that "Germandom in Poland experiences terror of the worst kind." The occupation of Denmark and Norway is merely noted in passing, as if it had been a little armed outing.

The movie's main part is titled "The Campaign." The summary of contents presents the following operations in terms of a heroic drama for which some optical shortcuts were justified:

> The major advances in the West in May and June 1940; the German armies move against Holland and Belgium on a broad front; the fortress Holland is taken after five days; the Maas river is taken; the Maginot Line is pierced; the English Channel is reached; the encirclement of the Anglo-French troops is completed and triggers the chaotic flight of the British Expeditionary Force from Dunkirk; the king of the Belgians offers his country's capitulation; another major assault by the German army is prepared along the lower Somme river, the Oise-Aisne Canal, and the Aisne river; the Weygand Line is smashed; Rouen is taken; Paris surrenders on 14 June; the First Army attacks the Maginot Line along the Saar; it crosses the upper Rhine; fortresses are taken; the last major constructions of the Maginot Line are being occupied; France offers a truce; Compiègne becomes the site for truce negotiations.[163]

The actual combat scenes are as interchangeable as they are tiring, even though the most dramatic parts from a variety of newsreels are incorporated. The symbolic power of the Maginot Line, together with its fortifications, is to be destroyed by showing for several long minutes the artillery bombardment of this "complex defense mechanism." What the film tries to put across is that "the machine itself can never be the *deus ex machina* in itself;" even "the most perfect organization remains useless if it is not an instrument, but is viewed as an autonomous force by a decadent generation" of Frenchmen.[164] This sequence has no other purpose than to demonstrate that the Maginot Line represents what this quote asserts: that the German victory is also a victory of life over death, of the future over the past. Pictures of British POWs in a camp are accompanied by the popular British song "We will hang our washing on the Siegfried Line!", but set in a minor key to offer a telling illustration of "Perfidious Albion's" waning optimism that victory is on their side. When invading paratroopers are shown over Holland at a height of three hundred meters, the commentary proudly anticipates the sentiments of the moviegoers: "The world is holding its breath—Eben Emael Fortress has capitulated." However, the film makes one prognosis that did not come true, i.e., that this campaign "will decide the fate of the German nation for the next thousand years."

The verbal introduction of the main part is supported by a sterile sequence of faces of "typically German" heroes. Clips from captured newsreel material have been effectually edited into the film. They make up a patchwork of "enemy faces," with Senegalese soldiers being particularly in evidence to reinforce racial prejudices. Their "alien" ecstatic dancing is meant to be viewed as disgusting. The technique of contrasting montage is also used when German troops, parading to the tunes of dashing march music, are juxtaposed with columns of flabby POWs. All viewers are meant to realize that the emergence of the Germans as the master race is preordained by nature.

Still, the war against the French is depicted as chivalric. A "hygienic war," it spares the viewer from the sight of dead and wounded soldiers. Instead, death is turned into the decorative symbol of a double grave covered with flowers. A fresh bunch of flowers will reassure the moviegoer back home that fulfilling one's duty with fatal consequences will result in lyrical transfiguration: a noble death guarantees that the dead person will be taken into the Valhalla. The mourning of genuine loss is to be mitigated by sacralizing it.

In order to illuminate the prospect of an aesthetic transfiguration with greater theatrical effect, the camera repeatedly captures the diffuse light of dusk and heavily clouded skies. This enables the directors to move all the more impressively through the vapors that hint at impending calamity toward the light of victory. Conversely, the unreal morning fog of another scene is designed to mitigate looming dangers. To perfect their scenario, the skillful engineers of viewer moods include backlighting in their drama to give the impression that danger is merely threatening the dark shadows they have produced. After all, there is no space in this moribund backdrop for individuals who have become heroes. They disappear as extras; they submerge among Hitler's anonymous supernumeraries who are destined to die. The theatrical hocus-pocus on the battlefield in the middle of enemy country endows the heroic struggle of the German "community of fate" with the mystical flair of the unreal, helping the viewer in the cinema back home feel that both fronts are one. The tragic death has been deleted from the script; in Hitler's world theater, only the death that is draped in heroism gets a warm exit, as in an epic of classical antiquity. Whatever the pictures fail to transfigure is left to opera-like music: "Yes, the flag is more than death!"

The camera captures the tirelessly advancing German soldiers as engineers of action who, bursting with energy, march across bridges. Their eyes are fixed firmly on the other side as the goal that holds out victory, in a symbolic as well as a literal sense.

The notion of "home front" represents the qualitative equivalent of the front line. Those fighting for Hitler's victories are to be found at both fronts; they constitute an inviolable "community of fate" in their certain knowledge that they can mutually depend on each other. Clips from a German armaments factory show the intelligent and serious faces of German skilled laborers that reflect an unconditional confidence in their precision work. In the next sequence we are given, high above in the cloudless skies, a powerful impression of how reliably the technical production empire of Armaments Minister Fritz Todt is capable of operating. Relentlessly, dive bombers and heavy bombers are seen unloading their deadly cargo on military and civilian targets. With the target firmly pinpointed, *stuka* pilots dive to one hundred meters above the ground. Accompanied by a nerve-grinding, whining noise, the speeds they reach are endowed with a sensuous quality. Man and machine become a single unit. Effectively presented maps introduce the assault on the legendary *Chemins des Dames* fortress, designed to demonstrate the accuracy of logistical general staff work, in this instance personified by Colonel General Gerd von Rundstedt.

Of course, the German soldier is also permitted to relax between his victories. Even hardened old blades can be funny—or what the scriptwriters thought to be funny. Billeted on a farm and surrounded by cackling hens, men who have been through tough battles splash around in a tub of water that is much too small. The camera catches them getting a haircut, polishing their boots, brushing their horses, and writing letters. Meanwhile, the fire break notwithstanding, the commanding officer continues his sacred duties: he studies the map in preparation for the next attack. Who among those sitting in the theater would not like to be with those happy victors. The pulsating rhythms of march music then change to the more elegiac sounds of an organ-playing soldier. His mood is represented through a soft fade-over showing water in which a blond German woman back home rinses her laundry. As this scene intends to convey, it is to fight for her in order to preserve her happiness that the boys have crossed the

Maginot Line in their war against the "arch enemy." After all, *"Siegreich woll'n wir Frankreich schlagen"* ("Victoriously We Are Aiming to Beat France"). There now follows, neatly presented, a special announcement that promises victory: frame and consciousness are once again filled with pictures of the trenches.

If the verbal polemic against France is relatively restrained, the root cause for this is probably to be found in the fact that the Germans did not wish to offend unnecessarily the collaborating Vichy government and its aging Marshal Pétain. Accordingly, the cavalcade of riders on white horses on the Champs Elysées in Paris looks rather tamely anachronistic, as if this sequence had been taken from a historical feature film. Incidentally, Hitler was absent from this parade and only Colonel General Fedor von Bock attended. Meanwhile, the German flag flies from the top of the Eiffel Tower and above the monuments of Verdun and Compiègne, symbols of Germany's defeat in World War I.

The film culminates in a depiction of the capitulation ceremony in Compiègne Forest that is trotted out with gusto. After the French general has reviewed the German guard of honor, Hitler—shown here for the first time—and OKW chief Keitel receive the defeated enemy in the same railway car in which the Germans had been forced to sign the armistice in 1918, the historic requisite of the "German trauma."[165]

The finale shows Hitler, as *triumphator Germaniae*, and his entourage strutting through Reims Cathedral. The choral music from *"Lieb Vaterland magst ruhig sein"* ("Dear Fatherland, Rest Assured") reaches a crescendo. The viewers can now comfortably lean back in their seats. They knew they could rely on the Wehrmacht and its supreme commander Adolf Hitler.

In a concluding *tour d'horizon*, a final attempt is made to convince potential doubters of the justice of this German war. Accordingly, the most impressive scenes from the movie appear as a brief jumble, peaking in a clip of the inexorable advance of Germany's soldiers. The sequence resumes the opening theme: the hands of soldiers taking their oath to the flag stretched upwards into the sky—the symbol of utmost loyalty.

Up to this point, Herbert Windt's soldiers' song *"Auf den Strassen des Sieges"* ("On the Roads of Victory") has been skillfully mixed in with the visual material. Now the refrain becomes the movie's leitmotif, replacing the slowly moving swastika flag:

When German soldiers are on the march
No devil will stop them.
Then the war's die will be cast
Then the turn of world history will come
Together with the flags of victory.

Approaching the Downfall

Soldier, you are my buddy,
When our bones begin to fade,
The moon will shine upon us like blue smoke,
The monkey roars in the bamboo bushes.
Soldier, you are my buddy,
When our bones begin to fade.

Song by Klabund that was banned in the Third Reich

The regular peacetime cinema program consisted of a short movie, followed by a *Kulturfilm* documentary and the newsreel, and concluded with the main feature film. During the war and depending on availability, this program tended to be weighted in favor of the newsreel. Newsreel content was adjusted to times that had become increasingly darker. Offering humorous relaxation came to be frowned upon. As early as 1940, Goebbels warned against coloring the newsreels with too much optimism. His Ministry avoided giving the impression that the war had ended with the capitulation of France. When, at the end of 1941, the Russian campaign experienced its first crisis, Goebbels even admitted that psychological mistakes had been made. Until now, the population had been shielded from getting too much unpleasant news.

In the spring of 1942 the Propaganda Minister recorded in his diary that it was necessary to show the population the realities of warfare in the East. This would prevent them from falling prey to illusions, but also tell them that there is no difficulty that cannot, in the end, be overcome by human will power.[166]

Long after the end of the Thousand-Year Reich had appeared on the horizon, people quite naively continued to ramble on about the final victory. However, as the war wore on, Goebbels recognized that new and additional psychological difficulties kept arising. Thus, in May 1943 he wrote in his diary that with the lengthening of the war the problem of the newsreel would become more acute. He was no longer certain what should be shown.

Around this time, during the spring of 1943, the propaganda units of all the services totaled some fifteen thousand. As to film reporters, the army had about eighty-five, the navy, forty-two, the air force and the Armed SS, forty-six each. Every week they sent their roughs per express to the studios in Berlin where Goebbels personally supervised the editing with relentless energy, turning the interplay of text and context into masterpieces of propaganda. As we know from his diaries, he considered the newsreel to be one of the "really important means of propaganda that we have in war at this time." He added that it was hard work each week to put the newsreel together in such a way that it constituted effective propaganda. Overall, Goebbels appears to have applied to the newsreel what Musil said about literature, i.e., that it was its task to describe not what is, but what should be.

When the escalating campaign in the East resulted in an enlargement of the propaganda units, a special department was established in the OKW to take charge of their work. At this time the "Twelve Commandments for Film Reporters" were also drawn up. The first of these rules read: "Always remember that millions participate in world events through your personal commitment and that you must give present and future generations a truthful and lively description of the gigantic struggle for Germany's greatness."

Up to the bitter end, Goebbels continued to believe in the power of propaganda and in victory with the help of the images it produced. However, reality had long taken a different turn among the PK units and had destroyed all illusions that they had helped to create. From the end of 1944, all PK personnel that were "fit for the front" (*frontverwendungsfähig*) were ordered to join the combat troops. By October 1943 more than one thousand PK reporters had been killed in action or had been reported missing or wounded. In November 1943 Ufa's main office in which all newsreels were produced was heavily damaged by bombs. The newsreel studios were moved to a shack in Buchhorst on the outskirts of Berlin. Yet, Goebbels's optimism remained unshakable, even if at most one third of the regular personnel was still around. On 22 March 1945 he notes his surprise in his diary "that the German people still feel inclined to go to the movies. Nevertheless, this is the case to a very large extent."[167] It was on this 22 March that the last *Deutsche Wochenschau* was released—No. 755/10.

As matters went from bad to worse in the Reich, the desperate will to achieve final victory was nourished among the front line troops and at the home front by Goebbels's fanatical slogans to hold out. Veit Harlan, a man who was in a position to know, later characterized the Propaganda Minister as the "master of disinformation." Hitler and Goebbels had long begun to realize that they were driving the Germans into an abyss. The *ultima ratio* of their cynicism was precisely this: those "who would be left after the struggle would merely be those of inferior quality, since the good ones had been killed in action." According to Speer, Hitler is said to have opined on 18 March 1945: "If this war is lost, the German people will also be lost. This fateful outcome is inexorable." It was unnecessary, he thought, to take account of the Germans' needs for their survival under the most primitive conditions. On the contrary, it was better to destroy everything. This would then prove that the people had been too weak. The future, Hitler concluded, belonged exclusively to the stronger peoples of the East.[168]

Hippler had this to say in response to intermittent reproaches that the newsreel minimized total war and suppressed the extent of German losses from the perspective of the front soldier: the latter would be "the last to demand that the most gruesome war-related events be reproduced. It will be enough for him personally to experience the horrors of war.... The German soldier would object to the publication of pictures that showed a comrade being hit by an enemy bullet."

Deutsche Wochenschau No. 651/10/1943 (passed by censor on 24 February 1943): This edition of newsreel provides a good example of the demagogic power exerted by Nazi propaganda. It deals with the capitulation of the 6th Army at Stalingrad on 2 February 1943—a historic date that marks the turning point of the war. This defeat was reinterpreted as part of an offensive strategy; the war was now fought in an imaginary place, somewhere, and the moviegoer was not told where.

Newsreels like this one became famous not only because of the infamous way in which the propagandistic dialectic had been perfected in pictures and commentary, but also because of Goebbels's artful rhetoric. His address to the nation from the Berlin *Sportpalast* on 18 February 1943 must be counted among those macabre performances that hypnotized the German people and dragged them into the abyss of defeat. It documents the moment when Goebbels asked, "before our enemies who are listening to us at the side of their radio sets," what was probably the most fatally suggestive question of German history: "Do you want total war? Do you want it more total and more radical than we can imagine even today?" To be sure, the concept of "total war" was coined by Erich Ludendorff who gave this title to his 1935 study on the subject of patriotic sacrifice.[169]

The newsreel also records the response—the "Yes" shouted with great enthusiasm with which the invited representatives of the German people voted for the descent into total chaos. When Goebbels asked the question whether "your confidence in the Führer is greater, more deeply held, and more unshakable than ever before," the banner-carriers spontaneously raised their flags in order to give Hitler a noisy salute, albeit from great distance.

When Goebbels's speech culminated in the words: "Now, People, arise! And storm be unleashed!" the cameras succeeded in making such an impact with their pictures of ecstatically jubilant masses that this may explain why so many viewers found themselves in total agreement with the Minister's words. What happened at the *Sportpalast* is what Hitler had described in *Mein Kampf* as the "community of the great rally." To him, this was the rally at which the individual would fall under the spell of mass suggestion, at which the person who joined at the beginning, vacillating and vexed by doubts, left with firm convictions, having become by the end "a member of a community."[170]

In this connection, Erwin Leiser quoted from the reports of the Security Police (SD) that regularly monitored morale and public opinion in the Third Reich until the Nazi leadership stopped them because they had become too gloomy. When the newsreel was released, it is said to "have tangibly heightened the propagandistic effect of the *Sportpalast* rally and to have raised it even in places where skepticism had hitherto prevailed. Even more diffident circles of the population found it difficult to escape from the captivating impact of the speech that was now to be seen on film together with the response from those who attended it."

By this time the fate of the 6th Army at Stalingrad had already been sealed. Yet, the newsreel did not even hint at this defeat. On the contrary, it suggested that German troops were continuing their advance.

To be sure, Goebbels advocated a more realistic reporting on the military situation in the East so that *Deutsche Wochenschau* would not suffer a further loss of confidence among the population. But Hitler explicitly voted against putting the facts on the screen by showing starkly realistic pictures. As Goebbels recorded

in his diary on 21 January 1943, the regime had to begin to face up
to telling the population about Stalingrad. He himself had advocated this for some time, but Hitler had been opposed to it. It was,
Goebbels felt, dangerous to let matters drift and to inform the
home front only after the event.[171]

In the words of the postwar German writer Hans Magnus
Enzensberger, Hitler had never thought it possible that the impending catastrophe, captured on newsreel, might become "the only
propellant of history." What Hitler wanted was to present Nazi
ideas as *the* sensational news in optically interesting ways in order
to satisfy the hunger for "authentic reality"; and he did not plan to
achieve this by showing "corpses that had been flattened, cities that
had been laid in ruins, and ships that had been blown up." The
only authentic reality that the Führer wanted to display was a
National Socialist one; no other reality was even allowed to exist.[172]

As Peter Bucher has demonstrated in his comprehensive study,
the Nazi newsreel never again achieved the degree of credibility
that it had gained during the campaigns against Poland and
France. Instead, it "increasingly became an object of ridicule."
Bucher also quotes a contemporary source from the period after
the fall of Cherbourg in July 1944: "'For months on end the Newsreel showed us the invincibility of the *Atlantikwall*. Now the lovely
dream is over.'"[173]

After Stalingrad, the Germans who saw newsreels became witnesses to Hitler's gradual deterioration, which he tried to control
with iron discipline. *Deutsche Wochenschau No. 660/19* of 28 April
1943 provides an illustration of this. Officially devoted to his fifty-
fourth birthday, it was more concerned with his campaigns in the
Leningrad region, in the Ukraine, and around the bridgehead at
Kuban. Congratulating him on 19 April 1943, Goebbels had a fitting explanation for Hitler's outward appearance: "Working all
day and waking and worrying at night unmistakably inscribe
themselves in his face in weeks like these."[174]

The newsreels of the 1940–1943 period had been devoted to a
single theme: to secure the "final victory." Relying on the incapac-
ity of the people to make clear judgments, the psychology of
Deutsche Wochenschau had been completely fixed on this objective.
Against the background of the commentary, pictorial arguments
were geared toward activating the so-called will to hold out. Each
issue was directed to condemn as diabolical the "mortal enemy."
This enemy was denounced either as an "Eastern subhuman"
(*ostischer Untermensch*) or as an exploitative "decadent capitalist."

One of the hate-filled slogans that the newsreels spread systematically was the notion that Germans would be unable to live a worthwhile life in a world dominated by Jews. In the language of the Third Reich, Jews existed only in the plural or in the collective singular as "*the* Jew." There is no space here to enumerate all the cynical statements about Jews in their infinite variety.

The Normandy invasion by the Western Allies on 6 June 1944 accelerated the impending defeat of the Third Reich. Thenceforth, Nemesis was on Hitler's heels also in the West. *Deutsche Wochenschau No. 719/26* (passed by censor on 14 June 1944) focuses on this invasion that had been thought impossible until then. As *Film-Kurier* commented on this particular newsreel: "The German front is being jerked into action.... Fire is spewing from all guns.... The invaders run straight into the hell of the German defenses, into a symphony of blood and filth."[175] And: "The traces of annihilation, of the enormous losses in men and material that the enemy suffered in this hell are to be seen everywhere." We can hear Goebbels from the prompter's box.

Deutsche Wochenschau No. 746/1944 (passed by censor on 20 December 1944); *Deutsche Wochenschau No. 747/2/1945* (passed by censor on 4 January 1945); *Deutsche Wochenschau No. 749/4/1945* (passed by censor on 18 January 1945): In December 1944 the Soviets had begun to move into East Prussia and the Americans were approaching the German frontier in the West. And yet *Deutsche Wochenschau* spread the tale of an offensive German strategy. Thus, No. 747 reported that the Wehrmacht was taking building after building, village after village, and that the Allies' tank armies were being smashed.

In No. 746 the commentary's heroic tone is reinforced by the music in the background: "Bursts of fire scan the skies ... A battle of materiél of unimaginable proportions is raging on the ground. Walls of fire and steel are put up between the combatants on both sides and create a zone that appears to be impenetrable." Again, the handwriting was Goebbels's. Up to the middle of 1944, Hitler had still personally supervised the production of *Deutsche Wochenschau*; now, from the winter of 1944 that rang in the last phase of the chaos, he no longer showed an interest.

On 24 December 1944, the last Christmas Eve under Nazism, Goebbels's trivial pathos blends with a line from the "Forward! Forward!" song that, headed by the flag, promised to lead to eternity. It was the flag that would then also mean death to many in reality. Speaking on German radio, Goebbels is more derisory of the fallen heroes than he offers comfort to those who mourn them: "Forward across the graves! The armies of the dead are stronger than we are on land or at sea. They march ahead of us. They left us in the noisy battles of the war. They will return to us when the bells ring in a victorious peace. We owe them the Reich more than we owe it to all the living. That is the only mandate that they have left us. We are duty-bound to fulfill it. Let us keep our hands and hearts prepared for this. As the poet says, the world will then soon rejuvenate itself like a newborn child." In his movie *Hitler, ein Film aus Deutschland* (Hitler, a Film from Germany, 1978) Hans-Jürgen Syberberg used these cynical words to contrast them with pictures of the gas chambers at Auschwitz.

Deutsche Wochenschau No. 749 of the middle of January 1945 threw out the last anchor of hope. It deals with those miracle weapons for which the war-weary population had been prepared for months through the deliberate spreading of rumors. Goebbels tried desperately to propagandize the magic "V Weapons" as ready for deployment, although they literally were no more than empty shells: "We bring you the first pictures of the V-2 rocket on its flight to Britain. For security reasons they were taken from a distance, and therefore they provide no more than a faint idea of the actual size of the V-2." Hitler had personally reserved for himself all decisions concerning newsreel reports on this topic.

Meanwhile, Speer had told Hitler on several occasions that he considered this propaganda quite wrong.[176] On 2 November 1944 he added in a letter to Goebbels that he thought it "unwise to arouse hopes in the public which cannot possibly be fulfilled for a considerable time.... I would therefore request you take measures so that the daily press and technical journals refrain from alluding to future successes in our armaments production."[177]

Goebbels had announced the coming of the V-2 in *Deutsche Wochenschau No. 723/30/1944, No. 725/32/1944* and *No. 737/44/1944,* and for the first time in a speech in Breslau on 8 July 1944. *Deutsche Wochenschau No. 724/31/1944, No. 732/39/1944,* and *No. 735/42/1944* had also presented pictures of another miracle weapon, the "one-man torpedo."

In the meantime, the endless streams of refugees from the East could no longer be covered up. Faced with these pressures, Goebbels for the first time conceded that military defeat was a fact, though not an inevitable fate. He thus constructed the fiction of a bulwark that would bring about a last-minute turn of the tide. As newsreel No. 752 put it, it was upon the soil of the Reich that

"Germany must force a reversal in the fate of Europe." In newsreel No. 751 horrifying scenes are to be found of fleeing Germans who had "to give up their homeland and their belongings and to take refuge before the advancing Huns (*Mongolensturm*)." These pictures spoke a language that reflected reality.

Deutsche Wochenschau No. 753/8/1945 (passed by censor on 5 March 1945): "The newsreel that is shown of Berlin is incredible. It is my intention to turn the battle for Berlin into a hero's song. The Berliners deserve this. The entire Reich looks toward the Reich capital today with restrained expectation, but always also in the fear that the city is not up to the pressures. We shall demonstrate that these fears are groundless." It is worth remembering these words by Goebbels in connection with No. 753/8/1945 which, apart from "atrocities committed by Soviet soldiers" and "defensive battles" in the regions of Jülich in the Rhineland, Budapest, Ratibor, and Frankfurt on Oder, reported for the first time on the deployment of the *Volkssturm* (People's Army) in Berlin whose members—the very young and elderly draftees—were constructing barricades in the beleaguered Reich capital.

Deutsche Wochenschau No. 754/9 (passed by censor on 16 March 1945) will be recorded in the annals of journalism as an example of unbridled demagoguery. It turned every defeat into a victory and celebrated even the spasms of death as signs of recuperation. It also transformed a wage strike in the United States into a consolation for the German population's misery.

In movies like *Sieg im Westen*, Hitler's troops had in fact been victorious. Yet, in 1940/41 the commentaries tended to be much less euphoric than now during the last phase of the catastrophe and in the face of many deaths. As early as 1930 Ernst Jünger had predicted a German hour of fate that "possessed mythical dimensions." Only in Germany, he wrote, and "in the face of death was it possible that Germanic innocence was preserved in the hearts of the best."[178]

Of course, those who kept on producing the newsreels knew that all was lost. Nevertheless, they fabricated texts that, while they read like satire today, must have sounded to contemporaries, if not deadly serious, at least like pure cynicism. Goebbels had once wished to attract the Jewish satirist Robert Neumann to the *Völkischer Beobachter* "so that everyone would read the paper with interest."[179] Now it was mostly the Minister himself who beefed up the demagogic content of his propaganda. He ordered Hippler, the director of the Ministry's film department, to submit the roughs of every single newsreel edition. Goebbels then corrected it and accentuated its thrust and context. Above all, he changed the commentaries. At the beginning of each week, Hippler appeared before Goebbels with "the silent roughs" and later with the fully edited version. "We then discussed and decided whether and what should be modified and complemented."[180] Hippler added: "It was not a matter of 'objective' reporting, of well-balanced neutrality, but of [providing] optimistic propaganda that exuded confidence in victory and 'recognized our right.' [Our efforts] were designed to strengthen the spiritual potential of the German people to fight."[181]

It suffices to present four examples of this type of propaganda during the final phase of *Deutsche Wochenschau* and the Greater German Reich. What is significant about them is that they, too, do not say much about the actual situation. The first sequence of *No. 754/9/1945*, reporting on events in the United States, shows violent clashes between strikers and the police. In effect, these clips date from 1937 and were taken in Chicago. The commentary perpetrates several lies at the same time: "Workers protesting against low wages in an American industrial town are beaten up [by the police]. Since the seizure of power [in 1933], police clubs have disappeared in Germany." Indeed, Hitler's henchmen did not need clubs; they had concentration camps.

The next sequence suggests the advance of German troops in the West: "These are the mercenaries of an ambitious U.S. general who once again closely missed his target. He did not succeed in winning a Cannae [total victory] against the German troops. Just like in the East, German soldiers fight on stolidly for as long as they breathe. The bulk of the German army group has crossed the river with all its heavy weapons." What the newsreel did not say was that the Wehrmacht was crossing the river on its retreat.

The third sequence shows units of the "Committee for the Liberation of the Peoples of Russia" marching by, equipped with the "most modern weapons," which belonged to the collaborationist Vlassow Army. In the fourth sequence, Bolshevik soldiers are seen attacking the Kurland bridgehead in the Baltics no less than four times. And "four times their offensive was turned back with enormous losses in men and material." The commentator does not say who suffered those losses.

The fifth sequence depicts refugees trekking across the frozen *Haff* on the East Prussian Baltic coast "from dawn to dusk" to reach "the shelter of the Reich." The next sequence captures

SS-Obersturmbannführer Otto Skorzeny, who had been involved in the kidnapping of Mussolini in September 1943 and had become a popular hero. He is trying to spread confidence with swashbuckling words in the style of a mercenary: "Even Ivan can be beaten. Our bunch has proved it."

The commentary accompanying the seventh sequence exudes a victorious mood: "In tough fights, street after street is cleared out by tanks and infantry. Between burning buildings, grenadiers equipped with anti-tank guns slowly move forward to finish off the remnants of the retreating Bolsheviks. Just as in the West, the war has become more than ever a matter for the entire population in the Görlitz region [just west of Silesia]. Liberation of the City of Lauban: in the first days of March German tanks and grenadiers launch their counterattack with strong support from the air against this town outside Görlitz. After days of heated fighting, the Germans move into the town on 6 March." Goebbels is then seen decorating Wilhelm Hübner, a sixteen-year-old Hitler Youth with the Iron Cross "in the marketplace of Lauban that has only just been retaken."

The eighth sequence, dealing with Soviet atrocities, is designed to distract from the regime's terrible crimes against the Jews of Europe by denouncing the Russians: "In this field, too, the Bolshevik beasts have committed the worst crimes. All decent Germans see their blood pressure rise when considering the bestial activities of these subhumans. These are the allies of Roosevelt's Christian soldiers. Murderous deeds betraying a horrific sadism have once again demonstrated to the German soldier that there must be no retreat before, and no pardon for, this enemy.—A woman in chains who has been dragged to her death." This is where the newsreel followed Goebbels's advice from the time of struggle before 1933 literally: to keep the propaganda machine "intact … we must now appeal to the most primitive mass instincts."

In the ninth sequence Goebbels's neurotic rhetoric triumphs one more time. The camera discovers signs of hope on the gaunt faces of armaments workers and of exhausted soldiers as they listen devoutly to the Minister's words that will be quoted here only in their most typical key sentences:

> Our soldiers will know and offer no pardon when they now start their offensive in various parts of the eastern front. The divisions that have already begun their smaller offensives and will, in the course of the next weeks and months, launch major offensives, will enter the fight as if they are going to a church service. And when

they shoulder their arms and mount their armored vehicles they will have in front of their eyes nothing but the killed children and their raped women. And a shout for revenge will rise from their chests that will cause the enemy to turn pale. Just as the Führer has mastered the crises of the past, he will also master this one. He is firmly convinced of this. As he said to me only the day before yesterday, "I am firmly convinced that we shall overcome this crisis, and I firmly believe also that we shall beat and roll back the enemy once we throw in our new offensive armies; and I believe as firmly that one day we shall pin victory to our banners as I have ever firmly believed in something in my life." To our Führer Adolf Hitler: *Sieg Heil, Sieg Heil, Sieg Heil.*

As during the pre-1933 period, Goebbels, during the final agonies of the Nazi regime, transforms the faith in Hitler's invincibility into a "religion of success" (Carl Friedrich von Weizsäcker). For him rhetoric was argument, not enlightenment.

We can be certain that this newsreel promising victory by the side of the mass grave of the Third Reich, made with demagogic virtuosity and including Goebbels's speech, will be used in seminars to analyze paradigmatically his verbal, mimic, and gestural powers. Apart from providing an insight into his psyche, his Görlitz speech also offers a telling picture of the state of the (German) mass soul that the Nazis would have liked to preserve forever.

The tenth sequence of the newsreel shows Hitler for the penultimate time as a man who is a physical and mental wreck. Yet, the commentator announces him cheerfully: "The Führer is here! The joyful welcome of the soldiers is like an oath of loyalty of all fighters to the man who is holding Germany's and Europe's fate in his hands—and who will master it!" Once this man had been Germany's shining hero. Now the *Götterdämmerung* is determined more by the somber figure of that same man: slowly dragging his feet and bent forward by ill health, he walks up to a group of officers whom he greets with a handshake. Seated at a table, he makes a few jerky movements; his physiognomy looks nervous; he utters some hectic sentences that the newsreel does not reproduce.

Hitler walks past some soldiers toward the camera before he gets into his car. The whole scene leaves a ghostly impression, as if Hitler's final "exit" is to be hinted at. It is difficult to conceive of a starker contrast between Goebbels's strong words just earlier on in this newsreel. As the Propaganda Minister notes in his diary on 4 March 1945: "I noticed with dismay that the nervous twitch of his left hand has greatly increased."[182] A week earlier on 24 February when he met with Gauleiter Karl Wahl, Hitler made "the impression of a man who was visibly ill and at the end of his tether."[183] Although Hitler knew that the war had been lost, he nonetheless prided himself on his "success" in having exterminated the Jews of Europe. Thus, he wrote in his "Testament": "I, at any rate, have forced world Jewry to drop its mask; and even if our efforts have failed, that failure will merely be ephemeral; for I have opened the eyes of the world to the Jewish danger."[184]

The ten-part *Deutsche Wochenschau No. 755/10/1945* that was released on 27 March 1945 adds up to a fateful document not just because of the way it ends; it also contains the last clips of Hitler. Together with Reich Youth Leader Arthur Axmann, the Führer, marked by death and a psychic wreck, distributes the Iron Cross to twenty teenage Hitler Youths in the garden of the Reich chancellery. The last gesture that we have of him—his gentle stroking of the cheek of a thirteen-year-old *Pimpf*—was perhaps the only sign of humanity or even of reluctant emotion on the part of the Führer during his demise; but it also symbolizes the perversion of a war to the bitter end. Erich Fromm, the psychoanalyst, has argued that whoever wants to understand Hitler's personality, should realize that "the mask that covered the face of this restless man was that of an affable, polite, self-contained, and almost timid person."[185] Fromm, who had left Germany in 1934, did not know Hitler.

The other parts of the newsreel, reporting on the retreat along the eastern front from Breslau, Königsberg, and Stettin, give the impression that General Lasch and Gauleiter Koch are the masters of events and even of the offensive, as they lean over their maps. A screen-filling map does not offer any details about the location of the front line. German troops had abandoned the bridgehead around Stettin on 20 March 1945, the week before this newsreel was released. Another scene tells the viewer that half a million Germans were being "brought back into the Reich" by ship, while German warships are said to be delivering weapons to the Kurland region. Nor does this newsreel miss the opportunity to talk of Soviet atrocities, with plundering and murdering Russians raping sixty-year-old grandmothers, and—to be sure—in the most bestial and perverted manner.

According to this last *Deutsche Wochenschau* "the German people [continue to] fulfill their duty ... and one pressing need: to fight and stand fast." However, instead of fighting and standing fast, instead of "taking up position at intersections with anti-tank gun, machine pistol, and rifle," as Goebbels had written in *Völkischer Beobachter* on 24 April 1945 in a salute to the Führer's "genius," Hitler preferred to withdraw from his much-vaunted *Volksgemeinschaft* by committing suicide in his "Reich capital" a week later, on 30 April 1945. Goebbels followed him on the next day to where the flag in the Horst Wessel song had pointed both of them.

Hangmen Also Die is the title of the American film about Reinhard Heydrich, Hitler's man in charge of the Reich Security Main Office. Fritz Lang made it on the basis of a script by Bertolt Brecht to honor, together with the victims of the village of Lidice that had been razed to the ground after the assassination of Heydrich in 1942, the innumerable men and women who had been murdered by Hitler's stooges Himmler, Eichmann et al. Hans Eisler wrote a moving and thoughtful song for this movie that he called "No surrender." But it was no consolation for the victims of Lidice, Warsaw, Auschwitz, Buchenwald, and other places of terror that the executioners themselves died a violent death—Hitler and Himmler, Goebbels and Göring committed suicide; Eichmann went to the gallows.

The mass murderers do not occupy a hero's grave; no flag rustles above them. On the occasion of the victory celebrations in Moscow, the blood banners that had once been elevated to ponderous symbols were thrown into the slushy snow on Red Square.

Notes

1. F. Lampe, "Kulturfilm und Filmkultur" in *Das Kulturfilmbuch* (Munich, 1924), p. 24.

2. Rudolf Oertel, *Der Filmspiegel* (Wien, 1941), pp. 227f.

3. Nicholas Kaufmann, "Sein Feld ist die gesamte Welt" in: *Filmforum*, vol. 4, no. 11, 1955, p. 7.

4. E. W. M. Lichtwark in *Kulturfilm-Almanach* (Hamburg, 1948).

5. Nelson Goodman, "Kunst und Erkenntnis" in Dieter Henrich and Wolfgang Iser, eds., *Theorien der Kunst* (Frankfurt, 1984).

6. Oskar Kalbus, *Pioniere des Kulturfilms*, p. 27.

7. M. Pfeiffer in *Die Bedeutung des Films und Lichtbildes* (Munich, 1917), p. 33.

8. Oskar Kalbus, *Pioniere des Kulturfilms*, p. 27.

9. Leopold Gutterer, "Form und Gehalt. Die geistigen und materiellen Grundlagen der heutigen deutschen Kulturfilmarbeit" in *Der deutsche Film*, vol. 7, no. 8/9, 1942, p. 2.

10. Kurt Tucholsky in *Die Schaubühne Berlin*, 23 April 1914.

11. Alexander Elster in *Bild und Film*, quoted in Marlies Krebstakies, ed., *Die Ufa. Auf den Spuren einer grossen Filmfabrik. Berlin von 1920 bis 1945* (exhibition catalogue publ. under the auspices of the Bezirksamt Tempelhof) (Berlin, 1987), p. 30.

12. Oskar Kalbus, *Pioniere des Kulturfilms*, p. 46.

13. *Neue Sachlichkeit* (catalogue for an exhibition on German Expressionism at the Städtische Kunsthalle Mannheim, 14 June–13 September 1925), with an introduction by Gustav Friedrich Hartlaub (Mannheim, 1925).

14. Siegfried Kracauer, *Theorie des Films* (Frankfurt, 1964), English translation *Theory of Film* (London, 1965).

15. Ulrich Kurowski, ed., *Lexikon des internationalen Films* (Munich, 1975), vol. 1, p. 60.

16. Béla Balázs, *Der Geist des Films* (Halle, 1930), pp. 215f.

17. Adolf Hitler, *Mein Kampf*, p. 526.

18. Fritz Hippler, *Betrachtungen zum Filmschaffen* (Berlin, 1943).

19. Ibid.

20. Georg Lukács, "Gedanken zu einer Ästhetik des Kinos" in Peter Ludz, ed., *Georg Lukács. Werkauswahl* (Neuwied, 1972), vol. 1: *Schriften zur Literatursoziologie*.

21. Joseph Goebbels, *Der steile Aufstieg*, p. XIII.

22. Margarete Mitscherlich, "Triumph der Verdrängung" in *Stern*, no. 42, 1987, p. 32.

23. Thomas Mann, *Gesammelte Werke in zwölf Bänden* (Frankfurt, 1960), vol. 10, p. 394.

24. Leni Riefenstahl, *Memoiren* (Munich, 1987), p. 212.

25. Klaus Theweleit, *Männerphantasien* (Basel, 1986), vol. 2, p. 64.

26. Das deutsche Lichtspielgesetz vom 16.2. 1934, clause 2, para. 5 in *Reichsgesetzblatt*, pt 1, Berlin, 1934, no. 1894, p. 95.

27. Johannes Eckhardt, "Abbild und Sinnbild" in *Der deutsche Film*, vol. 3, no. 1, 1938, p. 44.

28. Alfred Kerr, "Kino" in *Pan*, vol. 3, 1912/13, pp. 553–54, repr. in *Kino-Debatte* (Tübingen, 1978), p. 76.

29. Anton Kutter, "Der 'utopische' Kulturfilm" in *Der deutsche Film*, vol. 7, no. 8/9, 1942, p. 18.

30. Heinrich Koch and Heinrich Braune, *Von deutscher Filmkunst* (Munich, 1943), p. 4 of photo section.

31. Susan Sontag, *Kunst und Antikunst* (Munich, 1980), p. 31.

32. Hans Richter, *Der Kampf um den Film* (Frankfurt, 1979), p. 37.

33. Peter von Werder, *Trugbild und Wirklichkeit. Aufgaben des Films im Umbruch der Zeit* (Leipzig, 1943), p. 10.

34. Bertolt Brecht, "Der Dreigroschenprozess, 1931" in Siegfried Unseld, ed., *Brechts Dreigroschenbuch* (Frankfurt, 1960), pp. 93f.

35. Rudolf Oertel, *Macht und Magie des Films* (Frankfurt, 1959), p. 75.

36. Friedrich P. von Zglinicki, *Der Weg des Films* (Berlin, 1965), p. 336.

37. Ibid.

38. Oskar Messter, *Mein Weg mit dem Film* (Berlin, 1936), p. 130.

39. Egon Friedell, "Prolog vor dem Film" in *Das junge Deutschland. Blätter des Deutschen Theaters Berlin*, vol. 2, 1912, p. 509.

40. Adolf Hitler, *Mein Kampf*.

41. Rudolf Oertel, *Der Filmspiegel*, p. 236.

42. Egon Friedell, "Prolog vor dem Film," p. 510.

43. Joseph Goebbels, *Rede des Reichsministers Dr. Joseph Goebbels bei der Eröffnung der Reichskulturkammer am 15. November 1933* (Frankfurt, 1933).

44. Charles Darwin, *Descent of Man* (New York, 1886).

45. Adolf Hitler, *Mein Kampf* (Boston, 1943), p. 184.

46. Andreas Hillgruber, "Imperialismus und Rassendoktrin als Kernstück der NS-Ideologie" in Leo Haupts, ed., *Strukturelemente des Nationalsozialismus* (Cologne, 1981), pp. 11–36.

47. Eberhard Jäckel, *Hitler's World View* (Cambridge, Mass., 1981), p. 81.

48. Siegfried Kracauer, *Von Caligari bis Hitler*, vol. 2, p. 339.

49. Idem, *Theorie des Films*, p. 220.

50. Quoted in Hermann Glaser, *Das dritte Reich* (Freiburg, 1961), p. 57.

51. Hans Traub, *Film als politisches Machtmittel* (Munich, 1933), pp. 26ff.

52. Sergei Eisenstein, "Perspektiven" in H.-J. Schlegel, ed., *Sergei Eisenstein. Schriften* (Munich, 1973).

53. Joseph Goebbels, "Rede vor den Filmschaffenden in der Kroll-Oper am 10. Februar 1934" in *Deutsche Allgemeine Zeitung*, 11 February 1934.

54. Sergei Eisenstein "Über den Faschismus, die deutsche Filmkunst und das echte Leben" in H.-J. Schlegel, ed., *Sergei Eisenstein*, vol. 2, p. 210.

55. Bertolt Brecht, *Gesammelte Werke* (Frankfurt, 1967).

56. Vsevolod Pudovkin, "Die grundlegenden Etappen in der Entwicklung des sowjetischen Films" in V. Pudovkin et al., *Der sowjetische Film* (Berlin-East, 1953), p. 16.

57. Ibid., p. 17.

58. Ulrich Kurowski, *Lexikon Film*, p. 121.

59. Thomas Mann, *Reflections of a Nonpolitical Man* (New York, 1982), p. 402.

60. Paul Rotha, *Documentary Film* (London, 1951), p. 142.

61. Hilmar Hoffmann, "Triumph des Willens" in *Rheinischer Merkur/Christ und Welt*, 29 May 1987.

62. Gert Kalow, *Hitler—Das deutsche Trauma* (Munich, 1974), p. 42.

63. Siegfried Kracauer, *Von Caligari bis Hitler*, p. 328 (appendix to new 1979 edition).

64. Siegfried Kracauer, *Theorie des Films*; cf. Hilmar Hoffmann, "Abfallhaufen des Kinos. Über Kracauers Theorie des Films" in *Nürnberger Nachrichten*, 10 October 1970, p. 18.

65. Martin Loiperdinger, *Rituale der Mobilmachung* (Opladen, 1987), p. 34.

66. Ibid., pp. 34f.

67. Siegfried Kracauer, *Theorie des Films*, p. 354.

68. Friedrich Nietzsche, *Human, All Too Human* (Lincoln, NE, and London, 1984), p. 51.

69. Pierre Bourdieu, *Sozialer Sinn* (Frankfurt, 1987), p. 127.

70. Ibid., p. 128.

71. Institut für den wissenschaftlichen Film, ed., *Publikationen zu wissenschaftlichen Filmen* (Göttingen, 1977), vol. 4, p. 15 (article by A. Tyrell).

72. Walter Benjamin, *Das Kunstwerk im Zeitalter seiner technischen Reproduzierbarkeit* (Frankfurt, 1969), p. 42.

73. Leni Riefenstahl, *Memoiren*, p. 222.

74. Walter Hagemann, *Publizistik im Dritten Reich* (Hamburg, 1948), p. 123.

75. Fritz Hippler, "Der Tod in Kunst und Film" in *Der deutsche Film*, vol. 6, no. 6/7, 1941.

76. Hans Traub, ed., *Die Ufa*, p. 165.

77. Ibid., p. 112.

78. Sergei Eisenstein, "Open Letter to the German Propaganda Minister Dr. Goebbels" in: *Literaturnaya gazeta*, 22 March 1934.

79. *Chronik 1938* (Dortmund, 1987), p. 70.

80. Sergei Eisenstein, *Ausgewählte Aufsätze* (Berlin-East, 1960), p. 207.

81. Ulrich Kurowski, *Lexikon Film*, p. 83.

82. H.-J. Schlegel, ed., *Sergei Eisenstein. Schriften*, vol. 2, p. 138.

83. Nicholas Kaufmann in Hans Traub, *Die Ufa*, p. 183.

84. Jay Leyda, *Film aus Filmen* (Berlin-East, 1967), pp. 24f.

85. Hilmar Hoffmann, *Marginalien zu einer Theorie der Filmmontage* (Bochum, 1969), p. 26.

86. Ibid.

87. Marcel Martin, cited in Georges Sadoul, *Dictionary of Films* (Los Angeles, 1972), p. 150.

88. Jay Leyda, *Film aus Filmen*, p. 104.

89. Hans-Magnus Enzensberger, "Scherbenwelt—Anatomie einer Wochenschau" in idem, *Einzelheiten* vol. 1: *Bewusstseins-Industrie* (Frankfurt, 1964), pp. 106–33.

90. Jean-Luc Godard, "Feuer frei auf die 'Carabiniers'" in Frieda Graefe, ed., *Jean-Luc Godard. Ausgewählte Kritiken und Aufsätze über Film, 1950–1970* (München, 1971).

91. Goebbels in a speech on 8 February 1942, repr. in Joseph Goebbels, *Reden*.

92. *Das schwarze Korps*, 3 July 1941.

93. Helmut Krausnick, *Hitlers Einsatzgruppen* (Frankfurt, 1985).

94. Christian Hacke, "So unschuldig war die Generalität nicht" in *Die Zeit*, 29 November 1985, p. 19.

95. Alexander and Margarete Mitscherlich, *Die Unfähigkeit zu trauern*.

96. Paul Celan, "Todesfuge" in idem, *Mohn und Gedächtnis* (Frankfurt, 1975), pp. 37ff.

97. Hans Zöberlein, *Befehl des Gewissens* (Munich, 1937).

98. *Film-Kurier*, 20 January 1941. Cf. Joseph Wulf, *Lodz. Das letzte Ghetto auf polnischem Boden* (Bonn, 1962).

99. *Deutsche Allgemeine Zeitung*, 29 November 1940.

100. *Illustrierter Film-Kurier*, 1940.

101. Michel Foucault, *Überwachen und Strafen* (Frankfurt, 1976), p.47, English translation *Discipline and Punish* (New York, 1977).

102. Albert Memmi, *Rassismus* (Frankfurt, 1987).

103. Ibid.

104. Joseph Goebbels in *Das Reich*, no. 27, 1941.

105. Paul Virilio, *Krieg und Kino* (Munich, 1986), p. 110.

106. Carl Cranz in *Der deutsche Film*, vol. 6/7, no. 42, 1941, p. 4.

107. Paul Virilio, *Krieg und Kino*, pp. 35f.

108. Antoine Saint-Exupéry, *Flug nach Arras* (Stockholm, 1942), English translation *Flight to Arras* (New York, 1942).

109. *Illustrierter Film-Kurier*, 28 April 1940.

110. Ibid.

111. Jay Leyda, *Film aus Filmen*, pp. 160f.

112. Johan Huizinga, *Im Schatten von morgen* (Berne, 1935).

113. Michail Romm, "Wer sich anpasst, altert rasch. Ein Gespräch aus dem Jahre 1965" in Friedrich Hitzer, ed., *Zeitzeichen aus der Ferne* (Hamburg, 1987), p. 91.

114. *Kinemathek*, no. 24, February 1966, p. 3.

115. Horst Knietzsch, *Film gestern und heute* (Leipzig, 1967), p. 444.

116. Michail Romm, see note 113 above, p. 99.

117. Hermann Herlighaus, ed., *Dokumentaristen der Welt* (Berlin-East, 1982), p. 62.

118. Richard Griffiths in Paul Rotha, *Documentary Film*, p. 310.

119. Cf. *Historical Journal of Film, Radio and Television*, vol. 3, no. 2, 1983, pp. 171f.

120. Richard M. Barsam, *Nonfiction Film* (Bloomington, Ind., 1973), p. 236.

121. Bundesarchiv Koblenz, R 109 III—Universum Film AG, letter of 25 July 1944.

122. Jan-Christopher Horak, *Anti-Nazi-Filme der deutschsprachigen Emigration von Hollywood, 1939–1945* (Münster, 1985).

123. Vsevolod Pudovkin quoted in Ulrich Kurowski, *Lexikon Film*, p. 76.

124. Hans Richter, "Der Film-Essay. Eine neue Form des Dokumentarfilms" in *National-Zeitung* (Basle), 25 April 1940 (supplement).

125. Quoted in Joseph Wulf, *Theater und Film im Dritten Reich* (Gütersloh, 1964), p. 300.

126. Kurt Wolf, "Entwicklung und Neugestaltung der deutschen Filmwirtschaft seit 1933," unpubl. Ph.D. thesis, Heidelberg University, February 1938.

127. Joseph Goebbels, *Reden*, vol. 1, p. 238.

128. Fritz Hippler, *Betrachtungen zum Filmschaffen*.

129. Joseph Goebbels, *Reden*, vol. 1, p. 250.

130. Fritz Hippler, *Die Verstrickung. Auch ein Filmbuch* (Düsseldorf, 1983).

131. Hans-Joachim Giese in *Leipziger Beiträge zur Erforschung der Publizistik*, vol. 5 (Dresden, 1940).

132. Liz-Anne Bawden and Wolfram Tichy, eds., *rororo Filmlexikon* (Reinbek near Hamburg, 1978).

133. Rudolf Oertel, *Der Filmspiegel*, p. 236.

134. *Film-Kurier*, 18 September 1936.

135. Siegfried Kracauer, *Kino* (Frankfurt, 1974).

136. Peter Bucher, "Machtergreifung und Wochenschau" in *Publizistik*, vol. 30, no. 2/3, 1985, p. 190.

137. Ibid., p. 193.

138. Ibid., p. 190.

139. Heinrich Mann, "Der Film" in Anton Kaes, ed., *Kino-Debatte* (Tübingen, 1978), p. 167.

140. Stefan Dolezel, ed., *German Newsreel, 1933–1947* (Munich, 1984), pp. 9f.

141. Hans-Joachim Giese, "Ganz gewusst" in: Joseph Wulf, *Theater und Film im Dritten Reich* (Frankfurt, 1983), pp. 363f.

142. Johannes Eckhardt, *Abbild und Sinnbild*, p. 44.

143. *Filmdokumente zur Zeitgeschichte*, No. 34, 1958: *Die Entwicklung der Wochenschau in Deutschland. Ufa-Tonwoche Nr. 451/1939. Hitlers 50. Geburtstag* (Göttingen, 1960).

144. Erich Kordt, *Wahn und Wirklichkeit* (Stuttgart, 1948), p. 152.

145. Georg Santé, "Parade als Paradestück" in *25 Jahre Wochenschau der Ufa* (Berlin, 1939).

146. Peter Bucher, "Wochenschau und Staat" in *Geschichte in Wissenschaft und Unterricht*, no. 11, 1984.

147. Heinrich Roellenbleg, "Von der Arbeit an der Deutschen Wochenschau" in *Der deutsche Film*, special issue, 1940/41.

148. Heinrich Koch and Heinrich Braune, *Von deutscher Filmkunst*, p. 3.

149. Joseph Goebbels, *Das eherne Herz* (Munich, 1943).

150. Esther Shub et al., *Dsiga Vertov. Publizist und Poet des Dokumentarfilms* (Berlin, 1960).

151. Fritz Hippler, "Fragen und Probleme der deutschen Wochenschau im Kriege" in idem, *Betrachtungen zum Filmschaffen*.

152. Rudolf Oertel, *Der Filmspiegel*, p. 237.

153. *Film-Kurier*, 25 August 1939.

154. Hans Bertram, "Wie der Fliegerfilm entstand" in *Jenaer Zeitung*, 11 April 1940.

155. Oskar Wesel in *Film-Kurier*, 8 August 1941.

156. Joseph Goebbels in *Der deutsche Film*, vol. 5, no. 11, 1940, p. 220.

157. Ernst Wisshaupt, ed., *Der grosse deutsche Feldzug gegen Polen* (Wien, 1940).

158. Felix Heseleit, "Die neue Wochenschau" in *Film-Kurier*, 11 July 1940.

159. Hans Spielhofer in *Der deutsche Film*, February 1941.

160. Hans-Joachim Giese, *Die Filmwochenschau im Dienste der Politik* (Dresden, 1940).

161. Alfred Rosenberg, *Blut und Ehre*, p. 280.

162. Hans Traub, *Der Film als politisches Machtmittel*, p. 24.

163. Cf. P. M. H. Bell, *The Origins of the Second World War* (London, 1986), pp. 268ff.

164. Siegfried Kracauer, *Kino*, p. 336.

165. Bundesarchiv Koblenz, NS 10, no. 44, "Aus der Persönlichen Adjutantur des Führers und Reichskanzlers."

166. Joseph Goebbels, *Tagebücher aus den Jahren 1942–43* (Zürich, 1948).

167. Joseph Goebbels, *Tagebücher 1945* (Hamburg, 1977).

168. Erwin Leiser, *Deutschland Erwache!* (Reinbek near Hamburg, 1968), p. 113.

169. Erich Ludendorff, *Der totale Krieg* (Munich, 1935).

170. Adolf Hitler, *Mein Kampf* (German original), p. 563.

171. Joseph Goebbels, *Tagebücher aus den Jahren 1942–43*.

172. Hans Magnus Enzensberger, "Scherbenwelt."

173. Peter Bucher, "Goebbels und die deutsche Wochenschau" in *Militärge-schichtliche Mitteilungen*, 2/1986, pp. 53–69.

174. Joseph Goebbels, *Reden*, vol. 2, p. 212.

175. Helmut Hagenried, "Dokument vom Kampf gegen die Invasion" in *Film-Kurier*, 20 July 1944.

176. Albert Speer, *Inside the Third Reich* (London, 1971), p. 549.

177. Ibid., p. 550.

178. Ernst Jünger, "Die totale Mobilmachung" in idem, *Krieg und Krieger* (Berlin, 1930).

179. Fritz Hippler, *Die Verstrickung*, p. 186.

180. Ibid., pp. 185f.

181. Ibid.

182. Joseph Goebbels, *Final Entries 1945* (New York, 1978), p. 40.

183. Karl Wahl, *Patrioten als Verbrecher* (Heusendamm, 1973), p. 155.

184. F. Genoud, ed., *The Testament of Adolf Hitler. Bormann Documents, February–April 1945* (London, 1962).

185. Erich Fromm, *Anatomie der menschlichen Destruktivität* (Stuttgart, 1974), p. 383, English translation *The Anatomy of Human Destructiveness* (New York, 1973).

SELECT BIBLIOGRAPHY

Albrecht, G. *Nationalsozialistische Filmpolitik*. Stuttgart, 1969.

Anderson, M. M., ed. "Siegfried Kracauer," special issue of *New German Critique*, 54 (fall 1991).

Baird, J. W. *The Mythical World of Nazi War Propaganda*. Minneapolis, 1974.

Balfour, M. *Propaganda in War*. London, 1979.

Bessel, R., ed. *Life in the Third Reich*. Oxford, 1987.

Bock, H.-M., and M. Töteberg, eds. *Das Ufa-Buch*. Frankfurt, 1992.

Bramsted, E. K. *Goebbels and National Socialist Propaganda*. London, 1965.

Bredow, W. von, and R. Zurek, eds. *Film und Gesellschaft in Deutschland*. Hamburg, 1975.

Cadars, P., and F. Coutade. *Geschichte des Films im Dritten Reich*. Munich, 1975.

Coates, P. *The Gorgon's Gaze*. New York, 1991.

Drewniak, B. *Der deutsche Film, 1938–1945*. Düsseldorf, 1987.

Elsaesser, Th. *New German Cinema*. New Brunswick, N.J., 1989.

Golsan, R. J. *Fascism, Aesthetics, and Culture*. Hanover, N.H., 1992.

Hake, S. *The Cinema's Third Machine*. Lincoln, Nebr., 1993.

Haxthausen, C. W., and H. Suhr, eds. *Berlin: Culture and Metropolis*. Minneapolis, 1990.

Hull, D. S. *Film in the Third Reich*. Berkeley, 1969.

Jarvie, I. *Hollywood's Overseas Campaign*. New York, 1992.

Kaes, A. *From Hitler to Heimat*. Cambridge, Mass., 1989.

Kershaw, I. *The Hitler Myth*. Oxford, 1987.

Kracauer, S. *From Caligari to Hitler*. Princeton, 1974.

Labanyi, P. "Images of Fascism," in: M. Laffan, ed. *The Burden of History*. London, 1988, pp. 151–77.

Lowry, S. *Pathos und Politik: Ideologie in Spielfilmen des National-sozialismus.* Tübingen, 1991.

Monaco, P. *Cinema and Society.* New York, 1976.

Petley, J. *Capital and Culture: German Cinema, 1933–1945.* London, 1979.

Peukert, D. K. *Inside Nazi Germany.* New Haven, 1987.

Plummer, Th. G., et al., eds. *Film and Politics in the Weimar Republic.* New York, 1982.

Rentschler, E. "Mountains and Modernity: Relocating the *Bergfilm*," in: *New German Critique*, 51 (fall 1990), pp. 137–61.

Romani, C. *Tainted Goddesses: Female Film Stars of the Third Reich.* New York, 1992.

Rosenberg, E. S. *Spreading the American Dream.* New York, 1982.

Saunders, Th. J. *Hollywood in Berlin.* Berkeley, 1994.

Spiker, J. *Film und Kapital. Der Weg der deutschen Filmwirtschaft zum nationalsozialistischen Einheitskonzern.* Berlin, 1975.

Thompson, K. *Exporting Entertainment.* London, 1985.

Welch, D. *Propaganda and the German Cinema, 1933–1945.* Oxford, 1983.

———, ed. *Nazi Propaganda.* Totowa, N.J., 1983.

Zeman, Z. A. B. *Nazi Propaganda.* London, 1973.

INDEX OF NAMES

INDEX OF FILM TITLES